...For Dummies
BESTSELLING
BOOK SERIES

Golf's Short Game For Dummies®

Cheat Sheet

Keys to the Short Game

Understanding and improving your short game is the fastest way to lower your golf scores. The following list gives you the fastest way to understand and improve your short game.

- **Practice:** The word *practice* doesn't have to be the opposite of the word *play*. Learn to love rehearsing chips, pitches, bunker shots, and putts through target-oriented, focused practice. When you get on the course, you'll experience the immediate satisfaction of confidence, improved play, and better scores.

- **Play with purpose:** Golf isn't supposed to be like work — it's supposed to be fun. But if you're not playing with purpose, your game will suffer, and that's not fun. Concentrate and take the time to adequately check your lie, read the green, and clearly visualize a shot before you play it.

- **Lay a solid foundation:** Begin a long, happy relationship with your 7-iron. Sure, you can hit a 7-iron 140 yards, but you can also hit it 14 feet! Learning to chip and pitch with your 7-iron from various distances and lies can simplify your short game and give you a solid base from which to experiment with more specialized clubs and techniques.

- **Identify your goals versus your expectations:** Goals are very different than expectations. Your goal can be to hit an approach shot close enough to the hole to need only one putt every time. But a more realistic expectation is to get the ball anywhere on the green and use two putts every time.

- **Play in the subconscious:** Develop an understanding of your short game options for any shot and practice your technique enough so that when it's time to hit a shot, you can forget all about the swing mechanics and instructions. You want your play to be natural and flow freely without a lot of mental chatter.

- **Stand as close as you can to the target line:** Open the toe of your front foot and your hips and shoulders so that you're virtually looking down the target line at the hole.

- **Develop a feel for each shot:** Grip the club lightly in your fingers so that you get nice feedback from the club and the ball at impact. This sense of touch helps you connect with the ball and develop a feel for each shot or putt.

- **Keep your swing speed consistent:** Swing speed is a matter of preference, but your best bet is to swing slowly. Most importantly, swing the clubhead forward at the same speed you took it back. Rhythm is helpful.

- **Obey the captain:** When it comes to the golf swing, for right-handed players, your left hand is the captain and the right hand is merely the first mate. Let your left hand lead the swing, and just let the right hand steady the club and go along for the ride (and vice versa for left-handed players).

- **Follow through:** Following through is the best way to make certain you don't decelerate at impact. Deceleration stunts the swing and sends the ball offline or an improper distance. Swing freely and fully and follow through to a big, high finish.

- **Get the ball on the ground:** It is much easier to judge the distance a ball will travel and how the ball will break when it's rolling rather than when it's flying through the air. Think bowling, not basketball.

For Dummies: Bestselling Book Series for Beginners

Golf's Short Game For Dummies®

Short Game Practice Session

Since 50 percent of your strokes during a golf round come from the short game, 50 percent of your practice time should be devoted to hitting short game shots. Yeah, it's fun to use the driver to hit the ball a long way, but it's not how you drive, it's how you arrive!

Time (Minutes)	Location	Activity
5	Anywhere	Warm-up
10	Putting/Chipping Green	Putts
10	Putting/Chipping Green	Chipping/Sand Practice
10	Driving Range	Pitching with Short Irons
25	Driving Range	Hitting with Longer Irons and Woods

Short Game Preround Warm-Up

A practice session is different than a preround warm-up. The 30 to 40 minutes you spend at the golf course before your round should be used for stretching, getting a feel for having the club in your hand and making contact with the ball, and building your confidence.

Time (Minutes)	Location	Activity
5	Putting/Chipping Green	Brief Stretching/Putts
5	Putting/Chipping Green	Chipping
5	Driving Range	Warm-Up Stretching
5	Driving Range	Wedge Shots
5	Driving Range	Hitting with Your Favorite Club
5	Driving Range	Hitting the Driver
5	Putting/Chipping Green	Putts
5	1st Tee	Swing Away!

Goals and Expectations

For the average player, reasonable expectations are achievable. Goals are important too, but achieving reasonable expectations builds the confidence necessary to strive for the goals. If your expectations are too high, you might be constantly disapointed, which wrecks your self-image and confidence.

Shot	Expectation	Goal
Chip	Get the ball on the green — anywhere on the green.	Sink the chip or get the ball close enough to the hole to need only one putt.
Pitch	Get the ball on the green — anywhere on the green.	Get the ball close enough to the hole to need only one putt.
Sand Save	Get the ball out of the bunker in one shot.	Get the ball onto the green and possibly near the hole.
Putt	Try to use only two putts, and never more than three.	One-putt from time to time and never use more than two.

For Dummies: Bestselling Book Series for Beginners

Golf's Short Game
FOR
DUMMIES

by Michael Patrick Shiels
with Michael Kernicki

WILEY

Wiley Publishing, Inc.

Golf's Short Game For Dummies®
Published by
Wiley Publishing, Inc.
111 River St.
Hoboken, NJ 07030-5774
www.wiley.com

For general information on our other products and services, please contact our Customer Care Department within the U.S. at 800-762-2974, outside the U.S. at 317-572-3993, or fax 317-572-4002.

For technical support, please visit www.wiley.com/techsupport.

Wiley also publishes its books in a variety of electronic formats. Some content that appears in print may not be available in electronic books.

Library of Congress Control Number: 2005920298

ISBN: 0-7645-6920-1

Manufactured in the United States of America

10 9 8 7 6 5 4 3 2 1

1B/RR/QS/QV/IN

WILEY

About the Authors

Michael Patrick Shiels: Michael Patrick Shiels displayed his woeful short game at courses around the world while maintaining his career as an international golf and travel writer. That is, until writing this book, during which his handicap improved five strokes.

Golf's Short Game For Dummies is his fifth book. The *Los Angeles Times* called his *Good Bounces & Bad Lies,* written with Emmy Award-winning golf announcer Ben Wright, "perhaps the best sports book ever," and a *Washington Times* review sardonically compared Shiels and Wright to Ernest Hemingway and F. Scott Fitzgerald. Shiels' first book, a biography of famed Detroit radio host J.P. McCarthy, was a regional bestseller that received praise from Jack Nicklaus, Larry King, and Frank Sinatra, Jr. Shiels also penned *Works of Art: The Golf Course Designs of Arthur Hills.*

His travel articles have appeared in publications such as *Golf Magazine, Travel + Leisure Golf,* www.pgatour.com, *Sports Illustrated, Northwest World Traveler Magazine, Bermuda Royal Gazette,* and the *Honolulu Star Bulletin,* and he's written scripts for The Golf Channel and ESPN. Shiels has traveled the world — from Thailand to the Middle East to his beloved ancestral Republic of Ireland in search of rich stories to tell. You can contact Michael at Mshiels@aol.com.

Michael Kernicki: A PGA member for over 25 years, Michael Kernicki has spent most of his career as a Head Golf Professional and General Manager at some of America's finest golf clubs. He was twice named Golf Professional of the Year by the Michigan PGA and has received other PGA awards. Kernicki has served as a member of the PGA of America National Board of Directors and on the Rules of Golf Committee, where he has administered the rules at 13 PGA Championships.

Noted for his knowledge of the golf swing, he has instructed at Teaching and Playing workshops around the country and has authored several articles about the golf swing and the short game.

Today Michael is the Head Golf Professional at one of the nation's most prominent country clubs, Indian Creek Country Club in Miami Beach, Florida. As a daily routine, Michael teaches the short game and the golf swing in the most simple and logical manner. His primary objective is for his students to enjoy the game while they improve and make golf a game for a lifetime.

Dedication

Michael Patrick Shiels: To my eight-year-old son Harrison Ambrose Shiels, a giant-hearted little boy who, at the age of two, aced his first-ever hole of mini-golf at Pirate Golf on International Drive in Orlando.

Michael Kernicki: To my father, Walter Kernicki, for the tools you provided for golf and life.

Authors' Acknowledgments

Thank you to Stacy Kennedy, the *For Dummies* acquisitions editor who envisioned the flight plan and got "Short Game" off the ground. Project editor Mike Baker was the architect with the shot clock, and copy editor Josh Dials put the finesse in our swings. Kennedy, Baker, and Dials are a "Wiley" bunch indeed! Photojournalist Ginny Dixon staged and shot the action at the famed Indian Creek County Club in Miami Beach, and you can see more of her work at www.ginnydixon photos.com. Finally, thanks to the legendary PGA professional Dick Stewart, who has long lorded over Kalamazoo Country Club, for serving as technical consultant.

Publisher's Acknowledgments

We're proud of this book; please send us your comments through our Dummies online registration form located at www.dummies.com/register/.

Some of the people who helped bring this book to market include the following:

Acquisitions, Editorial, and Media Development

Project Editor: Mike Baker

Acquisitions Editor: Stacy Kennedy

Copy Editor: Josh Dials

Technical Reviewer: Dick Stewart

Senior Permissions Editor: Carmen Krikorian

Senior Editorial Manager: Jennifer Ehrlich

Editorial Assistants: Hanna Scott, Nadine Bell

Cover Photos: ©David Madison/ Getty Images/Stone

Cartoons: Rich Tennant (www.the5thwave.com)

Composition Services

Project Coordinator: Emily Wichlinski

Layout and Graphics: Barry Offringa, Jacque Roth, Heather Ryan, Amanda Spagnuolo

Special Art: Ginny Dixon

Proofreaders: Leeann Harney, Jessica Kramer, Carl Pierce, TECHBOOKS Production Services

Indexer: TECHBOOKS Production Services

Publishing and Editorial for Consumer Dummies

    Diane Graves Steele, Vice President and Publisher, Consumer Dummies

    Joyce Pepple, Acquisitions Director, Consumer Dummies

    Kristin A. Cocks, Product Development Director, Consumer Dummies

    Michael Spring, Vice President and Publisher, Travel

    Brice Gosnell, Associate Publisher, Travel

    Kelly Regan, Editorial Director, Travel

Publishing for Technology Dummies

    Andy Cummings, Vice President and Publisher, Dummies Technology/General User

Composition Services

    Gerry Fahey, Vice President of Production Services

    Debbie Stailey, Director of Composition Services

Contents at a Glance

Introduction...1

Part I: Walking the Short Game 7
   Chapter 1: Sharpening Your Approach.......................................9
   Chapter 2: Discerning the Short Game Certainties.............................21
   Chapter 3: Gearing Up for the Short Game 33

Part II: The Long and Short of It:
Short Game Technique 51
   Chapter 4: Chipping Off the Ol' Block......................................53
   Chapter 5: Pitch, Pitch, Pitch...67
   Chapter 6: Climbing Bunker Hill 87
   Chapter 7: Putting Your Best Foot Forward 105

Part III: Short Game Strategies 123
   Chapter 8: Waging (and Wedging) a Ground Campaign 125
   Chapter 9: Selecting Putting Strategies and Remedies.....................137
   Chapter 10: Taking an Unconventional Approach 149
   Chapter 11: Flipping to Flop...163
   Chapter 12: Keeping Your Head in the Game............................169

Part IV: Short Cuts to the Short Game..............179
   Chapter 13: Warming Up to the Short Game............................181
   Chapter 14: The Games People Play 195
   Chapter 15: Tricks and Treats: Techniques and
      Tools to Improve Your Game.......................................203
   Chapter 16: Learning from the Stars 217

Part V: The Part of Tens.................................225
   Chapter 17: Ten Simple Secrets of Short-Shot Success 227
   Chapter 18: Ten Ways You Can Practice Off the Course...................231
   Chapter 19: Ten of the Greatest Short Shots Ever 239
   Chapter 20: Ten Great Short Game Golf Courses 249

Index...257

Table of Contents

Introduction *1*

About This Book 1
Conventions Used in This Book 2
What You're Not to Read...3
Foolish Assumptions 3
How This Book Is Organized......................................3
     Part I: Walking the Short Game 4
     Part II: The Long and Short of It:
        Short Game Technique.................................4
     Part III: Short Game Strategies 4
     Part IV: Short Cuts to the Short Game 4
     Part V: The Part of Tens 5
Icons Used in This Book..5
Where to Go from Here 6

Part 1: Walking the Short Game *7*

Chapter 1: Sharpening Your Approach 9

Approaching the Short Game Statistically.................10
Approaching the Short Game Athletically..................11
Giving Yourself the Best Shot 12
Making Practice a Priority 13
     Recognizing the importance of practice................13
     Developing a practice plan...............................14
     Keeping practice fun 15
Avoiding Common Misfires.......................................16
     Playing without purpose 16
     Being under-prepared 16
     Using the wrong club 17
     Maintaining unreasonable expectations..............17
     Over-thinking..18
     Aiming to displease 18
     Ignoring textbook technique.............................18
     Getting too far from your work 19
     Experiencing death by deceleration 19

Chapter 2: Discerning the Short Game Certainties.... 21

Recognizing the Peril and the Opportunity................22
     Re-evaluating the easy 22
     Dissecting the difficult 22

Viewing the Variables: Terrain and Conditions 23
Accounting for the obvious 23
Sensing the subtleties 24
Understanding Your Options 25
Weighing Your Goals and Expectations 26
Playing in the Subconscious 27
Zeroing In On the Target Line 28
Visualizing the target line 29
Standing close to the target line 29
Grasping the Importance of Feel 30
Obeying the Captain: Allowing Your Front Hand to Lead 30
Centering on Ball Position 31

Chapter 3: Gearing Up for the Short Game **33**

Going Short-Game Clubbing 34
Sorting Through the Short Sticks 35
Pumping irons 36
Weighing wedges 36
Deciding which clubs to use 39
Calling All Putters Great and Small 40
The traditional putter 41
The long putter 43
The belly putter 45
Finding the Putter That Fits You 46
Caring for Your Putter 48
Handle with care 49
Cover it up 49
Give it a home of its own 49
Keep it clean and dry 49
Get a grip 50

Part II: The Long and Short of It:
Short Game Technique **51**

Chapter 4: Chipping Off the Ol' Block **53**

Discovering the Chip 54
Choosing the Chip over the Putt 54
Picking Your Chipping Tool 55
Chipping Goals and Expectations 56
Mapping Out a Chip-Shot Strategy 56
Hitting a Chip Shot 56
Taking aim 57
Setting up your stance 59
Making your move 61
Too Close for Comfort: Paul Runyan's
Greenside Chip Trick 62

Chapter 5: Pitch, Pitch, Pitch 67

Distinguishing the Pitch Shot 67
Covering Distance and Avoiding Hazards............................68
Pitching Club Preference 69
Pitching Goals and Expectations 69
Planning Your Pitch-Shot Strategy..70
Hitting a Pitch Shot 71
    Determining your flight plan and velocity..................72
    Setting up your stance 72
    Taking a swing...74
Pitching a Fit over Additional Complications 76
    Pitching over water hazards and bunkers...................76
    Pitching high and low...77
    Pitching from a bare, tight lie...78
    Pitching from deep grass 79
    Pitching from uneven lies 82

Chapter 6: Climbing Bunker Hill.................... 87

Setting Your Bunker Goals and Expectations 87
Avoiding an Explosion..89
Hitting a Bunker Shot 89
    Assessing the sand variables 89
    Choosing your club 92
    Raising clubface awareness...92
    Taking your stance 92
    Picking a target and taking aim......................................94
    Taking a sand-sweeping swing 95
Executing Bunker Shots from Troubled Lies........................97
    Negotiating uphill and downhill lies...........................98
    Cooking the fried egg 100
    Facing steep situations 102

Chapter 7: Putting Your Best Foot Forward 105

Tossing Your Putting Prejudice Aside 105
Recognizing the Importance of Putting Skills 106
    Doing the math...106
    Getting in your opponent's head 107
Putting Goals and Expectations 108
    Setting goals: Holing putts in two...............................108
    Meeting your expectations...109
    Letting the misses go 111
Rolling with the Fundamentals...112
    Taking a stance...112
    Getting a grip..113
    Targeting a line...115
    Swinging the flatstick 116

Reading the Break of the Greens............................120
Examining all angles 121
Closing your eyes 121
Spilling a bucket of water 121
Looking into the hole 121
Watching other players' putts....................122

Part III: Short Game Strategies 123

Chapter 8: Waging (and Wedging) a Ground Campaign 125

Gaining an Advantage by Keeping the Ball Low.................125
Charting your course 126
Choking down for a knockout knock-down 127
Pitching and Running 129
Taking aim...129
Selecting your club....................................130
Getting in your stance................................130
Taking your swing......................................130
Discovering the Famed Texas Wedge 131
Holding the Green 133
Pulling the Pin . . . or Leaving It In?.......................134
From off the green 134
From on the green 135

Chapter 9: Selecting Putting Strategies and Remedies 137

Becoming a Great Putter 138
Settling on a Style...138
Make it or break it......................................139
Lag it or flag it 141
Watching Your Speed..142
Conquering Speedy Breaks.................................143
Defeating the Yips and Other Putting Maladies 144
Cataloguing the causes 145
Tacking some solutions 146

Chapter 10: Taking an Unconventional Approach . . . 149

Chipping with a 3-Wood 150
Putting from Bunkers 152
Putting without a Putter....................................153
Opening the rulebook 153
Making a decision 154
Playing from a Cart Path 154

Bellying the Wedge 155
Splishing After You Splash 156
Hitting Lefty (or Righty)..157
    Taking a backhand swing.................................159
    Flipping the blade 160
    Looking away..160
    Carrying an opposite-handed club in your bag 161
Rehearsing the Unconventional............................161

Chapter 11: Flipping to Flop. 163

Focusing On the Flop Shot....................................163
Choosing to Hit a Flop Shot 164
Playing a Flop Shot 164
Deciding Against the Flop Shot..............................165
    Knowing the flop shot's dark side 166
    Considering your other options 166

Chapter 12: Keeping Your Head in the Game. 169

Regrouping When the Wheels Come Off................170
    Regaining your tempo 170
    Overcoming paralysis of analysis.....................171
    Realizing that it ain't your fault 172
Weathering the Heat of the Moment.......................172
    Accepting the fear 173
    Ignoring the result 174
Practicing Visualization 174
Staying Positive with Self Talk...............................175
Dispelling the Clouds of Doubt 176
Pacing Your Swing with a Phrase...........................177

Part IV: Short Cuts to the Short Game...............179

Chapter 13: Warming Up to the Short Game 181

Limbering Up Before You Play or Practice 182
    Loosening the legs...182
    Working the upper arms and shoulders....................182
    Bending over backwards 186
    Readying your wrists and forearms 187
Practicing Like You Play..188
    Making the short game at home on the range..........189
    Spending time on the green...............................191
Preparing before a Round 191
    Utilizing the perfect pre-round warm-up 192
    Warming up under the gun................................194

Chapter 14: The Games People Play 195

Pitching for Dollars..195
"Horse-ing" Around...197
Bingo, Bango, Bongo (Jingles)........................197
Snake 199
Eight in a Row 200
First to Make Five..201

Chapter 15: Tricks and Treats: Techniques and Tools to Improve Your Game.................... 203

Riding the Range 204
Standing up for balance 204
Becoming a one-armed bandit 205
Tuning your swing with music...................206
Practicing in the Sand and on the Green 207
Bunker board...207
Chalk talk 209
Trench warfare...210
Dowel drill 212
Improving at Home 213
Stretching your putting skill........................213
Weighing in on weights 215
Asking your mirror, mirror 215

Chapter 16: Learning from the Stars 217

Feeling like Seve Ballesteros.............................218
Escaping (Not Sleeping in) Bunkers like Gary Player.........219
Living Hard and Playing Soft like John Daly 220
Scrambling like Lee Trevino 221
Putting like Ben Crenshaw 222
Finishing like Annika Sorenstam 222
Yipping like Johnny Miller 223

Part V: The Part of Tens.................................225

Chapter 17: Ten Simple Secrets of Short-Shot Success 227

Play in the Subconscious 227
Be Aware of the Clubface 227
Swing Along the Target Line 228
Maintain Consistent Speed 228
Salute the Lead Hand as the Captain..................228
Let the Ball Get in the Way...............................228
Follow Through 229

Keep Realistic Expectations 229
Roll the Ball on the Ground 230
Recognize that Every Putt is Straight..................................230

**Chapter 18: Ten Ways You Can Practice
Off the Course** **231**

Putt on Your Carpet 231
Watch Golf on Television 232
Get Attached to Your Wedge 233
Chip into the Drapes...234
Bulk Up 234
Visualize Good Shots 235
Review Your Scorecard 235
Clean Up Your Act 236
Play Other Sports and Games 237
Read This Book When Necessary 237

Chapter 19: Ten of the Greatest Short Shots Ever 239

Tway at the PGA..239
Mize at the Masters 240
Hail Hale! 241
Rocca Rocks the British Open..242
The Million-Dollar Ace..243
Watson Plunders Pebble 244
Leonard Lets Loose 245
Lanny Lands the Cup...246
One Small Shot for Mankind 247
Payne's Putts at Pinehurst..247

Chapter 20: Ten Great Short Game Golf Courses. 249

The Old Course at St. Andrews: Fife, Scotland...................250
Pinehurst #2: Pinehurst, North Carolina............................250
Stadium Course, TPC at Sawgrass:
    Ponte Vedra Beach, Florida..251
Ballybunion Old Course: County Kerry, Ireland.................252
Threetops at Treetops Resort: Gaylord, Michigan 252
Strategic Fox, Fox Hills Golf Club: Plymouth, Michigan.....253
Indian Creek Country Club: Miami Beach, Florida 254
The Ocean Course at Kiawah Island Golf Resort:
    Charleston, South Carolina 254
Augusta National Golf Club: Augusta, Georgia...................255
Club de Golf Valderrama: San Roque, Cadiz, Spain 256

Index *257*

Introduction

I f we mention the term *professional golfer* to you, what image immediately comes to mind? Most likely you envision Tiger Woods taking a vicious swipe at the ball or Greg Norman bravely sweeping through the ball with his blonde locks flowing out from under his hat. You probably think of strong Tour players hitting big, booming drives that soar through the sky like guided missiles.

But even professional, tournament golf has an old and trusty adage: "You drive for show, but you putt for dough." Often you hear a player who wins a tournament say, "I won because the putts just started falling for me this week." No player ever won a tournament by hitting the ball the farthest from the tee. Players win tournaments at the opposite end of the hole — by hitting the ball close to the flagstick and making putts.

Take it from the pros: You can win more of your amateur tournaments and friendly matches by hitting the ball closer to the hole and giving yourself better chances to make putts. And you can improve your enjoyment of the game by improving your performance. An improved performance results in lower scores. And you can most immediately improve your performance and your scores by improving your short game.

Although most average players place a great deal of emphasis on how long a player can hit a golf ball, you use the driver from the tee only 14 times per round on a golf course. By contrast, you use your putter and short irons for as many as 50 percent of the total strokes. Players who strive to break 90 have a much better chance of realizing their goal if they come to the realization that they can save many, many more strokes by improving their short games instead of placing so much emphasis on the long ball. Chicks may dig the long ball, but as any dummy can tell . . .

The secret of golf satisfaction is in the short game.

About This Book

Every player likes to bang the ball with a driver, just like the kid at the carnival who tries to hit the bell with the sledgehammer. But standing at the driving range and belting pills gets you one thing — blisters.

Tiger Woods and John Daly may slug majestic, rising drives over 300 yards, but the average player has trouble equaling that kind of prowess. For most of us, the short game is the great equalizer. Something that we can do as well as the pros. For all their power, long hitting players like Woods wouldn't be as successful without equally impressive short-game skills — skills that average players can, indeed, acquire. You've likely heard Woods being tagged with the best-short-game-on-the-planet label, and if you've watched Daly, you've listened to announcers marvel at his touch around the greens. That part of their games you can emulate and even equal!

Convincing people to spend time at the practice green rather than the driving range is a tall order, but a spoonful of sugar can help the medicine go down, and we've written *Golf's Short Game For Dummies* to serve as an invigorating elixir for players seeking to improve their golf games.

Because many instructional books are as boring as the thought of practice itself, we wrote this book to entertain and excite you about developing and showing off your short game. Soon after you open the book and hit the practice facility, you can start winning bets and impressing your opponents.

This book details not only the specific types of shots and how to execute them but also relives stories of some of the greatest short game shots ever hit and shows you what you can learn from golf's biggest stars.

You find drills, tips, secrets, visualizations, and bits of advice that you can use immediately and that inspire you to go back to *Golf's Short Game For Dummies* time and time again for refreshers.

Conventions Used in This Book

To help you navigate through this book, we use the following conventions:

- ✔ We use *Italic* for emphasis and to highlight new words or terms that we define in the text.

- ✔ We use **Boldfaced** text to indicate keywords in bulleted lists or the action part of numbered steps.

- ✔ We use Monofont for Web addresses.

What You're Not to Read

We dedicate most of *Golf's Short Game For Dummies* to improving your play by improving your short game. We put some of the other historical asides and stories in sidebars throughout the book. You don't have to read these asides to understand the text, but you certainly can: Reading them may inspire you or provide you with some vivid examples to help your visualization.

Foolish Assumptions

If you're reading this book, we assume you have more than a passing interest in golf and more than a little desire to refine your game and improve your scores. You probably have your own golf clubs and know the difference between a 9-iron and a 4-wood. You know what your favorite golf courses are and can recognize a tough hole or an easy green. You like to go out and play with some friends, and you want to get a competitive edge over them. You likely understand enough golf lingo to be able to handle any of the terms we use in this book.

If you're a true beginner, we can surely help you develop your short game. But you should also consider picking up *Golf For Dummies* (Wiley), written by Champions Tour player and CBS Television golf announcer Gary McCord. His text can familiarize you with the game and help if you're having trouble with golf shots outside of the short game.

How This Book Is Organized

We organize *Golf's Short Game For Dummies* so that you can look through the table of contents and immediately find the help or instruction you need to hit a specific type of shot. If you have trouble with bunker shots, you can flip directly to the bunker shot chapter and read all about the technique and execution needed to play effectively from the sand. We lay out the basic nuts and bolts for you in plain "golf speak" (admittedly, a variation of English!).

You can also delve into discussions on equipment, strategy, unconventional shots, drills, practice techniques, and philosophies about the short game by turning to other chapters of the book. We have chapters that tell you which golf stars to emulate and what golf courses are best to test your short game on! You can even read about how to stretch and limber up properly before any round of golf or practice session.

Part 1: Walking the Short Game

Part I of *Golf's Short Game For Dummies* is all about reintroducing you to the short game. We show you that it doesn't have to be all that complicated. With some practice, you can begin knocking strokes off your score in no time by avoiding some common mistakes we all make. We also present a new way of thinking about the short game — broken down into two parts: fundamentals and preferences. We conclude Part I by dumping out that bag and taking a closer look at the golf clubs you use for short shots. The short game relies on fundamentals and preferences, and you have plenty of options in terms of clubs and equipment.

Part 11: The Long and Short of 1t: Short Game Technique

In this part, we present the technique and execution of the fundamentals of approach shots via the short game: chipping, pitching, bunker shots, and putting. This part spells out the basics and gives you the fundamental techniques you need to improve your short game. The good news is an effective short game isn't as tough to achieve as you may think. This part shows you why.

Part 111: Short Game Strategies

Part III reveals the strategies behind the fundamentals of chipping, pitching, bunker play, and putting and also gives you fixes if your game has gone astray. What should you be thinking when faced with a certain shot? Can you use a more effective variation of the shot? How can you putt more efficiently and take your green game to the next level? Should you hit the ball high or keep it low? What can choking down on a golf club do for you? How can you shape the shot and affect its outcome? What are some unconventional short-game shots you may encounter or unconventional techniques you may want to work into your repertoire? We have the answers. Also, you can meet the infamous flop shot and receive a host of tips and tricks for getting your mind right and your head in the game.

Part 1V: Short Cuts to the Short Game

We're all about practice. But we're all about practicing with a purpose and making sure that practice stays fun. In this part, we help you warm up with proven pre-round and practice routines to get you prepared for the short game ahead. We provide a bunch of games you can play to keep things interesting while you practice and a number of practice implements and aids that you can use without spending a fortune on various gadgets and expensive equipment. We also help you transform time on the couch and time spent watching the game in person into productive practice time by outlining what you can learn from the stars.

Part V: The Part of Tens

Part V is a fun Dummies tradition — the Part of Tens. Here we outline 10 simple secrets for short game success, cover 10 things you can do off the golf course to improve your short game, relive 10 of the greatest short shots ever, and present 10 great short game golf courses.

Icons Used in This Book

The icons we use in this book are carefully placed little graphics to help you identify specific, important information in the text. You can flip through the book and read only the passages with icons to get a bare-bones cache of valuable short-game information. You find the following icons throughout the book:

The Tip icon signifies a passage that whispers sage advice into your ear. The info makes you smile, because a light bulb goes off in your head that inspires you and gives you immediate comfort. Try the tips for quick improvement and a crafty edge on the process.

The Remember icon signifies some simple advice that you can hang onto — like a life ring when you fall overboard into a turbulent sea. See it, read it, remember it, do it. You'll like the result!

The Hazard icon signifies the possible side effects of a technique or a possible downside or complication. It indicates a passage that deserves attention because of the risk involved in the shot — a risk that you should understand, heed, and factor into your decision-making.

The Technical Stuff icon signifies a passage that goes beyond the surface in an attempt to explain the physics of why a certain shot works. If you're not into angles, degrees of loft, and the mechanics of the clubhead making contact with the ball in the short game, you can give the Technical Stuff the short shrift.

Where to Go from Here

Golf's Short Game For Dummies isn't a book that you need to read "A to Zed." You can start anywhere you want and go directly to the information you find valuable or compelling. You can get yourself out onto the golf course and into the action by reading the techniques and trying them out. Go ahead and climb right into the saddle if you want. We advise practicing the techniques first, of course, before you challenge the club champion.

If you want, you can read the entire book for an overview of our full short-game philosophy and outlook on technique. All the shots — chips, pitches, bunker plays, and putts — are related to each other through motor skills and the fundamental of acceleration at contact.

Where to go from here? Anywhere you want!

Part I
Walking the Short Game

In this part . . .

Drop that driver! Come over from the dark side and experience the force of the short game. You'll be wielding your pitching wedge like a light sabre after you realize the importance of the short game and start improving yours. Part I gives you an overview of the short game universe and gets you geared up to practice and play.

Chapter 1

Sharpening Your Approach

In This Chapter

▶ Defining the short game through statistics
▶ Establishing your short-game repertoire
▶ Using the ground to your advantage
▶ Clearing your schedule for practice
▶ Sidestepping common short-game sins

Golf is a journey with no final destination — a series of trips up and down hills — but if you play long enough, you'll come to enjoy the ride. You discover nuances of the game as you go along, and sometimes you learn important lessons the hard way.

Players who seek improvement — and who tire of seeing three-digit numbers on their scorecards at the end of a round — often just want to have some consistency in their game. Who can blame them? What's worse than swinging a golf club and wondering where the ball will go or even worrying about making contact? Nothing we know of. Well, maybe swinging with these thoughts while wearing a Jesper Parnevik outfit.

Precision is never more important than when you get the ball close to the green or the hole, and as we convey in this opening chapter, the short game is the most complex and varied aspect of the game of golf. But lucky for you, the short game is also the area in which you can make the most immediate and significant improvement.

In this chapter, we take a look at the importance of the short game, the best way to approach it, and how to prepare yourself to hit the shots that can improve your scores. Improved scores give you a greater sense of enjoyment — and who could ask for more?

Approaching the Short Game Statistically

According to the National Golf Foundation, a fine group of folks who make it their business to study the business side of golf, as many as 36.7 million people play golf in the United States. (Of those 36 million golfers, about 45 percent are between the ages of 18 and 39, and 22 percent of all golfers are female.) In a year's time, these golfers spend about $25 billion on golf equipment and fees. That's *billion,* with a *B.*

But like the old saying goes, money can't buy you love. And it can't buy you a 72 either. Even with all the cash players currently spend, average scores have changed very little over the years. Only 22 percent of all golfers regularly score better than 90 for 18 holes. For females, who shoot an average score of 114, the number is just 7 percent; for males, who manage to shoot an average score of 97, 25 percent break 90. The overall average is an even 100.

But par, on almost all golf courses, is 72.

When asked what they want to shoot, most golfers say they'd be satisfied shooting 85.

Although critics and the media place a great deal of emphasis on how long a player can hit a golf ball, you use driver from the tee only 14 times on a golf course. By contrast, you use the putter and short irons for as many as 50 percent of the total strokes.

The secret of golf satisfaction is in the short game. No matter what your score is, half your strokes come from the short game. Statistics prove that 50 percent of your score comes from shots within 75 yards of the green — whether you shoot 120 or you shoot 67. The percentage includes your putts, your chips, your pitches, and your bunker shots.

For instance, say you go out and shoot that 67. You hit all 18 greens in regulation. You make five birdies with five one-putts to shoot 5-under. That means you hit 31 putts out of 67 shots. And to sink some of those one-putts, you had to hit the ball close to the hole. You probably had a wedge or some type of short iron in your hand to do that. You didn't miss any greens, because you used your short game to get into position. Adding six more strokes to the putts, you have half your strokes accounted for.

If you shoot 110, you surely didn't hit all the greens in regulation, because if you did, you would have used 70 putts (or four putts per hole) to shoot that 110 — a dismal result for even the worst of putters. More likely you missed some greens and needed to hit some short-game shots — all the more reason to improve your short game.

Approaching the Short Game Athletically

The short game, by definition, covers short shots. You hit short-game shots from 75 yards and in — which is also known as the *scoring distance*. The short game requires a shorter swing. A 100-yard shot, by contrast, is a full-swing shot.

The short game is all about scoring and precision — not distance and strength. You want to get the ball onto the green with a single approach shot and into the hole with two strokes. (See Chapter 2 to help set your goals and expectations for the short game.)

The short game is the great equalizer. Unlike in many other sports, and even in other aspects of golf, scoring doesn't rely on power. In golf, you need to hit the ball straight and with the proper distance. Success means making good decisions and doing your homework.

With this in mind, you can see why golfers use the term *approach shots* — and not *bang it over the hole* shots. Think of an aircraft on approach to its final destination. To hit the runway and land safely, the plane has to travel at the right speed and at the proper angle of descent. It can't be short, and it can't be long. It has to, through a carefully made plan and proper execution, glide perfectly onto the runway and roll to a stop.

Your short-game swing options typically include a

- ✔ **Chip shot:** A low running shot, measured in feet, that flies only a small percentage of its life before landing on the green or in front of the green and rolling toward the hole (see Chapter 4).

- ✔ **Pitch shot:** A shot that remains the air for about 70 percent of its life before hitting the green and rolling to the hole. You often use a pitch shot when you have an obstacle to fly over, such as a bunker, creek, or hill (see Chapter 5).

- ✔ **Bunker shot:** A shot needed to extract a ball from a bunker. You normally hit bunker shots with a sand wedge, which splashes through the bunker and sends the ball floating out on a pillow of sand. Bunker shots fly high and land softly near the hole (see Chapter 6).

✔ **Putt:** Putting the ball into the hole may seem like a simple act, and we have good news is: it can be! Finding a way to roll the ball into the hole after you land the green is a matter of feel and preference, but good putters seem to have a bit of magic with the flatstick (see Chapter 7).

✔ **Flop shot:** A high-flying, soft shot that lands near the hole and stops instead of rolling to the hole (see Chapter 11).

Giving Yourself the Best Shot

The short game, and all its variables, offers golfers a multitude of options for playable shots. Although you hit some of your short game shots from distances as far as 75 yards from the hole, you hit others from as close as a pace or two off the green. The variables include not only the distances of the shots, but also the club you use, the terrain, the weather, the locale, and the competitive situation. We cover many of the variables you must consider in Chapter 2 and in the individual technique chapters in Part II, but one piece of advice cuts through all the uncertainty:

If you want to play the percentages and improve your chances of having good results, you need to get the ball rolling. Get the ball on the ground as quickly as possible so that you max out the amount of time it spends traveling on the ground.

Trying to fly a ball to the hole invites too much possibility for error. For example, chipping and running the ball gives you more accuracy than sending the ball soaring through the air toward the hole.

Think about it this way: If you have to hit a shot from 50 feet away from the hole, and you have an opportunity to putt the ball, you should choose to putt it most every time. When you putt,

✔ You stand directly over the *target line* (where the ball needs to roll to go in).

✔ Your eyes are over the line.

✔ You have an opportunity to make a simple backswing and fol-lowthrough.

So the only real challenge you have is judging your distance and speed. But if you line up for that 50-foot shot and put a 60-degree wedge in your hand, you allow additional variables in, such as:

✔ How far the ball has to carry in the air

✔ The spin you generate by hitting behind or right on the ball

✔ The effect of the wind blowing the ball left or right, holding it up in mid-flight, or sending it soaring over the green

✔ Where you have to land the ball to stop it close

Do you really want to have to factor in all this technical stuff? Probably not. These variables make it much more difficult to get the ball into or near the hole if you play the ball in the air. You have a much better chance of getting it close if you get the ball on the ground and moving.

Naturally, you face times when you need to hit a high-flying shot, such as when you need the ball to carry over a bunker, creek, or hill before landing on or near the green or when you don't have much room on the green for the ball to roll. These situations occur, but the more you can avoid them through careful course management, the simpler you make your short game. And a simple short game makes for lower scores.

Making Practice a Priority

Although you can learn certain techniques and styles from watching the likes of Tiger Woods, Jack Nicklaus, and Annika Sorenstam (and we point them out in Chapter 16), it isn't wise to try to copy all their techniques. Face it: The people that play competitive golf for a living are in a very, very small percentage. They don't show up on television for nothing.

They work at golf because it's their job. Their "office" is the golf course, the practice range, the practice green, or the practice bunker eight to ten hours each day. They play and they practice, and they practice by playing. You don't have that kind of practice luxury (we assume), because golf isn't your job. Lofting a ball in the air and stopping it within three feet of the cup is a shot best left to the professionals.

You can't spend eight hours each day practicing like the pros do, but you can, with whatever time you have, practice in a professional manner. People don't like to practice the short game, but the value of doing so is something you can learn from the professional golfers.

Recognizing the importance of practice

What makes you go to the range and bang a driver? Sometimes you slice it. Sometimes it goes straight. But the results always intrigue us at some level. And what do you hear in television commercials about golf equipment? You hear about hitting the ball a long way — almost exclusively!

Most of us are competitive enough that we want to play golf to the best of our abilities. We want to realize our potential. We want to have our best score. We forget sometimes that golf is a game that starts at the tee markers and ends at that little hole. If you don't care how many strokes it takes you, and you go out to the links for the enjoyment, that's great. Why bother to practice at all? But the point is that most golfers don't feel that way. And because you're reading this book, we assume you don't either.

Some people may really get a thrill out of banging the driver a long, long way, and they go out and hit all these prodigious, long drives, but when they look down at their scorecard after a round and see a big 100, they aren't so pumped anymore.

Maybe your goal is to shoot 90. Maybe you want to crack 80. You can shoot 80 or 90 consistently if you start spending half your practice time working on your short game.

Golf shots have much more value around the green, and the precision you need to display is much greater than on a drive or even an approach shot. A hole may be 400 yards, and you may be able to drive the ball 250 yards. You cover more ground, but your target, the fairway, is 35 yards wide. Your 150-yard approach shot is to a green that may be 60 feet wide. Your target when you chip, pitch, flop, or putt the ball is the hole — only a few inches wide — or a small circle around it.

If you shave five putts off your score because of improved chipping, or if you cut down on three-putts by five a round, your handicap starts to reduce dramatically. Just these improvements take scores from 100 to 95 or from 85 to 80.

Developing a practice plan

Practice should be an overview to everything. If you have 30 minutes in your busy schedule to run over to the practice range, you do yourself a huge disservice if you spend that entire half-hour hitting drivers and 5-iron shots. Every practice session, whether you take five minutes or five hours, needs to have a choreographed plan. Always include a specific amount of time that you devote to the short game: pitching, chipping, putting, bunker shots, and 50- to 75-yard shots.

Don't try this at home

Ben Crenshaw, a two-time Masters winner and one of the best putters ever, once had the honor of golfing with Ben Hogan late in Hogan's life. On one hole, Crenshaw found himself in a pickle and wanted to hit a low shot around a tree from a tangled, troubled lie. Crenshaw stood behind the ball contemplating the shot.

"What are you doing?" Hogan asked him.

"I'm going to hook this ball low around the tree to the green," said Crenshaw.

Hogan asked, "Have you ever played that shot before?"

"No," Crenshaw answered.

"Then why the hell are you trying to play it now? Chip the ball out."

The point is, whether you're a 30-handicap, a 15-handicap, or a scratch player, why would you try to attempt a shot that you've never practiced and expect it to work?

You can't punch and run a ball or play any kind of shot effectively without knowing how, and knowing how comes with practice. When you assess different shots, you have more options in your repertoire. (To take a look at some of these options, including the punch shot, check out Chapter 8.)

 Because 50 percent of your score comes from strokes taken from 75 yards or closer to the hole, you should devote 50 percent of your practice time to the short game.

If you have two hours to practice, spend an hour of it on the short game. And make a plan to break down the hour. Divide the time however you feel comfortable, based on what part of your game needs the most work or on a new shot you want to practice. How much time will you spend chipping balls at a target? How many shots will you hit from the practice bunker? How many putts will you hit? From how many distance? How long will you try hitting flop shots over a bunker? In Chapter 13, we help you answer these questions by customizing practice and pre-round warm-up routines to fit your needs.

Keeping practice fun

It's an unfortunate and unfair use of verbs to say that people "play" golf and "practice" golf. "Playing" anything is fun. "Practicing" anything is a drag. All work and no play makes golf a dull sport. So our goal with this book is to show you how to be "at play" while you practice. In Chapters 14 and 15, in particular, we give you some ways to have fun while you improve your short game.

When you start hitting really nice short-game shots and taking pride in the improvement you make, practicing becomes more fun and rewarding.

Avoiding Common Misfires

Hitting the ball from the tee is easy compared to the short game. Heck, the ball sits up on a tee, you hit it with the same club most every time, and you can swing away and hit it as far as you want. The short game, however, presents you with shots of different lengths and shapes from different lies. More possible shots mean more possible miscues. Don't be daunted, though: Every short-game shot has a common denominator of acceleration and simple mechanics. The shot isn't as difficult as it seems.

You can start improving your game this very minute simply by identifying and avoiding the common miscues that we cover in the following sections. And be sure to check out Parts III and IV of this book, which offer concrete advice about how you can correct mistakes.

Playing without purpose

Despite what you see on television, you should golf at a brisk pace and not deliberately. Touring professionals play for hundreds of thousands of dollars and do so on closed golf courses in front of T.V. cameras. Although you should try to emulate their play, you shouldn't try to emulate their pace of play.

Without slowing up play, be sure to take the time to adequately check your lie, read the green, and clearly visualize a shot before you play it. Prepare for your shot while you walk to your ball or while other players hit their shots.

No matter what, don't hit a shot without having a crystal clear vision of it and deciding on a specific target. Play quickly, but don't just smack the ball around.

Being under-prepared

Practice the various techniques and types of shots before you confront them on the golf course. Practice helps you build confidence and widen your array of options. Your self-confidence tells you when you're ready to try a certain shot on the golf course.

Sometimes, just like with a rookie quarterback, you have to press a certain technique into service. Pressure presents the truest test, and you have to perform under fire — but make sure you prepare the shot enough times in practice to build up your confidence.

Using the wrong club

You can have a better short game, lower your score, and have more fun if you play shots you're comfortable hitting. If from 30 yards and in you feel comfortable hitting a 7-iron for every shot, and it works, do it. Tell yourself, "I'm comfortable doing this. I love hitting this club."

Tiger Woods uses a 60-degree wedge for every shot around the greens. He doesn't change. He doesn't punch 7-irons. He hits bunker shots with his 60-degree wedge. He doesn't need to use a bunch of wedges, because he has one wedge that he likes to hit every shot with. He hits an amazing flop shot with a full swing where the ball only goes 20 feet, and he hits a shot that goes 50 feet by skipping along the ground knee high. But he does it all with one wedge that he feels very comfortable with.

Comfort and confidence contribute as much to short-game success as practice. After you get comfortable with a particular club, and make it your go-to club, you can focus your practice sessions around shots hit with the club. Chapter 3 has more about stocking your bag for short-game success.

Maintaining unreasonable expectations

If you play with the reasonable expectation that from 30 yards and in all you want to do is get on the green and two-putt, you can be a better player! Problems arise when players think they have to get it close to the hole. They over-analyze, psyche themselves out, and end up missing the green; now they have to chip it on or play a bunker shot and drill an eight-footer for par.

Relax and play within your abilities. Have a clear, concise, reasonable expectation of what you want to do. From 30 yards away, Tiger Woods can reasonably expect to get the ball up and in, but it may not be a realistic expectation for you. You should make getting up and down your goal, but your reasonable expectation is to get it on the green and two-putt. See Chapter 2 for more information on developing realistic expectations and goals.

Over-thinking

The whole object of golf is to be comfortable, confident, and to play in the subconscious. Let it happen by letting the game come to you. Trust the lessons you've taken, trust the skills that you've developed on the conscious side, and just make the swing. All you can do is practice to develop a consistent swing and become confident with it. From there, golf is a matter of hitting a ball and walking after it. If you prepare yourself and don't take every second so seriously, you can enjoy the walk. Check out Chapter 2 for more information on playing in the subconscious and Chapter 12 for all things mental.

Aiming to displease

Short-game shots are all straight shots. Unlike other shots in golf, you don't hit short-game shots with the intention of curving the ball. You don't need to hook it or fade it in there. Just knock it straight. This may seem like a simple concept to grasp, but remembering it can help you tremendously with your aim.

If you have a 10-foot break from right to left on the green, you still hit a straight putt to try to make it; you just have to aim 10 feet to the right of the hole because of the break. You don't aim at the hole and try to push the ball out with your putter. You pick a spot for your target line and aim so that the green takes care of the work for you.

The same goes for a 30-yard shot over a bunker, or any pitch or chip from off the green. You may determine that the uneven green will cause the ball to break 10 feet from the right to the left after you hit your target, so you have to allow for that, but all you want to do is hit the ball straight to your target landing area.

Remove the curves and angles from your mind after you pick your line and focus on hitting the ball straight.

Ignoring textbook technique

In golf, you practice fundamentals, and you develop preferences (see Chapter 2). You have to adhere to the fundamentals to be successful; the preferences you can enjoy.

The trick is, you can't let a preference take over a fundamental, because you reduce your chances of success. It may feel good to stand a certain way when you putt, and being comfortable is great — but you can't be a good putter if your stance clashes with the fundamentals of putting.

For instance, you can't grip the putter with the toe in the air and stand far away from the ball and think you can be a good putter. If you do, the putter naturally comes off line. Your preference defies the fundamental that the blade should come straight back along the target line, come back down along the same line, and swing straight through toward your target.

Getting too far from your work

Fundamentally, if you put your eyes over your target line, keep your putterhead over the line, take the putterhead straight back on the line, and bring it forward straight through, you can be a good putter. The same goes for chipping. The closer you get to "your work," the easier it is to make good shots.

You won't find any magic that drives this premise, just simple physics and logic. Think of a dart thrower or a billiards player. They each face their target and toss the dart or slide the cue right on line toward the target or hole.

Golf's a little different from darts and billiards because you stand to the side of the ball, but you can improve your chances by getting as close to the line as you can.

Experiencing death by deceleration

Don't stop the club when it strikes the ball at impact. Never, on any shot in golf, should you decelerate. Let the club swing freely and through the ball to its natural completion, as if you're sweeping away dust with a broom or as the pendulum of a grandfather clock swings. Stopping at impact can only result in a flubbed shot that falls short of your target. Make sure you have confidence in the type of shot you want to hit and in the club you pull out of the bag. Most players decelerate because they don't want to hit the ball too far or because they don't have confidence in the shot. Commit . . . and hit!

Chapter 2

Discerning the Short Game Certainties

In This Chapter

▶ Finding opportunity in tight spots

▶ Tackling different types of terrain

▶ Cycling through your options

▶ Balancing your goals and expectations

▶ Maintaining an empty state of mind

▶ Focusing on specifics of the short swing

*T*he short game can be a very expressive part of golf. What type of shot you hit is completely up to you (unless you hire a controlling caddie), and you determine your short-game style through practice, experience, and your personality: Do you like to hit low, controlled shots, or are you more of the high ball, flamboyant type?

No matter your short-game style, you need to know the difference and relationship between preferences and fundamentals. You can use all your preferences, but you should build your preferences on solid fundamentals — what we like to call short game certainties.

In this chapter, we introduce the dependable fundamentals so that you can start developing your personal preferences. We talk about what you should be thinking in terms of how you view a situation and shot. We teach you, technically speaking, what to look for when you're sizing up the task at hand and considering which of the various types of short-game shots you need in your situation. We also consider your emotional and mental state in terms of goals and expectations. And we make the case that, after you consider all the factors, you should forget everything and swing naturally — play in the subconscious.

Recognizing the Peril and the Opportunity

Part of the joy of golf is that no two shots are alike, no two holes are identical, and the situations you face constantly challenge you. A round of golf contains many little decisions that compose a score.

Some folks say that the holes in a round of golf are like the links of a chain or a string of pearls — one bad link or one bad pearl can render the chain useless and rob the necklace of its value. A round of golf is more than a chain of unique holes, however.

 Think of a round of golf as a shot-by-shot test. The next shot you have to hit is what matters — not the previous shot (whether it was good or bad!) and not the putt that follows. Focus on the shot you're sizing up right now.

Some shots seem easy: a little chip to the hole from three paces off the back of green, for instance, or a chip-and-run up from 10 yards in front. Some shots seem very difficult, like a flop shot from high grass over a yawning bunker to a hole cut close to the edge. You need to recognize both the peril and the opportunity in these shots.

Re-evaluating the easy

The easy shot has plenty of evident opportunity. You feel comfortable over the shot, and no real obstacles stand between your ball and the hole. You should be able to get your ball up and down with relative ease.

 The peril of the easy shot may be minimal, but its peril remains. Be wise enough to take the shot seriously, no matter how easy it seems. Keep your mind focused: The greater the opportunity, the worse the disappointment if you misplay the shot. If nothing else, you can damage your confidence by blowing a good scoring chance!

Dissecting the difficult

In the case of the difficult shot, the peril is usually evident in the form of a bunker, a water hazard, or a narrow green that slopes away from you. (Not to mention the peril involved if you're competing in a match.) If you mis-hit the ball, it could end up in the bunker or the stream, fly across the green into the heavy rough, or run across the green into the woods. Dire consequences lie ahead! If you miss the shot, you may lose the hole to your opponent or even lose the match.

Less evident is the opportunity a difficult shot presents:

- ✔ **Put your practice to work:** A tough shot is an opportunity for you to test your skills and the techniques you've practiced. You have a chance to "show off." And, if you can pull the shot off, it may stun your opponent!

- ✔ **Build confidence:** Making a successful shot from a perilous situation helps you build confidence for the next time you face one. Tough shots present an opportunity to improve and gain experience.

Be aware of the hidden peril that each difficult shot presents. Notice the break of the green, the length of the grass, and any obstacles between your ball and the hole, and know the consequences of hitting the shot too short or too long.

Viewing the Variables: Terrain and Conditions

Before you can decide what shot to play and how to play it, you need to make a full and honest assessment of the situation. You should pay attention to a number of variables when you consider your strategy, decide on a shot, and execute it.

The following sections cover some of the factors that the "computer of your mind" has to process when preparing for a shot. You factor some of these variables automatically or subconsciously with your instinctive awareness of your environment, but you should know that all the factors play a role in affecting your short game.

Accounting for the obvious

Outside of putting, where the surface of the green is typically uniform and the terrain subtle, your short-game shots become more complicated due to varying terrain and other variables, including:

- ✔ **The immediate lie:** What's the length of the grass? Is your ball lying flat on the ground? Or is it in a divot or a depression? Is the ball lying on an uphill, downhill, or sidehill lie?

- ✔ **Obstacles:** Do you have to maneuver around trees and bushes? Do you have to hit the ball over water or a bunker?

Sure, sometimes you can chip a ball from short grass off a flat lie to an unguarded green. But sometimes you have to pitch a ball off the side of a hill from deep rough and fly it over a bunker.

Much of the time, the mere fact that you need to play a short-game shot (chipping, pitching, or a bunker shot in this case) means that you missed the green with your approach shot, and missing the green almost always brings challenges — uphill, downhill, and side-hill slopes, bunkers, longer grass, bushes, and trees — into play.

Shot variables demand your attention. Always take them into account when you analyze your situation, plan your strategy, and visualize the shot you're about to hit.

Sensing the subtleties

In addition to obvious variables, you face subtle factors on the course that can affect the flight of the ball, its direction, and distance it travels. You may be so caught up in your yardage, hazards between you and the hole, and the target that you forget to consider how the more subtle conditions can affect your shot:

- ✔ **Grass variations:** If the grass is longer, the direction the grass grows, for instance, affects your ball flight. Does the grass lean in the same direction as you intend to hit the ball, or is it growing against you? Grass growing against you fights your club as it passes through. Is the grass tangled? Is it wet? Is the ball sitting up in the grass near the tips of the blades or has it nestled down in?

- ✔ **Firmness of the ground:** The ground may be soft or muddy due to rain, which can slow your ball when it lands. Or the ground may be hard and dry, which propels your ball forward faster when it hits the ground. Dry ground also affects ball-striking, because a swing that brings the clubhead down too far behind the ball can bounce off hard ground and cause the blade to mis-hit the ball or even completely miss it.

- ✔ **Wind:** Are you hitting a shot with the wind blowing behind you? Is the wind blowing in your face? Maybe the wind is blowing from one side to another, which pushes the ball offline after it leaves the clubface. You know how the wind affects a high-flying, long drive from the tee, but your high-flying wedge shot, although it travels a shorter distance, spends a lot of time in the air and is therefore susceptible to the breeze. Check out the flag on the green. Is it dangling or whipping?

✔ **Lay of the land:** On some occasions, you may find yourself hitting a chip or a pitch uphill to an elevated green. Sometimes you can't see the hole or the green if the elevation is severe enough. And sometimes, especially on mountain courses, you may have to hit shots down to a green from an elevated position or a downhill lie. The lay of the land and where the ball lies in relation to your feet can force you to change your stance and, in some cases, affect your club selection. The ball reacts differently when coming off an uphill, downhill, or side-hill lie than it does from a flat position.

You should take all variables, even subtle ones, into account before you play a short-game shot.

Understanding Your Options

After you recognize the peril and the opportunity of certain shots and consider the variables that affect the short game, consider your options. All the information you gather (by reading the previous sections in this chapter) should help you decide how you want to play the shot — what style of shot the situations calls for and what style of shot you're comfortable playing — and why.

With each swing, you want to play the type of shot that gives you the most confidence and in turn the highest percentage of success.

Your options, when it comes to the short game, are typically a chip, pitch, bunker shot, putt, or flop, along with a handful of less-common specialty shots (which we outline in Chapter 10). But the options don't end there. You can play your many shot options with a variety of clubs. As we cover in more detail in Chapter 3, you normally play short-game shots with a lob, sand, gap, or pitching wedge; a 9-, 8-, or 7-iron; or a putter.

You use these clubs because of the high lofts they provide, which make the ball travel a short distance. Highly lofted clubs are also easier to hit because they lift the ball off the turf and propel it forward.

You use your putter for the shortest shots because it offers no loft (or sometimes a tiny fraction of loft). Of the short irons and wedges, the 7-iron is the least lofted; it propels the ball the farthest on the lowest trajectory. Working up, each short iron produces more loft, less distance, and a higher trajectory.

Weighing Your Goals and Expectations

Setting goals and expectations is important for players who take the game seriously, but you need to set attainable goals and realistic expectations. If you're unsure of the difference between the two, check out the following list:

- ✓ **Goals:** Your short-game goals can be lofty. You may want to make more birdies, which means you want to one-putt more often. That goal means you have to hit the ball closer to the hole consistently. Sometimes you achieve that goal, sometimes you fall short of the cup. But lofty goals often translate into hard work.

- ✓ **Expectations:** An expectation is something that you want to make happen all the time. For the average player, a good expectation is to make more pars or to improve your short game so that when you miss greens with your approach shots, you can occasionally save par or at least minimize the strokes needed to complete the hole.

Goals are important, but achieving reasonable expectations for each short-game situation builds the confidence necessary to strive for the goals. If your expectations are too high, you may be constantly disappointed, which wrecks your self-image and confidence. In Table 2-1, we outline suggestions for goals and expectations for the average golfer to keep in mind.

Table 2-1   Goals and Expectations for the Short Game

Shot	Expectation	Goal
Chip	Get the ball on the green — anywhere on the green.	Sink the chip or get the ball close enough to the hole to need only one putt.
Pitch	Get the ball on the green — anywhere on the green.	Get the ball close enough to the hole to need only one putt.
Bunker Shot	Get the ball out of the bunker in one shot.	Get the ball onto the green and as close to the hole as possible.
Putt	Use only two putts, and never more than three.	One-putt from time to time and never use more than two.

Work on your short game enough so that getting the ball on the green with one shot and then hitting no more that two-putts is a reasonable expectation. If you consistently meet your expectations, holing a chip shot or hitting the ball close to the hole with one shot and needing only one putt becomes an attainable goal.

You can break down your goals and expectations depending on your distance from the pin. If you stand 50 yards away, your realistic goal may be to get the ball into the hole in three shots. But the closer your ball is to the green, the more you can realistically heighten your goals and expectations. For example, when faced with a short chip from just off the green, you may expect to get the ball into the hole in two strokes — a chip and one putt. (When you line up a short chip or short pitch shot, draw a mental five-foot circle around the hole.)

Short game goals and expectations can also change as you make your way toward the hole. If you stand 50 yards away, and your goal is to get the ball into the hole in three shots, flubbing your first shot into the bunker costs you big time. Being in a bunker changes your expectations. You may make it your goal to hit it out of the bunker and close enough to the hole to one-putt to keep on pace with your original plan, but it isn't a realistic expectation. A reasonable expectation is to hit your bunker shot and two-putt. Make sure you minimize your mistakes.

It seems simple, but breaking down the short game by setting goals and expectations illustrates why the short game is the best place to save strokes, and the best way to improve your scores is to aspire to improve your short game. You have to get more precise with your short game and eliminate costly mistakes caused by unrealistic expectations.

You can expect to land a ball onto the fairway far more often than you can expect to drop a shot within 10 feet of the cup from 50 yards. You can expect to hit the ball onto the green more often than you can expect to hit the ball close to the hole. You can expect to two-putt more often than you one-putt. Your goals may be to hit fairways, hit greens in regulation, and hit the ball close to the hole and one-putt. But accomplishing reasonable expectations helps you build confidence and go a little easier on your psyche.

Playing in the Subconscious

The only thing you should think about during a swing is the target. After you perform all your analysis and consider the conditions, the variables, the perils, the opportunity, the percentages, the options, the statistics, and your goals for the shot, all your focus should be on the target.

The game of golf, whether you're hitting a driver or a 75-yard sand wedge, is best played subconsciously. Your conscious mind is where you develop your skills and technique and analyze the situation, but after the preliminary practice and thoughts, you want to turn your mind off and make the shot subconsciously.

Basically, you want to play like you're Forrest Gump — like you don't even know what the heck is going on! Do you think he over-analyzed a ping-pong shot or a long run for a touchdown? Don't think so. You get too discombobulated if you play in the conscious mind. The golf swing is complicated, and the variables are many.

Different people use different techniques to turn their minds off when the time comes to play the shot. Some folks use breathing techniques. Some use a repeating preshot routine, and others take a practice swing to relieve tension and reassure themselves about how they want to hit the shot. And some golfers choose to become very focused on the target. (We cover these mental aspects of the short game and others in Chapter 12.)

The fundamental technique to quiet your mind during the swing that can serve you well in the long term is to build confidence through practice, which allows you to swing the club consistently and purposefully as opposed to a making a mechanical move toward the ball. You've hit the shot before countless times, you know how to do it, you know how it feels; now let your body and sporting instincts take over.

Zeroing In On the Target Line

The object of golf is to propel the ball — via a putt, chip, pitch, or full shot — toward the hole. When the ball sits on a tee or lies at rest in the rough, fairway, or on the green, the hole is often the target. Sometimes, such as on par-5s or dogleg par 4s, or when the hole is tucked in a difficult spot on the green, you strategically aim at an area away from the hole.

According to simple physics, the shortest distance between two points is a straight line — in this case, the target line. The direction and distance between the ball and the target (which is usually the hole) is the *target line*. It extends from the ball to your target.

(Actually, the target line should extend back through the ball and on to infinity.) The better you can visualize this imaginary line, the better chance you have of aiming properly and executing your shot with accuracy.

Visualizing the target line

We've known golfers to use all sorts of techniques to visualize the target line. The key is to pick a visualization method, any method, and get into the habit of employing it each and every time. You want to visualize the line so that you can draw your club back straight along the line. At the climax of your backswing, you swing the club forward, through the ball, and along the target line after contact.

The target line should extend 12 to 17 inches past the hole so that your putts are certain to reach the hole and not stop short.

The simplest way to help clearly "see" the target line is to stand behind the ball and position it directly between you and the target. Look at the ball and up the target line toward the target and draw yourself a mental line.

For some extra mental reinforcement, some folks advocate picturing the target line as a blazing line of fire or dramatizing it as a trench dug in the ground. Some take their club and point it at the target as part of their pre-shot routine.

Standing close to the target line

The object of the short game is accuracy, and to be accurate you have to get the club as close to the target line as you can. The farther you step away from your line, the more your swing and the clubhead begin to go around your body, which adds more power through centrifugal force. The longer the shot, the farther you have to step from the line. Thusly, the longer irons, like the 3-, 4-, 5-, and 6-irons, have longer shafts for more torque.

When your choice of iron gets shorter, and your swing becomes more vertical, you need to step closer to the line. Not to worry: Short shots aren't about power.

The fundamental act of propelling the ball forward in a straight fashion is easier when you take the clubhead straight back and straight through. Think of playing horseshoes — you stand right on the target line and even face the target when tossing the shoe. Stand close to the line, and the swing becomes more vertical and straighter on that line.

Grasping the Importance of Feel

Hold your club with a normal grip — the same one you use to hit full shots. Grip pressure on short game shots should always be soft. Hold the club lightly in your fingers. You may find it difficult to have a good short game if you choke the heck out of the club.

Loosening your grip helps you feel the weight of the clubhead, because your fingers are more susceptible to the touch. You want to feel the weight of the club to improve your clubhead awareness. If you feel the clubhead, you can understand the mechanics of the swing, and in the short game, being aware of your swing leads to confident and controlled strokes. Your distance control improves, and you can experiment with different clubs and different shots knowing that as long as you can feel the clubface, you can hit any type of shot.

Feel is important. Judging your distance and direction is an easier task if you have an awareness of the face through *soft hands* — meaning light grip pressure on the club.

Obeying the Captain: Allowing Your Front Hand to Lead

In all short-game shots, the face of the club needs to be square and straight to the target. If the face stays straight and contacts the ball straight, the ball can't go anywhere but straight.

What controls the face of the club? In chipping, pitching, putting, bunker shots, and in every other short-game variation imaginable, the hands control the face. More precisely, your non-dominant hand controls the face: If you're a right-handed golfer, the left hand controls the face. (Vice-versa if you're left-handed.) The back hand is only a guide — a supporter of the lead hand, the captain of the ship.

If you have trouble getting the feel for letting your front hand lead the swing, go to the practice tee and hit some chip shots with a 7-iron with your back hand firmly stuck in your pocket. You'll begin to see how the back hand is almost superfluous in the swing.

Centering on Ball Position

The average player should maintain a ball position in the center of the stance for normal short-game play. With as many variables as you face when it comes to a short shot — distance, speed of the green, loft of the clubface, length of the club, hazards, terrain, and wind, to name a few — keeping the ball in the center of your stance helps simplify and standardize at least one part of your technique.

You need to move the ball up or back in your stance in some extreme situations caused by the terrain and wind, and we address those situations in Part III.

Ben Hogan's real secret

The great American player Ben Hogan, who won every major championship and prided himself on practice and the search for perfection, was often asked what his "secret" was. Hogan is now deceased, but a number of people claim to know what Hogan's secret was. The truth is debatable, but Hogan did offer those close to him one piece of advice that people rarely talk about and that certainly qualifies as a useful Hogan secret.

From time to time, as many people do, Hogan would awake in the morning for an early starting time with swollen or puffy hands. Hands in that condition are certainly a detriment to the short game, which requires touch and feel.

Whether you swell up because of arthritis or perhaps a bit too much imbibing the night before a round, you may try the same, simple remedy Hogan used: a pint of ginger ale, which reduces the swelling, before a morning round!

Chapter 3

Gearing Up for the Short Game

· ·

In This Chapter

▶ Celebrating your wealth of wedges

▶ Knowing what wedges are right for you

▶ Courting your putter-mate

▶ Browsing through the many different putter types

▶ Giving your clubs your tender love and care

· ·

*Y*ou play golf at various lengths, over tumbling terrain or on table-flat land, on grass of different lengths, and in weather that varies from calm and warm to windy and cool. In addition to these variables, you play the game with clubs of different lengths and degrees of loft! Plus you can add in all the models and styles of putters now offered in golf shops, each touted as the latest big thing.

The old saying, when you need an excuse for a poorly struck a golf shot, is to "blame the carpenter, not the tools!" Nonetheless, you often see golfers who hit poor shots examine the blades of their irons as if somehow they'd broken in mid-swing or were responsible for the misfortune. That's okay as an ego-defense mechanism, but choosing the right club and, in this case, the right type of club can help you hit better, more precise shots. If nothing else, choosing the right club removes a variable from the golf shot for you to ponder when you're wondering what you did wrong (or right!) when the ball comes back to earth.

Some players carry more wedges than woods, which creates many situations when they must wonder — which wedge when? And other players (or perhaps the same players, for the truly experimental) may switch from putter to putter in an attempt to find the magic one that sinks every putt for them. This chapter can help you get your gear straight, so that you can stick it in your bag and forget about it.

Going Short-Game Clubbing

The rules of golf dictate that you can only carry 14 clubs in your bag during a round. The typical set you buy from a retailer consists of three woods and nine irons (including two wedges). Throw in the requisite putter that players often purchase separately, and you're up to 13 of your 14-club limit.

But no rule states which 14 clubs you can or should carry. And just because certain clubs come in a set doesn't mean you can't mix and match to customize your golf bag with clubs you see fit to carry. Check out Table 3-1 for a rundown of the more common clubs and their typical lofts.

Table 3-1	What's in Your Bag?
Club	*Loft*
Driver	8.5 to 11.5 degrees
3-wood	16 degrees
5-wood	21 degrees
3-iron	22 degrees
4-iron	25 degrees
5-iron	28 degrees
6-iron	32 degrees
7-iron	36 degrees
8-iron	40 degrees
9-iron	44 degrees
Pitching wedge	45 to 50 degrees
Gap wedge	50 to 54 degrees
Sand wedge	54 to 56 degrees
Lob wedge	58 or 60 degrees

What you don't see in Table 3-1 is a column listing average distances you can expect to get from each club. We know that many books on the subject at hand include such information. But we see things a little different. We're wary of listing average yardage for clubs and especially of assigning lengths between men and women. We don't want to focus on the averages too much because each player is an individual and very different.

Assigning "average distances" can make folks feel like something's wrong with their game if they don't meet the average. You shouldn't try to measure up to some predetermined "average." Whatever club works for you from a distance is fine. If you want to take a snap shot of where your game is at in terms of distances, head to the range and work your way through your bag of clubs.

Sorting Through the Short Sticks

Short game equipment runs the gamut from irons and wedges to putters. And a key consideration is the loft of each club (see Table 3-1). *Loft* refers to the angle of the clubface. A steeper face angle (more degrees of loft) means more lift when you strike the ball. But the loft of each club actually affects two important aspects of the short-game shot:

- ✔ How far the ball travels
- ✔ How high the ball travels

Irons range from the 1-iron up to the 9-iron and from a lob wedge to a pitching wedge, and you choose what club to hit depending on how far and how high you want to hit the ball. The 1-iron, in theory, provides the lowest and longest flight path, and a lob wedge (60 degrees) or sand wedge provide the highest and shortest trip. (Very few average golfers ever carry a 1- or 2-iron, because it takes great skill to hit these low-lofted clubs consistently well.)

Irons perform differently for every player, but you can assume about a 15-yard difference in length as you work your way up the iron scale. A well struck 8-iron should make the ball fly 15 yards farther than a similarly struck 9-iron, and so forth.

Unlike the standard variances in the angle of the blade in irons, individual wedges come in many different degrees of loft, and those degrees allow for much more precise distance than the 15 yards between the irons.

You can find wedges with blades that feature 45 degrees of loft all the way up to 62 degrees — and everything in between (see Figure 3-1). You can buy a wedge or have one custom made at almost any launch angle you prefer.

Figure 3-1: Wedges typically range in launch angle from 48 to 60 degrees.

Pumping irons

Wedges aren't the only "short irons." The 7-, 8-, and 9-irons are also among the family of short irons. How and when you use these clubs is a matter of preference, but fundamentally speaking, you typically use a 7- or 8-iron to chip (see Chapter 4) and the 9-iron and pitching wedge for pitches with higher trajectory and shorter distance (see Chapter 5), along with their normal full-swing uses of course.

Weighing wedges

Before golf equipment makers starting adding varied wedges, they produced only pitching wedges (PW) and sand wedges (SW) with every set of irons they made. Equipment makers and players never thought about offering or carrying wedges with varied degrees of angle and loft.

But as players became increasingly skilled and golf club technology improved, player demand, plus the opportunity for more product and profit, caused golf club manufacturers to create more clubs with varying degrees of loft. Now *wedges* is a generic term.

In the following sections, we provide you with some background information on four of the more common wedges, and in the "Deciding which clubs to use" section later in this chapter, we help you make some decisions about what to stick in your bag.

Pitching wedge

A typical male player of average skill can expect to hit a pitching wedge 90 to 110 yards at the longest (or about 10 yards shorter for the typical female player of average skill), but you can, of course, shorten your swing to hit much shorter shots when necessary.

The pitching wedge, the next step beyond a 9-iron, is typically lofted between 45 and 50 degrees. The club also has a *bounce,* or flange, that runs across the bottom of the blade to give it weight. Because the face is angled so much, the club has more room on the bottom edge for a flange.

The pitching wedge should produce a high, arching shot. High wedge shots roll forward a very short distance after they hit the green and will sometimes, especially when hit with high swing speeds and by skilled players, spin back from the spot upon which they land if they hit the green with enough backspin (see Chapter 5 for pitching mechanics).

The club produces *backspin* when the ball rides up the clubface. The grooves in the wedge help to impart backspin as the ball stays on the face longer, and the ball stays on the face longer when the angle of attack is steeper — more vertical and striking down on the ball. As for club speed, you want to maximize the time that the ball spends riding up the face when you want to create maximum backspin. A slower but consistent speed with the club at the correct angle is the best way for most golfers to produce backspin.

A quick release of the hands increases the speed of the club and can maximize backspin; however, you should use this motion only for certain situations.

Sand wedge

You use the sand wedge, in its most literal purpose, to extract the golf ball from sand bunkers (see Chapter 6). But many golfers use the sand wedge just as they use any lofted wedge, from greenside rough or even the fairway.

Enough practice with the sand wedge can give you confidence with it from anywhere, but practicality and simplicity dictate limiting its use. Better to choose a club of appropriate loft for the yardage needed than to try to force or muscle a sand wedge.

The sand wedge has a very short shaft and is usually the heaviest of the short irons, weighing nearly 40 ounces. Sand wedges have a typical loft angle of 54 to 56 degrees. The blade of a sand wedge splashes through the sand and through grassy lies, sending the ball a short distance on a high trajectory.

Lob wedge

Lob wedges have extremely angled blades and typical lofts of 58 or 60 degrees. (Some touring professionals actually have wedges with more loft than that!) Striking the ball with this club causes it to "lob" up high, travel only a short distance, and fall steeply onto the target.

A lob wedge comes in handy when you need to hit a high shot that travels a short distance and stops quickly, such as when you're greenside and you have a bunker between your ball and the hole and you don't see enough room on the green for the ball to roll to the hole.

You may want to leave the lob wedge to advanced or highly skilled players unless you have the time to practice with one and really get to know it. The margin for error (and the margin of success) with a lob wedge is very small, because the face angle is severe and because the ball doesn't roll much after it lands. The flop shot, which we describe in Chapter 11, often requires a lob wedge.

If you decide to add a lob wedge to your golf bag — and to your golf game — consider doing so only after you feel comfortable with your pitching wedge and the other short irons.

Most golf retailers allow you to hit the various lob wedges they sell into a practice net or on a range. Just as with choosing any club, hit some of them until you find one that looks good, feels good, and gives you the results you like — a confident, effective shot.

Gap wedge

Because pitching wedges typically have a loft from 45 to 50 degrees and sand and lob wedges go from 54 to 60, the gap wedge poetically fills the "gap" in loft. Again, it all depends on which wedges you carry, and what loft they offer, but if you feel the need to have a short iron with a loft in between those that you already have, you can select a gap wedge to bridge that distance.

You have to be an excellent short game player with terrific awareness of how far and high you hit the ball to require wedges with "in-between" lofts. Work hard enough on your short game and you can gain the feel, touch, and imaginative shot making that make a gap wedge useful to you.

Golf retail shops and your golf club's PGA professional can show you gap wedges with varying degrees of loft. After you run the numbers and figure out what degree of loft you want your wedge to be, choosing one is a matter of preference and performance.

Necessity was the father of invention

The late Gene Sarazen was one of golf's most beloved and accomplished players. He won 32 PGA tournaments during his competitive career, which took place just as golf started taking hold in America. Sarazen, a World Golf Hall of Fame honoree, was one of the first players to win each of what are now considered golf's "grand slam" of major championships: The Masters Tournament (1935), the U.S. Open Championship (1922 and '32), The British Open Championship (1932), and the PGA Championship (1922, '23, and '33.) But Sarazen may never have won the British Open title without a little ingenuity.

The golf courses of England and Scotland, on which the British Opens are held each year, are known for their fearsome pot bunkers. Sarazen, in hopes of improving his chances to escape effectively from these menacing craters, invented the sand wedge in 1931 and used it to win his British Open title at Sandwich, England in the summer of 1932.

Sarazen's crafty little tool was more than a strategic curiosity — it became one of the most revolutionary pieces of golf equipment in the history of the game! Widespread use of the sand wedge dropped average scores dramatically, brought about the remodeling of golf courses, and forced golf course architects to reconsider how they constructed bunker complexes and greens.

Average scores dropped because players became more proficient at extracting their golf balls from bunkers and began doing so with much better accuracy. Golf course architects were able to build more bunkers into new golf courses and use them in an expressive fashion. Southern Dunes Golf Club, outside Orlando, for instance, has over 180 bunkers on the course! These stylish, sandy touches, designed by Steve Smyers, provide beautiful contrast to the eye and also help frame the holes. Before the sand wedge, a golf course like Southern Dunes would have been unplayable!

Deciding which clubs to use

Now that you know about the various options you have available, you may be dizzy from too much information. But don't worry; we can simplify things.

Average players on down to about the 8-handicap players have the ability to play golf only a certain number of times in a given week. When you watch The Golf Channel or various tournaments and you think about using the same equipment as the Tour players, remember that they're experts who have every measurement of their equipment taken to tailor specifically to their bodies and swing types. The best players in the world know the huge difference between hitting a 56-degree club and a 52-degree club. An average player with a 22-handicap just isn't skilled enough to know the difference between these degrees.

Only hours and hours of practice and frequent play can help you develop enough clubface awareness to sense the difference between a few degrees of loft based on feel and ball flight.

And when you practice or play golf a limited number of times per week, you use the same set of golf clubs. You store the clubs in the trunk of your car or maybe in the bag room at the golf club. The clubs of an average player don't change. You likely either play at your golf club or you jump around the local area to different tracks at resorts or clubs. The conditions for different courses are always different. The grass is different, the sand is different, the length of the course is different — but you play with the same set of golf clubs.

What do the guys on the PGA Tour or the women on the LPGA Tour do? They may change wedges every week depending on the conditions of the upcoming course. For instance, when they go to Miami for a yearly stop, they know what the sand is like, and they may want a wedge with a certain degree of loft to deal with the fluffy beach sand or the tangled Bermuda grass. Maybe later in the season in Michigan, where the sand may be firmer and the Bentgrass a bit thicker, they take a wedge with less bounce or loft. Professional golfers may change each week to wedges of the same brand but with different lofts.

But should you do that? No way. Don't even think of it!

Use whatever wedge you feel most comfortable with everywhere you play golf. You likely don't have the luxury of the sort of club changes the pros make, and you don't want to introduce fruitless variables into your game. Getting to know your clubs intimately so that you have an idea of what the ball does when it leaves the clubface, how high it flies, and how far it rolls allows you to play in the subconscious. When you play in the subconscious, you have a much better chance of effective, confident wedge play.

Calling All Putters Great and Small

More than any club in your bag, the type of putter you use is a personal choice. Although you see many brands of drivers and irons available on the market, most manufacturers turn out woods and irons that all have essentially the same look, shape, and specifications. Putters, however, come in all shapes, sizes, styles, weights, and lengths.

Putters are designed to put a good, straight roll on the ball, and when it comes to physics, they essentially accomplish that when the face strikes the ball. But the way you grip them, their length, how heavy they are, the manner in which you swing them, and the way they look vary wildly. Some putters seem expressive, some look classic, some are very futuristic, and some are very plain. Some even sport school colors or personalized logos.

 You can splurge on an expensive putter, or you can settle on one for as little as $10. But no matter if it looks like a spaceship or a mallet, choose the putter that works best for you. But, if you're new to the game, using a putter with a line indicator on the top may make aiming down the target line easier for you.

The traditional putter

The earliest putters in golf's modern era (say, starting in the 1960s) were all very similar. They had comparable lengths, looks, styles, and weights. The shaft was upright and attached to the *hosel,* which connects the near end of the putterhead. The putterhead was typically a *blade,* which is to say the putter looked very much like any of the irons, only with a steep face designed to roll the ball on the ground.

The traditional putter is the most popular, conventional type of putter and is widely used among average players and touring professionals alike. These putters become the shortest club in your bag — rivaled only by the lob wedge. Traditional putters are steel-shafted, and their putterheads can be made of any number of materials, including wood, aluminum, copper, and stainless steel. They can be metallic and unfinished in appearance, or they can look like smooth, shiny metal. Sometimes they come painted, and sometimes they have colored or non-colored materials inserted into the sweet spot of the face to help the player feel the ball make contact and set the ball rolling properly.

Blade putters

Golf's original *blade putter* is still in wide use, although, in most cases, manufacturers have thickened and widened the blade and put a line across the top to aid in alignment. Phil Mickelson, playing on the PGA Tour, uses a putter similar to the original blade putter —

very minimalist. Tiger Woods, on the other hand, uses a traditional-style blade putter that he has modified (or modernized) and milled to be thicker, heavier, and sometimes perimeter weighted.

"Feel players," who rely on honing their touch and feeling the ball come off the putterhead, favor blade putters. If you believe putting is more poetry than science, and you like to feel as if you're finessing the ball into the hole rather than simply lining up and banging it in, you're a touch and feel person, and the blade may be for you.

Mallet putters

Putters of traditional length may not always be blade putters. Mallet-shaped putters, and modernized variations of them (see Figure 3-2), have become popular.

Figure 3-2: Hitting the green with a traditional mallet putter.

Like blade putters, mallet putters spring from the earliest golf clubs, but instead of being modeled after the irons, mallet putters closely resemble woods. The putterhead is rounded in the back and has some heft behind the face. Imagine a tiny 5-wood and you essentially picture a mallet putter.

The modernized versions of the mallet putter are produced in various shapes, and many of them use various measures to balance the putter — sometimes resulting in a futuristic appearance. The ball "pops" stronger off a mallet putter than it does off a blade putter because of the extra weight behind the blade. With larger putterheads, club makers have more flexibility in moving around the club's center of gravity.

A mallet putter has some heft to the blade. If you're a player who likes to get some "hop" on the ball when putting it toward the hole, and if your approach to putting is akin to lining things up and shooting, try a mallet putter.

The long putter

The long putter has been a subject of controversy from the very beginning of its existence. Instead of being the shortest club in the bag, the "broom handle" or "polecat" long putter is the longest club in the bag — longer even than the driver! (See Figure 3-3 for a glimpse at its length.)

Form follows function, the end justifies the means, and demand creates supply. So what's the purpose of the long putter? Golfers have various reasons for preferring the long putter, ranging from steadying their nerves to taking stress off their backs.

Some players turn to the long putter because they can putt — and practice putting — without having to bend over. The upright position puts less strain on the back, which appeals to older golfers with back concerns.

Other players turn to the long putter because they struggle with their nerves — especially over short putts. Players who are too "wristy" with their putting stroke or suffer from the yips find that the grip needed to swing the long putter stabilizes their wrists and arms and allows them to swing the putter in a pendulum fashion. You can't really swing the long putter without letting it flow freely, and that free motion eliminates pulled or pushed putts.

Because the long putter is so tall, the most popular way to grip it is to anchor the top, butt-end of the putter to your chest with your left hand (for righties) and then lightly grip the putter farther down below with the right hand (see Figure 3-3). The weight of the putterhead can swing almost freely and directly back and forth on the line of the putt, almost like the pendulum on a grandfather clock. Your shoulders have a difficult time turning, and you don't provide a chance for your wrists, elbows, or lower body to affect the stroke and the swing path of the blade.

Figure 3-3: Long putters keep your shoulders from turning and allow the putterhead to swing along the putting line in a pendulum fashion.

Because the long putter is legal and accepted by golf's governing bodies, the USGA (in the United States) and the R&A (the rest of the world), the real question isn't whether they create an unfair advantage (see the "Considering the long-debated controversy" sidebar), but rather are they sensible and to *your* advantage to use? The long putter is definitely worth a try for older players or players who suffer from the yips or nervous maladies.

Rocco Mediate was the first player to win on the PGA Tour with the long putter when he won at Doral. It was a tender back that drove Mediate to the long putter, and he later stated that if the long putter were really an easier and better way to putt, everyone on tour would use it. As of now, only a handful of players in the top 500 in the world employ it. Some of the touring professionals are simply wary of the stigma of stocking such an unconventional putter, because others may view it as a concession to weakness. Others, of course, are just so nimble and skilled that they don't need to use the long putter.

Considering the long-debated controversy

The controversy about the long putter being a fair piece of golf equipment continues, and some have called for the United States Golf Association (USGA) to ban it from tournament play. Players and critics often site two reasons:

✔ **Unusual equipment:** Some see it as unusual equipment because of its unconventional design and how far removed it is from the intended spirit of putting. After all, golfers can't putt croquet-style by swinging a putter between their legs, nor can they use the putter like a pool cue, so why should they be able to simplify their putting stroke to the degree that most of the challenge and skill is removed? Anchoring part of the club to your body, some argue, is unfair and defies the spirit of the golf stroke.

✔ **Extra relief:** Another reason that the USGA regularly considers banning the long putter is because it can help in the application of a completely unrelated rule. When taking relief from an unplayable lie, hazard, ground under repair, or other situation from which relief is allowed, players are granted, depending on the situation, one or two club-lengths of relief (no nearer the hole). Any player who carries a long putter (whether he actually putts with it or not) can use it to measure off two club-lengths of relief, which is an advantage over anyone else in the field who doesn't carry the long putter. (Most drivers, however, are roughly within an inch or two in length.)

The belly putter

The belly putter is golf's latest, greatest idea — a compromise between the advantage of the long putter and the practicality of the traditional putter. The belly putter is longer than the traditional putter and shorter than the long putter.

You grip the belly putter, just as you may imagine by the image the name conjures up, by anchoring the top, butt end of the club, literally, into your belly (see Figure 3-4). By anchoring the putter in your belly, the motion of the stroke becomes simpler and more reliable — a pendulum effect, just as with the long putter.

Vijay Singh, the man who, in 2004, unseated Tiger Woods as the world's top-ranked player, popularized the belly putter more than any other player. Ironically, when Singh took the top ranking from Woods, he'd recently switched back from a long spell with belly putter to a traditional putter. (Even one of the top golfers in the world over-analyzes sometimes!)

Figure 3-4: The belly putter encourages a reliable pendulum putting motion, which even entices younger golfers.

Finding the Putter That Fits You

In the wide world of putters, choosing the flatstick that best suits you can be as daunting as courting a spouse. Face it: You have to spend about as much time with your putter as you do your spouse if you want to get better. You use it for more strokes than any other club in your bag, so it must be dependable — through the good times and the bad. Confidence is a hugely important aspect of your putting game, and you must have total confidence that the putter in your hand is capable of getting the job done. It's not how the putter feels in your hand; it's how it feels in your stomach!

We know of a fellow who had three putters in his bag that he rotated through, even during the round. He couldn't understand why his putting failed him on a regular basis. Every time he missed a putt he felt he should have made, he switched putters. In total frustration, he finally took all the putters out of his bag and bought the most expensive putter he could find at his local golf shop. Now, in his mind, he'd eliminated all the variables that hampered his putting performance. In his mind, because he bought an expensive name brand putter, he could no longer blame the putter. This caused him to focus on the weaknesses in his technique and, perhaps more important, allowed him to putt with more confidence. His putting improved immediately.

Most people don't choose a putter based on the expense, but as the story illustrates, you should choose a putter that you're comfortable with and that you can count on. Commit and simplify.

 But how to choose among the spectrum of bold mallets, shiny blades, and snazzy gunmetal putters? Try and try again. Many golf-specific retail shops have an artificial putting surface, and the larger ones may even have a real grass outdoor practice green. The golf shop at your local public golf course or country club, often referred to as a "green grass shop," is ideal, because you can grab a handful of putters and spend an afternoon on the practice green trying each of them out. What should you look for during your practice sessions with probable putting mates? Go through the following points:

- Have a look-see at the putters and decide which ones fit your look and idea of style (operating on the "look good, play good" theory).

- Give each putter a fair shake by making some long and short putts of similar lengths.

- Don't necessarily judge a putter by how many putts you sink. Don't even worry about making the putts — just get a feel for each of the putters and how the ball rolls.

- Hit some putts with your eyes closed to get a feel for the weight of the putter and how it feels when it makes contact with the ball.

 When it comes to the longer, less traditional putters, consider scheduling a putting lesson with your local PGA professional. He or she can show you how to grip and swing each of the putters.

At some facilities, you can arrange to take one or two of the putters onto the golf course for a practice round. What better way to find out how a putter feels in the heat of the action?

 Ultimately, choosing your putter comes down to a combination of physical and psychological factors: how the putter feels and how you feel about it. After you make your decision, run with it and don't look back. The best way to have confidence in your new putter and help it perform well is to spend as much time as possible practicing with it (and as much time as you need choosing it — if you have to live with it, you shouldn't make your choice a quick wedding trip to Vegas).

Showing devotion to your putter

Superstition in sports is a time-honored tradition. Hall of Fame baseball manager Sparky Anderson, for instance, made certain not to step on the chalk baseline every time he left the dugout to make a pitching change. Some professional basketball players make certain to bounce the ball the same number of times before every foul shot. Golf is no exception — especially when it comes to putting. Tales of golfers and their devotion to putters are legendary. Some clean and polish their putters regularly and lovingly. Some golfers cuddle with their putters in bed. And at the other end of the spectrum, some golfers punish their putters by removing them from the bag and banishing them to the darkness of the car trunk. One tale speaks of a golfer that tied his putter to the back bumper of his car, dragging it for miles at a high speed to teach it a lesson. Of course, more than one player has deep-sixed a putter in a greenside pond or broken it over a knee during a fit of rage.

Some of the great players in the history of golf have had long, warm relationships with their putters. Robert Tyre Jones Jr., possibly the greatest amateur ever (he's the only player to win the "grand slam" of the U.S. and British Amateur and both Open Championships in the same year), had a very successful partnership with his putter "Calamity Jane." South African Gary Player was long loyal to his dull, black, blade putter. Player bought the putter for only a few yen while in Tokyo in 1961, but he used it to win over 100 tournaments — including each of the four modern major championships.

Jack Nicklaus made putters famous by winning major championships. He won with a putter he named "White Fang" and, in 1986, a startling looking putter called "Response" that had a massive black putterhead — one of the largest ever made! Sales of the Response soared after Jack's win.

Scott Hoch surely helped sales of his futuristic putter by winning the PGA Tour event at Doral with it, despite the fact that he laughed about the bizarre appearance of the putterhead by saying that it looked like a "potato masher!"

Caring for Your Putter

Your putter and driver are the clubs that receive most of your attention — the stars of your team, if you will. If your driver is like a baseball team's home run slugger, your putter is like an ace closer. The driver gets attention for belting the ball a long way, but the putter comes in and does the precision work to close out the hole or save par. So you should give your putter the "star treatment."

Handle with care

Missed putts, especially short ones, can cause a lot of frustration. Do what you can to resist the temptation to take out your anguish on your putter. Tossing, flipping, or ramming your putter back down into your golf bag can damage it, as can the time-honored tradition of bending or breaking it over your knee. Remember, you can no longer use a putter, or any club for that matter, that you bend or alter during play, according to the rules. Too much "putter punishment" may leave you without a putter to finish the round with! (But in case you succumb to temptation as many a golfer has, check out Chapter 10, where we give you some pointers on how to putt when you suddenly find yourself without a putter.)

Cover it up

A putter cover, which slips easily on and off the putterhead during a round, helps protect your putter blade. Putter covers are soft and padded with fluffy insides, which help them serve a dual purpose: They clean and dry your putterhead each time you slide the snug cover back on the putter (helping to ward off rust), and they help prevent nicking and chipping caused by the other irons in the golf bag.

Some covers come with the putter upon purchase, but you can also buy them at golf courses and resorts. They can be nice souvenirs that put a little color and expression into your golf bag!

Give it a home of its own

Some players take the extra precaution of keeping the putter in a separate part of the golf bag or even outside the golf bag. Some newer golf bags have an individual compartment designed to hold just the putter. Some golf bags even have a clip on the outside that secures the putter for easy removal. This spares the putter shaft from all the abrasive action of removing and replacing woods and irons from the bag during the course of a round and from the clanging abuse you or the golf cart can cause.

Keep it clean and dry

As with the rest of your clubs, take measures to keep your putter clean and dry. Sometimes golf club staffers give your clubs a swiping with a towel following a round, but you should give your clubs some special attention from time to time. Make certain you properly clean and polish them. Depending on the design of the putter, water and a mild detergent or soap usually do the job. Be sure to dry the putterhead thoroughly after washing.

Get a grip

You should replace the rubber or leather grips of your woods and irons on a regular basis — how often is a matter of how much use they get and how they stand up to the elements. Give the same attention to your putter when you feel the time is right. Of course, touch is so important when it comes to putting that you may get comfortable with the feel of an old, worn grip, but if the putter grip feels hard and dried out or slippery, you should consider a new grip.

Go to a golf shop and take the time to try out and evaluate the many types, shapes, and sizes of putter grips available, just as you did when choosing your putter. You can find rubber, leather, wrapped, round, paddle, corded, and other types of grips available in all sizes and thickness. Your PGA professional and your own good sense of touch and feel help you choose the grip that best suits you.

Part II

The Long and Short of It: Short Game Technique

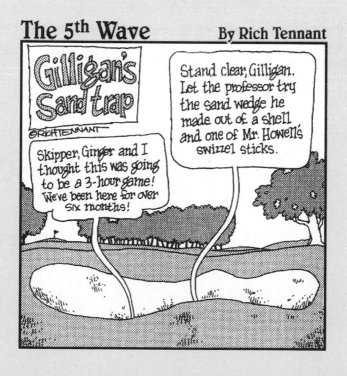

The 5th Wave   By Rich Tennant

Gilligan's Sand trap

Skipper, Ginger and I thought this was going to be a 3-hour game! We've been here for over six months!

Stand clear, Gilligan. Let the professor try the sand wedge he made out of a shell and one of Mr. Howell's swizzel sticks.

In this part . . .

Welcome to the "nuts and bolts" owners manual for you and your short game. We've come to help *you* become a "do-it-yourself" short-game artist. Chipping, pitching, bunker shots, and putting — we explain all the shots right here in Part II. Tuck this book under your arm, grab a 7-iron, and head out to the practice green!

Chapter 4

Chipping Off the Ol' Block

In This Chapter

▶ Leaving your putter in the bag

▶ Using the right tool for the job

▶ Laying out your chipping blueprint

▶ Hitting your chips close

▶ Finding chip-trick magic with the Runyan

A statistic often analyzed and discussed on the PGA Tour is *greens in regulation* (GIR). Hitting a green in regulation means that you hit your ball onto the green in a prescribed number of shots based on the par value for the given hole. Hitting a green in regulation, by definition, leaves a player with two putts to make par, which means you land the green in one shot on a par-3, two shots on a par-4, or three shots on a par-5.

Hitting greens in regulation makes the game of golf much easier. In the case of the average golfer, however, hitting greens in regulation is a goal more than an expectation. You may find your ball on the collar of green or in the rough just off the green. You may have to play from the fairway just in front of the green or maybe a close-cut collection area behind it. So close to GIR glory!

Now is when the chip shot comes in handy. In this chapter, we show you how the chip shot can help you overcome missing greens in regulation and tell you how to play the shot effectively. The chip shot, which may seem like a little, unglamorous type of shot, is the foundation on which you can significantly improve your short game.

Discovering the Chip

Technically and literally speaking, you hit a *chip shot* when you're close to (but off of) the green. When we say close, we're talking within 10 feet of the green.

A bit of comparison is in order: A chip shot is shorter than a pitch shot. As you see in Chapter 5, a pitch shot is more like throwing the ball up in the air — pitching it from farther out. If you're talking yards, you're talking about a pitch. You refer to chip shots in feet. With a chip shot, you literally chip the ball off the old block like you're carving a wood chip. The shot may seem small in that way, but the chip is a hugely important skill to have. It saves you many strokes in the long run and helps offset the reality of missing greens in regulation.

The following are the general characteristics of the chip shot:

- A chipped ball doesn't have much loft.
- The ball pops off the club, making a chipping or flicking sound.
- The ball streaks through the air but not in the arc of a high lob. It flies in a low, tight manner, propelled more forward than up.
- The ball covers only a short distance in the air. It should spend 20 percent of its duration in the air and 80 percent on the ground.

A chip is the best way to keep the ball low, keep it on the ground, and get it rolling as soon as possible. As we advise in Chapter 1, you have a much better chance of getting the ball close to the hole if you roll it as opposed to hitting it through the air. You can lower scores, because judging the distance of a shot rolling on the ground is easier than estimating a shot that flies through the air.

Choosing the Chip over the Putt

A chip shot is the next best thing to putting because of the amount of time the ball spends rolling along the ground (and you don't always have the luxury of putting the ball). Consider using the chip shot when you miss the green with your approach shot and you're almost close enough to putt. Although you face occasions when you can use the putter from off the green (see Chapter 8), you also face plenty of situations when strategically it isn't wise to putt your ball:

- Your ball may lie in longer grass around the green.
- Your ball comes to rest between a bunker and the green.

> ✔ Your ball must travel over a hill before it reaches the green.
>
> ✔ Your ball may be only a few feet off the green, but the hole may be a long way from your ball.

Evaluate your situation. On most courses, fairway grass gives way to an apron of longer grass that circles the green before you get to the fringe of shorter grass. If you have 20 feet between your ball and the hole and you want to try to putt, the chances of your 20-foot putt rolling through the fairway, over the collar, and finally onto the green and close to the hole aren't nearly as good as your chances of chipping it over that grass, landing it on the green, and letting it roll close to the hole.

Some courses, especially in Scotland and Ireland, have the same length of short grass leading to the green, and the ground is very firm, so you can putt the ball if you're more comfortable with that shot. That, however, is a best-case scenario. Chipping is often the best-case scenario for accuracy.

Picking Your Chipping Tool

The club you use to chip the ball determines how the ball flies and rolls. If you're close enough to the hole to use a chip shot, you don't need to loft the ball into the air for a long time, so grab a less-lofted club to play the shot.

As long as you follow the fundamentals of execution (see the "Hitting a Chip Shot" section later in this chapter), what club you use is a matter of preference. But keep in mind that hitting a chip shot with a highly lofted club reduces your chances of getting close to the hole. Getting a less-lofted clubface solidly on the ball at contact is easier, and a less-lofted club creates more roll after the ball lands the green.

Players enjoy the highest percentage of success with a 7- or 8-iron. Those two clubs have less-lofted clubfaces, making them more accurate chipping tools, and they roll the ball nicely. You can use those clubs for every chip, no matter how many feet lay in front of you, by simply taking a longer backswing. If you forced us to pick, we'd say the best club to chip with is a 7-iron. Plus, choosing a 7-iron and sticking with it helps remove one variable from the chip shot — club selection.

Chipping Goals and Expectations

For every golf shot you hit, you should have both goals and expectations for the result. Knowing the difference and how to push and prepare yourself for each shot allows you to start lowering your scores — and your blood pressure. What do you want to accomplish with each chip? What do you consider an acceptable result? A reasonable expectation?

> ✔ **Setting a goal:** Go for the green! An ambitious goal for your chip shots is that you chip every one close enough to the hole to tap-in or need only one putt to finish the hole. Granted, you can hole a putt from anywhere if you get lucky, but a chip shot that results in a nice, comfortable short putt is a great success and should be a goal you aspire to.

> ✔ **Meeting your expectations:** An easily attainable expectation for your chip shots, with reasonable practice, is that you hit the ball onto the green every time. Regardless of how close the ball is to the hole after your chip, you should expect to get the ball onto the green and hit no more than two putts every single time.

Mapping Out a Chip-Shot Strategy

Because a chip shot shouldn't cover much distance through the air, and because you use a less-lofted club like a 7- or 8-iron, you want to run/roll the ball most of the way to the hole. So you have to calculate the length of the shot, the speed of the green, and the direction the ball will roll after it lands. See the shot in your mind before you play it.

The quicker you get the ball onto the ground, the more it can roll to the cup. You should try to roll the ball for about 80 percent of the distance it travels. If your ball rests 20 feet from the hole, and you choose to chip the ball, you should try to land the ball about four feet in front of you to make it roll bout 16 feet.

The ball should pop over the grass between you and the green before rolling out.

Hitting a Chip Shot

Simply put, hitting a chip shot is a matter of physics. The following list breaks it down into a few easy steps. You can use this list as checklist for your setup and your chipping practice, along with Figures 4-1 and 4-2:

1. **Take out your 7-iron.**

2. **Stand close to your target line.**

3. **Keep your weight in the center of your stance.**

4. **Open your front foot and shoulders toward the target so that you can virtually face the hole.**

5. **Grip the club lightly.**

6. **Pick a suitable spot where you want to land the ball.**

7. **Draw the club back low to the ground, keeping your wrists firm and turning by rotating your shoulders**

8. **Keep your legs and lower body still and out of the swing.**

9. **Swing the club back along the target line and then forward through the ball.**

10. **Watch the ball hit the spot and roll toward the hole.**

Taking aim

Your first task is to pick an intermediate spot where you want to land the shot. The ultimate target, of course, is the hole, but first you have to deal with the initial 20 percent of the shot that flies through the air and lands on your target.

You consciously determine the spot that rests 20 percent of the way between you and the hole while you walk up to the shot, evaluate the situation, and read the break of the green. Is the shot uphill? Downhill? Will the ball roll to the left after it lands on the spot? To the right?

The spot you pick must allow for the unevenness and break of the green after the ball hits and rolls. If you think the green will break 10 feet from the right to the left, pick a landing spot 10 feet to the right of the hole as your landing area. (Check out Chapter 7 for tips on reading greens.)

Don't try to curve the chip shot — you want to hit it straight to your landing spot and let gravity and the green naturally roll the ball toward the hole. (Take a look at Figure 4-1 to see how you hit straight toward the target, no matter if you're aiming at the flag or off to one side.)

All you can do is pick a spot and hit it — the rest is up to the green and nature. You can't think about the hole. After you commit to the landing spot, turn off your brain and play in the subconscious. You've done your work! Hit the ball as if it were on a straight railroad directly to the spot.

Figure 4-1: When chipping, the clubface has to swing straight back along the line and straight through.

Setting up your stance

You hit a chip shot by taking a stance that puts you close to your line — close enough so that you can get your eyes almost directly over the target line, as you can see in Figure 4-1a (and see Chapter 2 for more on the target line). If you're close to the target line, you have a better chance of taking the club straight back along the line (see Figure 4-1b) and making it go straight through to the target (see Figure 4-1d).

Your stance is largely a matter of preference (we detail fundamentals and preferences in Chapter 2). What feels good to you? What makes you comfortable? As long as you're comfortable and in balance, you can let the club do all the work.

A preference that may make you feel more comfortable is to slightly open your stance. Opening your stance allows you to see down the target line and may make it easier for you to swing the clubhead at the target. Being comfortable enhances your confidence. If you're right handed, you may want to drop your left foot back a few inches behind your right and point your left toe about 45 degrees out toward the direction of your target (see Figure 4-1). Instead of your feet being parallel and pointing out in front of you, your left foot should angle a bit outward.

Positioning the ball

Keep the ball in the middle of your stance for chip shots (see Figure 4-2a). This makes it simple for you to swing the clubhead along the target line, and the angle of attack at which the clubface comes through the ball holds true. Generally speaking, moving the ball back in your stance makes the ball fly lower (and moving it forward pops it higher), but you needn't move the ball back or forward for standard chip shots, no matter which club you use.

Reviewing weight distribution

When playing a chip shot, put your weight in the center of your stance, right below your backside. This balanced position makes it easier to open yourself to the target — that is, to point your front toe and shoulder a little left or right of where they normally face when you address the ball.

In general, the higher you need the ball to fly, the more weight you should place on your front foot. The more weight you put on your left side (for righties), the more the club swings up rather than back and low to the ground. When a righty plants that left side, the club arch becomes more vertical, and swinging a club vertically makes the descending blow steeper, which makes the ball fly higher.

For most chip shots, you want the ball to fly low and run, so keep your weight in the middle of your stance throughout the swing. You don't really need leg power at all for the shot. Swing around your legs. If you have trouble with a too-active weight shift, hit some practice chips with your feet together to work on your balance or imagine that you're riding a horse and position your legs like you're in the saddle, which keeps them quiet and evenly weighted.

Figure 4-2: Position the ball in the center of your stance, keep steady, and let your left wrist keep the clubface straight to the target.

The chipper of days gone by

Golf club manufacturers used to produce and sell a club called a *chipper*. It looked like a putter, but it had the loft of a 4-iron. Why did it have the loft of a 4-iron? Because in the olden days of Ben Hogan, Sam Snead, and Byron Nelson, players hit chip shots with 4- and 5-irons. The grass was firmer, dryer, and longer then. Golf courses weren't as long and lush. Nelson, for instance, played on burned out, non-irrigated grass in Texas, so he could keep the ball very low without having grassy areas to carry. He also needed to propel the ball forward. In Scotland, course operators didn't irrigate until about 10 years ago. Tiger Woods now plays on lush, long grass, and so do you, in most cases.

Setting your shoulders

Your shoulders will naturally open or angle just left of the target if your stance is open (see Figures 4-1a and 4-2c). You should be close enough to the ball so that you can almost look right over it and right down the target line (so you virtually face the hole).

If you have trouble visualizing this stance, stand in front of full-length mirror. Put a ball down, keep your eyes over your line, and then look up in the mirror and notice where your head position is, where your eyes are in relation to your line, and how your shoulders face slightly toward the target. See how close you are to the line. Imagine a target between you and the mirror, about 10 feet away. Chip a ball to the corner of the bedpost or the dresser. Seeing yourself and how you stand in relation to the ball and the target line gives you a good awareness of your body and the mechanics that go into the chip shot.

Gripping the club

A standard golf grip is fine for the chip shot (see Figure 4-2a). You may feel pressure to get the ball close to the hole, but be aware that pressure can produce tension. So try to resist. Keep a light grip on the club so that you can feel the ball hit the blade. A light grip gives you a better chance of propelling the ball the proper distance. The chip isn't a power shot — you need to focus on touch. Let your hands feel the shot by keeping a light grip.

Making your move

The distance of the shot and the velocity with which you need to swing the club to reach your target landing spot determine how far you take the club back. The chip shot relies on feel, and feel comes with practice. You're not born with feel. You're born with touch, perhaps, and vision.

Swinging the club to hit a chip shot is like drawing back the string on a bow to shoot the arrow (see Figure 4-2b). You must judge how far back you have to draw the club to shoot the ball over the fringe and onto the green, propelling it to the hole.

Tracing the length and shape of the swing

The easiest way to understand the chip swing is to think of it like the hands on a clock. The bottom of your swing is six o'clock. The top, therefore, above your head, is 12 o'clock. If you swing the club back along the target line from a staring point of six o'clock, and your backswing stops at three o'clock, for example, the swing along the target line after you strike the ball shouldn't stop until the nine o'clock position. In chipping, the appropriate times on the hands of the clock of your swing vary depending on the distance you need. (See Figures 4-2b and 4-2d for an illustration.)

Draw the club back low to the ground along the target line and then forward through the ball. Finish the swing pointing at the target, at the same distance that you took the club back. Don't stop when you hit the ball. Keep the club moving with your front wrist leading, which keeps the face on the target line (see Figure 4-2c). Players who stop the club when they hit the ball are left to wonder why the ball didn't make the green. You never see the professionals take a big swing and stop at the ball. They may take a big swing, but the followthrough is just as big after the ball sails away — and with good reason: simple physics!

Talking about speed

If anything, you should slightly accelerate your club through the ball. You can't take the club back at 10 miles per hour and then hit the ball at 5 miles per hour and expect to have success. You can take the club back at 10 miles per hour and swing it through at 10 miles per hour and have a tremendous amount of success. You can even take the club back at 10 miles per hour and swing it through at 20 miles per hour and have tremendous success. But you can't decelerate the club at impact.

Too Close for Comfort: Paul Runyan's Greenside Chip Trick

The late Paul Runyan is well known as a two-time PGA Championship winner (1934 and '38) and revered for his short game prowess. The Hall of Famer won more than 50 times on the PGA Tour despite being one of the shortest hitters of his time.

From time to time, Runyan gave short game lessons and tips for PGA professionals to teach their students. One of the specialty shots he recommended is a shot that we'll call "The Runyan," because he certainly deserves to have his name on it!

When you find your ball very close to the hole (as in Figures 4-3 and 4-4) and just off the green, you don't want to putt the ball through a longer or grainy grass fringe. Trying to putt a ball through longer greenside grass or grainy grass is an unpredictable venture, because the wiry or lush grass slows the shot and perhaps knocks your ball offline. But the prospect of chipping the ball through the long grass can also be daunting because the grass can grab the club and turn the face when you try to swing through it. And if the hole is cut close to your ball, an errant swing may send the ball much too far past the hole.

If you face a tough situation and your practice time hasn't built up your confidence in the conventional chip shot, the time to use "The Runyan" has arrived. Here's how:

1. **Take your putting stance with your front foot open a bit.**

2. **Stand close to your target line.**

3. **Hold the club (a 7-iron works best) in a vertical fashion, like a putter, so the club stands up on its toe with the heel off the ground. (See Figures 4-3a and 4-3b.)**

4. **Grip the club like you grip your putter (see Figure 4-4a).**

5. **Position the ball in the center of your stance or a little toward the back, which de-lofts the club (see Figure 4-4b).**

6. **Swing straight back and straight through in a pendulum fashion, as if you're putting, keeping the clubhead low to the ground. Swing mostly with your shoulders and arms. (See Figure 4-4.)**

The toe of the club, which is the only part that sits flush to the ground, makes contact with the ball (see Figure 4-3c). The toe deadens the hit a little bit. Because you employ little loft, the ball rides the face of the club slightly, giving the ball some overspin so it rolls forward.

The ball hops out of the grass low (see Figure 4-3d), just like a regular chip shot (depending on how hard you swing), and then rolls out softly to the hole. Just like with conventional chips, you want the ball to roll for about 80 percent of the shot. Putting imparts overspin — you want the ball to turn over and roll. With the Runyan, the ball rides up the face of the club, spins, hits the green, and skips a bit before it releases and starts to tumble and roll forward.

Figure 4-3: With the heel of the club elevated, take the club straight back and straight forward to produce a Runyan roll.

The advantage of playing The Runyan shot is that only the toe of the club goes through the grass. If you hit the shot normally, more of the blade would try to fight the course blades of grass. What happens when the grass grabs the blade? The clubface closes and knocks the ball offline. If the club catches in the grass, your shot goes kaput! But if you put only the toe through the grass, you reduce the chances that your club will catch.

Under certain situations, because of the long rough a few feet off the green and a close-cut pin, you face a very difficult shot. You can try to hit The Runyan shot with a sand wedge. The ball comes out soft, bumps like a knuckleball, and trickles out. Because you hit it with only the toe, the ball comes out deadened and harmless. Just make sure to bring the club back far enough to get the ball close to the hole and accelerate through the swing.

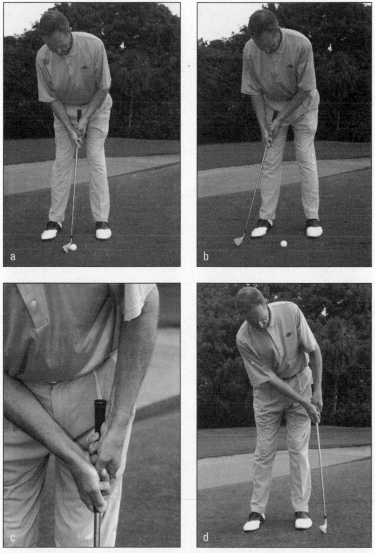

Figure 4-4: The Runyan resembles a lofted putt you hit with a 7-iron. Get close to your line and bump the ball with the toe. No wrist action required.

The Paul Runyan shot is accurate, because you stand over the ball like a putt, you use a putting grip, your eyes are over your line, and you take the club straight back and straight through. The loft of the club gets the ball out of and past the long grass, and the rest of the ball path rolls out like a putt.

As with every technique, be sure to spend time practicing The Runyan before you try to use it on the golf course.

Chapter 5

Pitch, Pitch, Pitch

● ●

In This Chapter

▶ Recognizing the difference between a pitch and chip

▶ Knowing when to pitch in

▶ Choosing your pitching-weapon of choice

▶ Formulating a pitch-shot strategy

▶ Executing the pitching fundamentals

▶ Landing the green from undesirable lies

● ●

The pitch shot is an exciting example of the precision and drama of golf. A pitch shot is fun to watch — especially if you're the one hitting it — because a well-struck pitch flies majestically through the air, hanging up until it lands on the green and hops near the flag. While in mid-flight, a pitch shot provides suspense and gives you time to enjoy the view. Of course, you also have time to second-guess yourself and wonder if the shot is as good as it seems. Will it reach the green? Will it carry the bunker? Will it stick or bounce off the back? "C'mon baby, be as good as you look!" Yeah, a pitch shot leaves you time to beg, too.

A pitch shot falling to the earth can cause you to gasp or curse: a gasp caused by the pleasant surprise of how close the ball falls to the hole, or the curse as the ball plummets into the front bunker.

In this chapter, we breakdown the pitch shot and tell you how to hit nice, controlled pitches that hit the green and stay there. Hitting these exciting, airborne flyers is simpler than you may imagine. Soon you'll be providing the drama shots on the golf course yourself!

Distinguishing the Pitch Shot

A *pitch* is a shot that you hit to the green from anywhere within 75 yards. By way of comparison, a pitch shot is longer than a chip shot (see Chapter 4), stays in the air for much more time, and, after it lands, rolls less. The techniques of both are similar. The best way to get a handle on the difference between a chip shot and a pitch shot, as we discuss in Chapter 4, is to discuss the length of a chip in feet and the length of a pitch in yards.

The following are the general characteristics of the pitch:

- A pitch shot has a good amount of loft and flies through the air in the arc of a high lob.

- A pitch shot is a mini-version of the full swing and an extended version of a chip shot.

- The ball travels most of its distance in the air and then stops near the hole with perhaps a little roll.

- A pitch shot should spend at least 70 percent of its duration in the air and 30 percent or less rolling on or up to the green, depending on the type of pitch you hit.

The pitch is a vital shot to have in your repertoire, because hitting the green from up to 75 yards out is essential to good scoring. You want to have confidence in both your pitches and chips, but you don't want to use them both on the same hole and put pressure on your putter.

Covering Distance and Avoiding Hazards

You need to pitch when your ball rests far enough away from the green that you have to fly the ball up and onto it because you can't chip it on — too much real estate to cover with a chip shot. And if you need to hit the ball high and have it land steeply without rolling much after it hits the green, the pitch shot is for you. In addition to distance and having a small amount of green to work with, you may face other troublesome features that stand between your ball and the cup:

- A bunker may loom between your ball and the green.

- You may have to carry the ball over a creek or pond.

- You may have to avoid a grass bunker.

- A hill or mogul may guard the green.

A pitch shot allows you to fly your ball high through the air, over the trouble, and onto the green.

Pitching Club Preference

The pitching stick you pull from your bag depends greatly on how much yardage lies between you, the green, and the hole. As long as you follow the fundamentals of execution when you hit the shot (see the "Hitting a Pitch Shot" section later in the chapter), the club you use to hit a pitch is a matter of situation and preference.

Fundamentally, you want to choose a club that, when struck, sends the ball flying far and high enough to cover all the land and landscape features you need it to. You also need to bring the ball down with a suitable trajectory so that it stops on the green or perhaps near the hole.

Your pitching wedge may seem to be the obvious choice, and fundamentally, it is. But the short game offers plenty of room for preferences. Some players may prefer to hit pitch shots with anything from a 9-iron to a sand wedge.

 Practice pitch shots with your short irons on the range so that when you get onto the golf course, you have a good sense for the trajectory and distance each short iron produces. Make sure you hit all types of pitches — low liners that stay under the wind or high flops that clear bunkers — with different clubs to account for any situation you may encounter. (See Chapters 8 and 11, respectively, for more on these types of shots, and Chapter 13 for tips on taking your short game to the driving range.)

Pitching Goals and Expectations

For every golf shot you hit, you should have both goals and expectations for the result. The pitch shot is one of the most pleasing and exciting shots in the game of golf when properly executed. A range of emotions can occur when you see that you've hit a good pitch shot. The best of them are sure to draw a smile from you and a grimace from your competitor. What do you want to accomplish with each pitch? What's an acceptable result? A reasonable expectation?

✔ **Setting a goal:** Go for the green! An ambitious goal for your pitch shots, just as it is for your chip shots, is that you pitch every one of them close enough for a tap-in or one putt to finish the hole. Yes, you can hole a putt from anywhere if you get lucky, but a pitch shot that results in a nice, comfortable short putt is a smashing success and a great goal.

✔ **Meeting your expectations:** An easily attainable expectation for your pitch shots is that you hit the ball onto the green, *anywhere,* every time. Avoiding creeks, bunkers, or other hazards is a major part of this expectation because avoiding the trouble is more important than getting the ball close to the hole.

Planning Your Pitch-Shot Strategy

Visualizing and planning are vital to the success of your pitch shot. You need to consider the situation at hand before you pick your target line and your landing target. Ask yourself the following questions before you pitch and run (to the green):

✔ **Although your ultimate goal is getting the ball into the hole, should the hole really be your target?** Is the hole cut in a difficult spot, such as tucked behind a bunker or dangerously close to the edge of the green? Would aiming for the larger, middle part of the green be a safer, more sensible target?

✔ **How far do you need the ball to fly before it lands on the green?** This information is important for club selection, because you need to factor in the wind, the obstacles, and your desired ball-trajectory.

✔ **Is the green tilted in such a way that your ball may roll off the green or toward the cup?** If so, pick your target line and target landing area accordingly.

✔ **Do you expect the green to be hard or soft? Will the ball hit and stick or will it bounce and roll?** Take into account the conditions of the greens you've seen on previous holes or on the practice-putting surface, the recent weather (wind hardening the surface or rain softening it), your shot trajectory (high shots may stick, lower liners may roll), and the slope of the green.

✔ **Will strong winds affect the ball while it sails through the air?** Pick your club, your target line, and your trajectory accordingly.

✔ **Do you have a good lie, or is the ball on an uneven spot, divot, or long grass?** Remember to swing accordingly. For right-handers, a ball above your feet tends to pull to the left *(draw),* and a ball below your feet fades to the right *(slice).* (Vice-versa for lefties.) Be sure to stay down and swing through divots.

✔ **Where do you stand in your match? Are you in a situation that justifies taking a bold chance?** You may have to take on that tight pin placement if you come to the 18th one shot back, but if you're nursing a one-shot lead, pick a safe spot in the middle of the green and go for the two-putt.

Consider all your options and available information before you choose a target, but when you do choose a target, make it very specific, like the flagstick, a ridge on the green, the line of a bunker, or the flat opening in front of the green. This helps you focus your mind, gage the length of the swing, and be precise with your aim.

Hitting a Pitch Shot

Hitting a pitch shot is a matter of swinging the right club with the proper amount of force, allowing the loft of the iron and the speed of the clubhead to send the ball in the air toward the hole. As the old saying goes, "Let the club do the work." The following points break the pitch shot down into a "how to" list that you can come back to for reference, along with Figures 5-1 and 5-2 (and see the following sections for a detailed discussion of the pitch swing):

1. **Visualize the shot by picking a spot on which to land the ball.**

2. **Choose the club that can carry the ball through the air the proper distance.**

3. **Keep more of your weight on the front side of your body.**

4. **Open your front foot by withdrawing it about six inches from the target line.**

5. **Grip the club lightly.**

6. **Keep your head and body still.**

7. **Swing the club back along the target line and then forward through the ball in a smooth fashion.**

8. **Follow through straight toward the target.**

9. **Use the result of the shot to improve on your next pitch.**

   Where did the ball land in relation to your target? Did your highly lofted club put too much spin on the ball? Did the wind knock it down? Take all info into account.

Determining your flight plan and velocity

The peril in hitting a pitch shot is that you can't just swing away like you can with a driver or some of your long irons. Because the pitch shot places a premium on distance control within 75 yards, it requires that you hit the ball the proper length. You may have some wind to deal with, and you should account for that too. Unless you face a truly strong wind, however, you shouldn't be concerned with its effect on the distance or direction of the golf ball.

After you select the club you're comfortable with, the trick is to match the length of your backswing to the distance you want the ball to fly:

- ✔ If you don't take the club back far enough, your instincts can cause you to try to add some force on the downswing, which results in an uneven swing without a smooth or flowing motion.

- ✔ If you swing the club too far back, you may decelerate the club on the downswing in an attempt to feather the ball up to the hole. Deceleration, in any type golf swing, is death.

Pick a suitable spot where you want to land the ball. Remember, you want the ball to fly over any trouble, such as a bunker or creek, and then land on the green near the hole.

Setting up your stance

Your stance for a pitch shot isn't much different from the stance you use for a full golf swing. When you hit a pitch, however, you open up your stance a little bit by opening your lead foot about six inches forward from parallel (with your back foot), and you stand closer to the target line (see Chapter 2 for more on the target line). You should feel as though you're partially facing the hole. Your waist and shoulders should naturally follow that open toe (see Figure 5-1a). An open stance allows you to be target oriented (with your lead foot aiming at the target) and to finish your swing facing the target.

Positioning the ball

The pitch shot fundamentals lie somewhere between the full swing and the chip shot. Therefore, the ball position for a pitch shot is almost the same as it is for any other shot — the longer the club, the more toward the front of the stance the ball should be. For pitch shots, you're likely to use a sand wedge, pitching wedge, 9-iron, or 8-iron, so you should play the ball in the middle of your stance (see Figure 5-1b).

TIP

You can try putting the ball about an inch farther back than normal, which puts your hands a little more forward and creates a steeper swing arc. This type of swing makes your clubhead come through the ball on a more downward fashion, creating a sharp blow that puts backspin on the ball. That backspin helps the ball stop quickly when it hits the green on the fly.

Figure 5-1: Keeping your front foot and body open and target-oriented, swing along the target line with good weight balance to pitch it close.

Distributing your weight

When playing a pitch shot, you should put your weight in the center of your stance or, if you prefer, shifted more onto your front leg. The more weight you put on your front side, the more the club swings up to provide a descending blow.

A steeper swing makes the ball fly higher, so the higher you need the ball to fly, the more weight you should place on your front foot.

Getting the right grip

As with most short-game shots, you need to grip the club lightly. For the right-handed golfer, put the club a little more toward the palm of the left hand, and keep the back of your left hand pointing at the target. Your left hand should always lead; you let the right go along for the ride and offer guidance to the swing (see Figures 5-1c and 5-2c).

Taking a swing

Club selection determines the length of your backswing. Because a pitching wedge is more lofted than a 9-iron, a ball pitched with a pitching wedge flies higher but not as far as a ball stroked with a 9-iron. In order to cover the distance you need, your pitching wedge swing needs to be a touch longer than your 9-iron swing.

Take the club back as far as you need to, and then make a swing with a smooth, easy tempo. Draw the club back low to the ground, keeping your wrists firm and turning by rotating your shoulders. Swing the club back along the target line (see Figure 5-1b) and then forward through the ball (see Figure 5-1c). Make sure you accelerate through the ball and follow through. If you decelerate, you'll flub the shot and leave it short of the green.

The distance you need to cover determines the length of your backswing. For a longer distance, swing back up to 11 o'clock (see Figure 5-2b) and forward up to 1 o'clock (see Figure 5-2d). Keep your legs and lower body still, but allow a small weight shift if you need distance.

Don't be so eager to see the result that you take your eyes off the ball and look up too early. You've chosen your club and made your strategic decision, so now you can swing confidently and follow through straight toward the target. (See Figure 5-2d.)

The only way to know how far back you need to draw the club in order to fly the ball to the green is to practice hitting pitch shots. Sure, some of the equation comes from touch, talent, and instinct, but if you spend time on the range hitting shots of varying length

(75 yards, 50 yards, 25 yards, and so on), you know how far back you need to draw the club. When you face a 50-yard pitch shot on the golf course, you want to recall hitting that shot on the practice range. That way you can look at what may otherwise be a daunting shot full of indecision and say, "Yeah, I've got that shot."

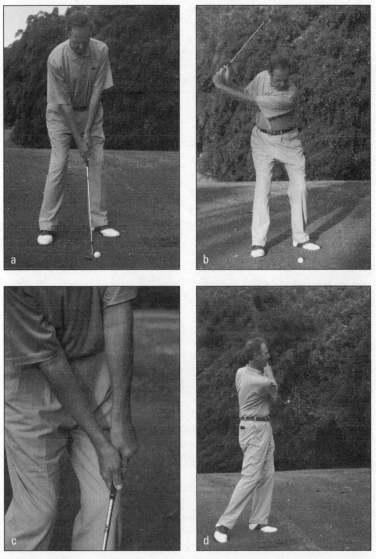

Figure 5-2: Make your backswing proportional to the distance you need to cover and let your lead hand carry the load.

Pitching a Fit over Additional Complications

In the previous section, "Hitting a Pitch Shot," we provide you with the fundamental building blocks for executing a classic pitch. But over the course of 75 yards, many additional issues and obstacles can interfere with pulling off the perfect pitch. Man-made obstacles, natural obstacles, and varying lies can make a difficult shot in terms of distance control that much harder. But don't get your knickers in a bundle just yet; we give you tips to overcome hazards in the following sections.

Pitching over water hazards and bunkers

Sometimes you have to fly your ball over obstacles in order to reach the green. If you have to hit a pitch over a bunker, creek, or hillock, your shot may seem more daunting. The stakes are higher, because a ball landing in a bunker or creek costs you precious strokes.

When facing a hazard or bunker between you and the hole, no matter how much you want to hit your pitch shot close to the cup, your most important priority is to make certain that the ball clears the obstacle.

Sometimes the hole is cut close to the edge of the green and you don't have much space between the obstacle and the hole to work with. You may be tempted to hit a very delicate, high-flying pitch shot that falls steeply, lands softly, and stops near the hole. As exciting as it is to successfully execute a shot like that, you feel even more disappointed when you watch your ball fall short and plug into a bunker or splash into a creek. (But you can check out Chapter 6 for all your sand needs and Chapter 10 for tips on when to pass on playing from a water hazard and when to take a stab at it.)

If the hole is close to the edge of the green, you have plenty of green to work with beyond the hole. Use it. After you become more skilled at hitting pitch shots, you can try to stop your ball close to the hole or to fly it beyond the hole and use backspin. But first and foremost, get your ball over whatever hazard you face.

If you're not comfortable playing your pitch shot over the hazard, or if you don't have enough green behind the hazard to stop your ball, don't be ashamed to play your pitch shot away from the trouble — even if it means playing away from the hole. If the cup is tucked on a small part of the green behind a bunker, you can opt to play your pitch shot to the larger, unguarded part of the green — a much safer option with less risk. Let your maverick playing partner mock you; you can mock him when he's standing in a creek with his pants rolled up trying to save a shot.

Give the hazard its due, but at the same time, don't be too intimidated by the bunker or stream. Consider the lie, the shape of the land, the wind, the distance you need to carry the ball, the amount of land you have to stop it on, and the necessary height of the shot. After you analyze all the factors and make your decision, forget about the creek or bunker. Don't let fear restrict your swing or the obstacle intimidate you into making a timid pass. Of course, the more you practice, the more confidence you'll have in your ability, and the less intimidating obstacles and hazards will seem.

Pitching high and low

Although pitch shots are conventionally considered to have a standard, high trajectory, you may come across occasions when you need to craft a pitch of a certain height. You may need to hit a high pitch to fly over a tree, or you may need a low pitch to go under a tree branch or to keep the ball out of the wind. This kind of crafty control is sometimes called *creative shot-making,* and although creativity is good, make certain that you know how to play these types of shots by practicing them on the range.

The varied irons in your golf bag have different trajectories (the higher the number, the higher the shot), and the built-in loft of your club provides the desired trajectory and height of the shot. But you may find that you need to hit the ball the typical distance the given club provides with more or less loft than the club usually offers.

Being able to hit the ball at various trajectories with different irons is something you can work on after you feel you have a great grasp on fundamental pitch shots. Advanced players have mastered these types of shots, and you can too, but make certain you master pitch shots with your appropriate short irons before you begin experimenting with high and low trajectories with other clubs.

Here are some ways to alter the trajectory of a pitch shot.

Changing the ball's position

You can move the position of the ball in your stance:

- **Lower trajectory:** Put the ball farther back in your stance at address, nearer your back foot.

- **Higher trajectory:** If you put the ball closer to your front foot at address, near the front of your stance, you add more loft to the club.

Spinning the club

You can add more loft to the club or take away some of the loft by spinning the club in your hands and changing the angle of the iron's face:

- **Lower trajectory:** If you spin the clubhead more closed, you de-loft the club.

- **Higher trajectory:** If you spin the clubhead more open, you increase the loft.

In either case, keep your hands even or slightly in front of the ball position and open or close the clubface as needed.

Getting hands on

Your hands can also affect the height of your shot:

- **Lower trajectory:** Keep your wrists firm and don't let them hinge until your followthrough after the ball is gone. The ball gets plenty of bounce off the clubface — you don't need to "help it" into the air by releasing your wrists.

- **Higher trajectory:** If your hands release or begin to flip through the ball early, you make the trajectory of the ball higher. If your hands stay in front of the ball when you pull the club down from the top, the clubhead doesn't catch up at impact and the ball flies on a low trajectory.

Pitching from a bare, tight lie

A pitch shot is challenging enough from a good fairway lie or from the light rough, especially when you have to carry a bunker or a water hazard and land the ball softly. But from time to time, you must face one of the toughest shots in golf — a pitch shot when the ball sits on a bare, tight lie or from any firm ground. In places like Texas or anywhere that endures a dry spell, the ground can become dry and cracked. On the short grass of links courses in Britain and Ireland, your lies may always be firm and tight.

The challenge in pitching from a bare, tight lie is that bad contact can add strokes to your score quickly. You can skull the ball if the club hits the ground first and bounces into the ball. Or, in an attempt to avoid such a fat strike, you may overcompensate and top the ball by trying to pick it off the hard surface.

Although you may be tempted to hold on for dear life, your best bet to hit a good pitch in this situation is to grip the club very lightly. Don't try to help the ball into the air. Let the club do the work by maintaining a light grip pressure as you swing through impact. Let the weight of the clubhead fall through the ball under its own momentum by keeping your hands and arms soft and loosening your shoulders. Trust your swing and, as always, play in the subconscious.

Pitching from deep grass

If you regularly miss greens with your approach shots, you often find your ball in all types of lies and ground conditions. Long grass is one of the more common challenges you face, so you should be sure to practice hitting the ball from deep, grassy conditions.

When the ball rests down in the grass (see Figure 5-3), the lie requires a steeper swing (see Figure 5-4) than you use for a normal pitch, so take out one of your lofted clubs, such as the lob wedge, sand wedge, or pitching wedge.

The steeper swing that lofted wedges automatically produce (because the clubs are shorter) lessens the amount of grass that can come between your clubface and the ball, because the clubs come down at a steeper angle.

Don't short yourself. Use a long enough club to be certain your ball can reach the green. Although you want to get the ball near the hole, your most important mission is to get the ball onto the green . . . anywhere on the green! A highly lofted club stops the ball quickly.

Figure 5-3: Spin the face open to add loft and keep your hands forward.

After you pick your pitching tool, follow these steps to escape the deep rough and get on in one:

1. **Play the ball in the center of your stance (see Figure 5-3.)**

   You want to give yourself enough loft, but the thick grass also requires some distance.

2. **Swing the club back smoothly (see Figure 5-4a) and let your wrists hinge up or bend if it feels like they naturally want to because of the weight of the clubhead**

   Keep your lower body quiet — a pitch shot from rough requires "handsy-work," meaning your clubhead falling through the ball propels the shot. You don't need the leg power a driver or long iron requires.

3. **On the downswing (see Figure 5-4b), shift your weight forward, which creates a steep descent and provides clean contact (see Figure 5-4c).**

4. **Follow through fully.**

   Turn through the ball so that at completion, you face the target (see Figure 5-5).

Figure 5-4: Not allowing your lead wrist to change keeps the face open and produces maximum loft on an already steep swing.

Figure 5-5: A full finish with your body facing your target is an essential ending to a perfectly executed shot.

Pitching from uneven lies

Course designers like to present more challenges as you get closer to the pin, so within 75 yards of the green, you're likely to find your ball lying on an uneven lie from time to time. As scary as it may seem, you need to be able to hit effective pitch shots from side-hill, uphill, and downhill lies.

Staking out side-hill lies

If you find your ball on a side-hill lie in which the ball sits above your feet (see Figure 5-6), you can count on the ball drawing rather than flying straight. Gravity and the angle of the hill when the club makes contact conspire to pull the ball after impact. Account for this by adjusting your target line a bit more to the left or right than you may normally aim.

Figure 5-6: Adjust your normal aim to account for the natural draw that comes with a side-hill lie where the ball sits above your feet.

If you find your ball sitting a side-hill below your feet (see Figure 5-7), you can count on the ball slicing rather than flying straight. The same forces that pull the ball when it rests above your feet conspire to push the ball after impact. Account for this by adjusting your target line a bit more left or right than you may normally aim.

Dealing with downhill and uphill lies

The tricky part about hitting a pitch shot from a downhill lie is hitting the ball with the clubhead before it strikes the ground behind the ball. Make no mistake — this is indeed a tough shot!

When you come upon a downhill lie (see Figure 5-8), put most of your weight on your front side at address and keep it there throughout the swing. Because the hillside tilts you to your front, you naturally de-loft the angle of the clubface. The ball will come off the club flying lower and perhaps longer, so you may want to take a more lofted club or shorten your backswing accordingly. Make certain you swing through the ball, and let the clubhead extend down the slope of the hill on its swing path to keep from topping the ball.

Figure 5-7: Adjust your target line to account for the slice that results from the side-hill lie where the ball rests below your feet.

Doing your repair duty

If you execute well and hit the green with your pitch shot, or any shot for that matter, be sure to find and repair the mark you make. Because a pitched ball flies high and lands on the green at a steep angle, it often leaves a quarter-sized indent in the green called a *pitch mark*. Soft greens after rains are especially susceptible to pitch marks.

Nobody likes to have a putt derailed by an ignored pitch mark. And not only do pitch marks wreak havoc for putters, but they also take weeks to grow back. Most golf courses either provide or sell divot repair tools in the clubhouse, so you have no excuse for failing to carry one in your pocket!

To repair a pitch mark, put the sharp edges of the divot repair tool into the perimeter of the indentation and push the edge toward the middle. Don't try to push the ground in the middle back up. Just go around the perimeter a few times and push the sides toward the middle and then flatten the raised ground with the bottom of your putter.

For uphill lies, you want to let the clubhead follow the ground contour, just as you do with downhill lies. Because the ball lies on an uphill slope (see Figure 5-9), the angle effectively increases the loft of the club, causing the ball to fly higher and shorter after impact. Choose a longer club than you would normally use and/or lengthen your backswing to account for the lost yardage. The angle of the hill, depending on its severity, also affects your balance by forcing your weight onto your back side and perhaps causing you to pull up or even fall back out of the shot. Guard against this by keeping your weight on your front foot and keeping the ball in the middle of your stance.

Figure 5-8: When you face a downhill lie, put most of your weight on your front foot and position the ball more toward the back of your stance.

Figure 5-9: When you face an uphill lie, keep most of your weight on your front foot and try not to fall back out of the shot.

Chapter 6

Climbing Bunker Hill

In This Chapter

▶ Knowing what to expect out of the bunker

▶ Replacing *blast* with *splash* in your bunker vocab

▶ Executing a fundamental bunker swing

▶ Assessing the condition of the sand

▶ Keeping your mind on the clubface

▶ Escaping troubled bunker lies

They lurk, yawning like hungry monsters and gleaming in the sun like happy beaches. Their long, delicate fingers, sweeping faces, and geometric balance belie the trouble they can cause your scorecard. Bunkers add both artistry and complexity to the golf course.

Bunkers guard the fronts, sides, and backs of greens, catching the timid, the bold, and the off-line shots of players that miss the target. Flagsticks hide behind them, tempting players to hit shots over the bunkers or provoking enough fear to have them steer shots away from the hole to vacant portions of the green.

Some bunkers are deep and some shallow; some are simple and some complex. Make no mistake, however: Bunker play is an art as refined and as thoughtful as the very design of the splashy hazards themselves. This chapter helps you to both appreciate the danger of bunkers and to demystify their desperate, desert spell.

Setting Your Bunker Goals and Expectations

Well-executed bunker shots are a beautiful sight. The sand bursts up in all directions, looking like a splashy fireworks show, and from this cloud emerges the ball, which soars high to its apex and lands softly on the green, checking up and stopping near the hole.

If you're an average player, your expectation and goal should be one in the same: Get the ball out of the bunker and onto the green in one shot. From there, make two-putting your new expectation and consider the outcome a success. If you happen to hit it close to the hole and make your putt — a lofty goal — enjoy your wild success.

Your objective is to blast the ball out of the bunker in one shot and make a true escape. You can enjoy the beauty of turning a bad situation, like a ball buried in a bunker, into a good one, like a ball very near the hole. If you play golf long enough, you'll hit some splendid, beautiful shots from time to time, and you'll feel great. Hitting a ball from a bunker onto the green and then making the putt is characterized in statistics as a *sand save*. Your pals in a friendly game may call this occurrence a "sandy." Enjoy sand saves when they happen, because they rarely occur for the average player.

Special beach rules apply

Bunker play boasts its own set of rules. A bunker is considered a hazard, and a ball is in a bunker when it lies in or touches any part of the bunker. Before you make your stroke from a bunker, you can't

✔ Test the condition of the hazard

✔ Touch the sand with your hand or your club

✔ Touch a loose impediment in the bunker

This means you must be very careful not to let your club touch the ground when you take your stance. If you take a practice swing, don't hit the sand. The penalty for violating this rule is the loss of the hole in match play or two strokes in medal play.

Some golf courses have large, sandy areas defined as *waste bunkers*. These scrubby areas aren't raked or maintained, and they often have shells and pebbles in them. You can ground your club and take practice swings in waste bunkers, which aren't considered hazards, just as you normally do anywhere outside a hazard on a golf course.

Check your scorecard, which typically identifies these waste areas, or ask the PGA professional in the clubhouse before your round to alert you to waste bunkers. When in doubt, consult with your competitor before you ground your club in what you think is a waste bunker.

Avoiding an Explosion

Somehow, over the years, the term "explosion shot" has become attached to bunker shots. Although it may look like a blast to you when the clubhead hits the sand and the ball flies out, thinking of a bunker shot as an explosion is a harmful comparison.

Explosion means "bang!" It means a bomb went off. Rather than explosion, think "splash." Splash says, "Hey, I'm having fun here playing in the sand. Sand is my friend. I'm just splashing around." It may seem like a minor issue, but as we discuss throughout this book, short-game success is all about the mental. Splash takes the aggressive, violent connotation out of your mind — and therefore out of your swing.

Hitting a Bunker Shot

Although you can easily be intimidated by the complexity of a bunker shot, it isn't unlike hitting a pitch shot or a flop shot (see Chapters 5 and 11). The key is to splash the sand with your club before it makes contact with the ball.

Assessing the sand variables

Not all bunkers are alike, and neither is the sand that forms them. You need to make a perceptive, smart assessment of the type of bunker your ball lands in, the lie you have to deal with, and the bunker's sand type. Of course, the ball isn't technically trapped, because you have plenty of methods to help it escape after you plot your exit strategy.

Determining the shape you're in

The size of every bunker is different. But, generally, you encounter two extremes:

- **Sand scrapes:** Some bunkers may be shallow but expansive, so although you may not need to fly the ball extremely high, you have to hit it a longer distance forward to escape the bunker. In this case, be certain to use the proper amount of clubhead speed to propel the ball forward and not just up and out. A longer backswing and a closed clubface can propel the ball farther. (See Figure 6-1 for an example of a shallow bunker.)

✔ **High lip:** Some bunkers are small, circular pot bunkers that may be deep but not large in circumference. If you have to negotiate a big lip between the ball and the green, make certain that the ball gets up quickly: Take the club back steeply and follow through. Open the clubface and maintain that position through the shot. (See the "Facing steep situations" section later in this chapter and the accompanying figure for more information.)

Regardless of the bunker shape you're in, you have to account for the variables of height and distance:

✔ How far does the ball have to fly in order to escape the bunker and land on the green?

✔ How high does the ball have to fly in order to clear any high side or rising lip that extends up in the bunker?

The more upright your swing, and the more open the clubface becomes, the higher and shorter the ball will travel.

Adjusting to the sand

The sand that one golf course uses in its bunkers may be very different from the sand another course uses. Some courses have bunkers with fine, soft sand, and others put in firm sand. You see some bunkers with more sand than others, and the sand can be fluffy or wet and hard-packed.

Although the rules dictate that you can't test the nature of the sand before you play a shot from a bunker, take the time to be aware of whether the sand looks wet and hard or light and fluffy. Different conditions call for different techniques:

✔ **Soft sand:** If the sand in the bunker is soft and fluffy, you need to put a bit more speed in your swing, because cushy sand slows the club down as the clubhead goes through. So feel free to be aggressive and make a strong swing.

✔ **Hard sand:** When the bunker sand is firm or wet, you need to slow your swing speed down, which means not taking the club back as far. The ball comes out quicker because you don't have as much cushy sand between your ball and the clubhead. But make sure you don't decelerate your swing and leave the ball in the sand.

Checking out your lie

Examine the ball and the way it lies in the sand. Is it sitting on top of the sand or is it buried? If you have a clean lie, consider yourself lucky that the ball isn't buried or lying in a footprint. A ball partially buried is to be expected, but if it looks like you need a shovel, the "Executing Bunker Shots from Troubled Lies" section later in the chapter can help. Figure 6-1 features a perfect lie in a bunker with seemingly soft sand that calls for a bigger swing.

Figure 6-1: Dig your feet in with an open stance and splash through the sand with your natural swing.

Choosing your club

Greenside bunker shots often require you to fly your ball high through the air over a short distance. The height you have to fly your shot in order to escape the bunker is more important than the distance you need to cover; therefore, to play an effective bunker shot, you should use the shortest, most lofted club in your bag. The most lofted club in your bag is likely your sand wedge; you may also have a 58- or 60-degree club. Note the amount of loft of the wedge in Figure 6-1a.

Raising clubface awareness

To be an effective sand player, you must be aware of what's going on with the face of the club. You select a highly lofted club to play the shot, and the clubface needs to remain lofted as it scoops through the sand and sends the ball skyward. In other words, when you take your grip and swing the club, you shouldn't do anything that could de-loft the clubface or change its angle, such as breaking your wrists or trying to help the ball into the air. In Figure 6-1, you can see that the clubface doesn't change from the address (Figure 6-1a) through impact (Figure 6-1c) — a product of the lead wrist position at impact, which isn't broken.

Your grip shouldn't be tight, either, in an effort to keep the loft. The harder you grab, the more tension you put into your arms and hands, and if you have tension in your grip, you can't feel the clubhead. You always want to feel the clubhead and maintain its lofted state.

Taking your stance

When you set up to hit a bunker shot, you stand virtually the same way you stand to hit a pitch shot (see Chapter 5). When you take position over the ball, your lead foot should point open 45 degrees, and your body and shoulders should open to that same 45-degree angle facing down the target line and toward the target (see Figure 6-2a). Put more of your weight on your front foot to keep from swaying and make sure to keep your knees flexed.

Digging in and staying level

You do have to deal with one major difference between your pitch stance and your bunker stance, and it stems from the conditions of the shots. Unlike a pitch shot, when you hit the ball off the ground and brush the grass with the clubhead, a bunker shot requires you to make contact with the sand *behind* the ball on the downswing at impact, forcing the ball in front of a cushion of sand. You don't strike the ball. Because the clubhead needs to splash through the sand below the ball, you, naturally, have to get lower.

To make splashing the sand easier, when you open your lead foot and take your stance, dig yourself down into the sand (see Figure 6-1b). You should bury the soles of your shoes. If you stand level, you have to reach down unnaturally during your swing to make proper contact with the sand. You want your swing to stay consistent, and the only way to do that is to lower yourself down by digging your feet in. This way, you can take your natural swing.

Choosing your ball position

Generally, when you stand over the ball, you should position it in the middle of your stance (see Figure 6-1a). As an average player, you should keep the ball in the middle of your stance for all bunker shots — a way to go about playing the shot that allows you develop your touch and feel by keeping it simple.

Advanced players do some creative things with ball position, but you should play the ball in the middle, and practice with it there, until you feel as though you've mastered the bunker shot — to the extent that it can be mastered, that is. When you step into a bunker without fear and are confident that you can get the ball out of the bunker and reasonably close to the hole with one shot under any conditions, you've come as close to "mastering" the sand as you can.

Sometimes, however, the circumstances you find your ball in dictate that you move the ball from the center of your stance no matter what your skill level is:

- ✔ **Uphill bunker shot:** Move the ball a little bit forward of center to make certain you hit the sand in front of the ball.

- ✔ **Downhill bunker shot:** Move the ball a little behind center in your stance to make certain the ball flies up, as gravity naturally pulls it down.

Read more about particularly troublesome lies in the "Executing Bunker Shots from Troubled Lies" section later in this chapter.

Figure 6-2: To become a sand sniper, open your stance, aim a bit left of your target line, splash the sand, and produce a big followthrough.

Picking a target and taking aim

Because your ball comes out higher as a result of the highly lofted face of the club you use for bunker shots, it doesn't roll as far. If you never de-loft your open clubface and splash the ball out, your ball comes out high, lands in a soft, vertical fashion, and rolls only a short distance after it hits the green.

In numerical terms, your ball should roll for only about 40 percent of its life — so 60 percent of the shot takes place in the air. After you become an efficient bunker player, you can pick a spot to aim at, but if you're an average player, don't concentrate on a particularly small spot. Your expectation should be to get the ball out of the sand and onto an area of the green. You don't want to have to hear any lame beach jokes from your partners as you scrape sand all day.

As you read in the section "The shape of the backswing" later in this chapter, your bunker swing should be steeper than your natural swing, and therefore you can't go straight back along the target line (see Chapter 2 for an introduction to the target line). And because your clubhead comes across the target line, you have to aim a little bit to the left of the target when you set up (see Figure 6-2).

Taking a sand-sweeping swing

You have to understand that, as odd as it sounds, you don't try to hit the ball during bunker shots. A well-executed bunker shot sends the ball flying out of the bunker on a platform of sand (see Figure 6-2c). The impact the club makes on the sand, and the reaction of the sand, is what propels the ball out of the bunker. Do you try to dig the ball out or blast it out with a boatload of sand? No. You try to send the ball out on a cushion of sand.

Pick a spot two inches behind the ball. Concentrate on that spot and swing the club through it. When you practice and work on your bunker shots, imagine the ball sitting on an area of sand that you want your club to sweep — or splash — through.

Imagine another golf ball lying in the sand directly behind yours — that's about how far behind the ball your clubhead should enter the sand. Attempt to hit the second imaginary golf ball in order to move the real one.

Don't "help" the ball out of the bunker and into the air. Anytime you try to do so, your weight transfers to your back leg, and you raise up as you try to scoop the ball. The more your weight stays on your back side, the more likely you are to belly the ball by hitting it with the bottom of the club and skulling it across the green or into the side of the bunker. Keep your weight in the center of your stance and minimize any leg action or transfer of weight.

The shape of the backswing

The shape of your takeaway and backswing should be a very upright, vertical motion. Your backswing should be steeper because the angle of attack needs to be steeper in order to get the ball up sooner and higher than normal. (For an example of a really upright vertical backswing, check out Figure 6-5.)

The angle down, when you swing a golf club through a ball, actually translates as up — in terms of the ball's response. If you swing down with your club, the ball goes up.

But also consider that the steeper you take the club back, the shorter the distance the ball can travel because of the emphasis on height. Your club goes vertical, you swing slowly, and the clubhead is lofted, so the ball simply can't go very far.

To swing the club back more vertically, use your hands to swing the club more than your arms. To get the backswing steeper, you need to get wristier by cocking your wrists a little more than you normally do. When you cock your wrists, the club may wander off the target line some, but you should stay focused on the face and keep your grip loose. You swing the clubhead though the ball just as you normally do, but you swing at a steeper angle.

The length and speed of the backswing

We're talking distance control here. With a bunker shot, the length of your backswing determines how far the ball flies after it leaves the bunker.

If you just have to get the ball out of the bunker and the flagstick is cut close to your side of the green, you can't take the club very far back or you'll send the ball a long way. But no matter how far you judge that you need to take the club back, be sure to swing all the way through and follow through to a complete swing (see Figure 6-2d). Take it back halfway if you need to, but be sure to finish fully! (Check out the next section for more on the followthrough.)

Depending upon your lie and the density of the sand, the speed of your swing is also a factor. Think of this like driving your car: the faster and harder you swing, the farther the ball will go, but you also have more margin for error — just like driving too fast!

Try to maintain a consistent swing speed all the time to achieve success. The speed should be smooth and slow enough so that you can feel the clubhead. If you play a course with harder sand, you can swing easier (or harder in the case of softer sand), but always keep the clubhead speed the same during the round. To vary the distance of a bunker shot, vary how far back you take the club. The speed takes care of itself.

The followthrough

One of the biggest mistakes players make during a bunker shot is failing to follow through after they make contact with the sand and begin to move the ball forward.

A bunker shot requires a big finish. No matter how short your greenside shot is, it requires the *chorus line finish* — a big, full fol-lowthrough, not the *nine o'clock to three o'clock* finish of a chip shot or pitch shot (see Chapters 4 and 5, respectively).

The reason for the big followthrough is that the sand slows your clubhead down at impact. Metaphorically, if this is a 10-mph swing, the clubhead can go through the ball at 12 mph or even 15 mph, but it shouldn't go through at 5 mph. Your goal is to get your down-swing to go the same speed as your backswing — or a bit faster. You slow the downswing by decelerating the clubhead, which kills the momentum of the swing.

Hitting off grass is different. The club goes through the grass easily, so you can swing the club easier. Shorter grass doesn't really catch on the blade too much. But the minute you try to hit through the sand, the clubhead slows down. Therefore, you have to make sure that you constantly maintain good clubhead speed, and in order to maintain good speed, you need that big finish. Concentrating on making that finish ensures that you don't inadvertently slow down the clubhead on the downswing or at impact. The bigger the finish, the better your chances of escaping the bunker.

You may be tempted to quit on a bunker shot and not make the big finish out of hesitation or lack of confidence. If you stop the club just after you hit the ball, you've decelerated — and you never want to decelerate! Deceleration is the short-game kiss of death, no matter the shot.

Executing Bunker Shots from Troubled Lies

As if bunker shots aren't difficult enough, sometimes you encounter a situation where the ball doesn't lie on perfectly flat sand.

Blame the sheep for that pot bunker

Although it may seem like bunkers were created specifically to complicate your trip around the golf course, that bit of Machiavellian self-pity isn't always warranted. The original golf courses — treeless, seaside links courses in Scotland — only featured bunkers because the resident sheep dug the holes to escape the wind and "bunker down" at night. Indeed, caddies and sometimes even roustabout golfers have been known to seek refuge in the bunkers of the Old Course at St. Andrews.

Because the sheep cared little about golf strategy, their placement of the bunkers on golf's original courses and the shape of them had no real reason to their rhyme, and very often they weren't even visible to the golfers who hit shots into them. These pot bunkers were deep and deadly, and therefore course managers gave them names such as the famous "Hell Bunker" or "Principal's Nose," "Coffin," or "Sahara."

Modern golf course architects have been much more strategic in their placement of bunkers, although some still end up with dastardly names, such as the "Church Pew" bunkers at Oakmont CC and "Hell's Half-Acre" at Pine Valley. But architects don't merely place bunkers in precarious spots to make golf holes tougher. Knowing what the designer had in mind can help you play the course more effectively. Listen to the language of a golf course when you play and take time to notice how the bunkers are positioned. Most architects repeat their styles and philosophies on each hole on a given course, and recognizing what the designer had in mind can help improve your strategy.

Architects design bunkers for aesthetics, to frame the hole, or to give it style. Bunkers also serve as aiming points or directional devices to show the player where to aim the ball. In some cases, bunkers are designed to "save the players from themselves," in which case the bunkers may catch a wayward ball that would otherwise roll into a pond or down the side of a cliff. You may find that a short hole has many bunkers defending the green. Only fair, wouldn't you say?

Negotiating uphill and downhill lies

One of the most intimidating and difficult bunker shots you encounter occurs when you find your ball halfway up the face of the bunker (as in Figure 6-3) or halfway down the back of a bunker (see Figure 6-4).

If you think logically about an uphill or downhill lie in a bunker, you understand that

- ✔ When you have an uphill lie, the ball comes out higher.
- ✔ When you have a downhill lie, the ball comes out lower.

Figure 6-3: Put the ball forward in your stance and make your shoulders parallel with the slope of the bunker for an uphill lie.

So, what to do about it? When you have an uneven level, you must adjust your shoulders, at address, to mimic the slope of the hill:

✔ **Uphill shot:** Your shoulders need to tilt until they rest parallel to the ground (see Figure 6-3). If you don't make your shoulders level to the hill, your swing smashes into the hill. You also make it difficult to get through the hill into your big followthrough; you end up with the clubhead stopping and a ball that can't go anywhere. You don't want the club getting caught in the sand because you swing right smack into the hill. The clubface should square, not open, because the incline already adds loft.

✔ **Downhill shot:** Your shoulders need to tilt again, this time so they mirror the downhill slope of the bunker (see Figure 6-4). Tilting back on a downhill bunker shot causes you to bury the club in the sand too far behind the ball or top the ball. The angle becomes unnaturally severe and inappropriate. Keep your weight on your front side and swing the club vertically.

If you tilt your shoulders to match the hill, you make plenty of room for your swing. Tilting for the downhill or the uphill lie naturally allows you to swing normally, splash through the sand, and rotate into your finish because you swing with the slope of the hill. Simple physics, we suppose, but you don't need a physics course to improve your sand game.

Figure 6-4: Put the ball in the back of your stance and tilt your shoulders forward to match the slope of a downhill lie.

Cooking the fried egg

A ball that lands in soft sand and buries itself gives you what's called a *fried egg lie*, because the ball lies in the middle of a round depression in the sand with only the top of the ball visible. The ball looks like the yoke and the circle of sand the white part of a sunny-side-up fried egg.

What you have is a challenging shot. But if you make adjustments to your standard sand swing, you come out okay:

✔ **Dig in deeper:** If you find your ball buried in a fried egg lie, the ball usually rests an inch or two below the surface of the bunker. Therefore, the first thing you need to do to play it successfully is to dig your stance in even lower so that you can start from a lower point. You still want the clubhead to splash below the ball, but the ball is even lower than normal. So, if the ball is two inches lower, you have to get two inches lower as well, which is tougher than you may think. Get in as deep as you can and get set.

✔ **Get the club lower:** You can get the club lower into the sand if you allow the leading edge to dig more. Close the clubface up a little at address and de-loft it to make the club dig easier.

✔ **Swing faster:** To play the buried lie, the club has to go into the sand two inches lower, and you have to splash much more sand, so the club slows down much faster. You also have to deal with more shock on your hands. In this case, you need to use a speedier swing. Not a harder swing, just a faster one. Instead of powering up, increase your club speed so that you can keep the club moving.

We know: Earlier in the chapter in "The length and speed of the backswing" section, we stress the advantages of not messing with the speed of your swing. But the fried egg is an extreme lie, and extreme lies call for extreme measures. Swinging faster than normal is an extreme measure and hopefully you won't frequently find yourself with fried-egg lies.

✔ **Pick a closer target:** The ball has no backspin when it comes out because of the buried lie. It comes out like a knuckleball and turns over. Try to hit it a couple of feet shorter — this shot rolls more than a typical bunker shot and has over-spin because so much sand rests between the clubface and the ball.

Your best bet is to close the clubface a little and get that ball out — anywhere out — and onto the green. Don't think too much about the buried lie. Experimenting and practice help your confidence immensely.

Facing steep situations

You may stumble upon occasions when you find your ball up against a severely steep sod face or lying under an extremely high, looming lip. You may stand over your ball and look up at the wall of the bunker or the lip and think, "I can't get this ball up fast enough to get it over that lip and land the green." If that thought enters your mind, you're almost always right! You probably have such a bad lie that the ball can't physically come off the club at a sharp enough launch angle to allow it to clear the face of the bunker or the lip.

What are your options? Check out the following pointers:

✔ In the face of overwhelming odds, you may want to take a swing at the ball anyway, which can lead to terrible repercussions: The ball could hit the lip or wall and fall back into the bunker in the same spot or in an even worse position; you could plug the ball into the face of the bunker or the lip; or, even worse (and this happened to Jeff Maggert in the Masters Tournament), the ball could bounce back off the wall or lip and hit you, putting you in danger and causing you to incur a two-stroke penalty.

✔ You can declare the ball unplayable, take a one-stroke penalty, and drop the ball within two club-lengths of where it lies but no nearer to the hole. The downside of this option is that the ball must remain in the bunker.

✔ Perhaps the least desirable but wisest option is to play the ball out of the bunker — backwards. Play the ball out of the bunker at the easiest point of escape, and then play it to the green with your next shot. Such defeatism is against the nature of every golfer; you don't want to hit the ball backwards up a fairway or away from the hole, but sometimes you have to take your medicine and go the smartest, safest route.

If you decide to give it a go in the face of the odds, open your clubface as much as you can (see Figure 6-5a), take a very vertical, upright back swing (see Figure 6-5b), and then let your lead hand take the clubhead through the sand (see Figure 6-5c). Try to ignore the result so that you can swing the clubhead all the way through to a big, full finish (see Figure 6-5d).

Figure 6-5: When faced with a steep bunker face, make sure your clubhead speed is consistent and accelerate into a big followthrough.

Chapter 7

Putting Your Best Foot Forward

In This Chapter
▶ Becoming confident on the greens
▶ Acknowledging the magnitude of the putt
▶ Setting putting goals
▶ Adjusting your expectations
▶ Working on putting fundamentals

*I*n the world of golf books, entire "bibles" have been written about putting. You come across countless putting grips, techniques, styles, philosophies, strategies, and even types of putters. You can research mental keys, so-called secrets, and even scientific theories concerning putting. In this chapter, you work on the fundamentals of making putts and becoming a good putter, and you also discover that your putting technique is very much a result of personal preference.

Tossing Your Putting Prejudice Aside

Players at all levels of golf often overlook putting as an integral part of golf. Seems ridiculous, right? Well, with most people, the mention of golf conjures up visions of long tee shots and powerful ball striking long before it provokes images of elegant putting.

Putting is the culmination of every golf hole. After you hit your tee shot as far and as straight as you can, and after you negotiate and execute an approach shot that flies from long, heavy rough through the air, avoids the bunkers, hits the target, and lands on the green, you're ready to calmly roll the ball with deft precision and touch with a club that looks unlike any other in your bag.

Even the word "putt" seems to be a hapless little runt of a word —
so much less intriguing than drive, flop, punch, or stroke. Putt.
Very old men putt around in the garage. A slow moving motorboat
putters by. Putt-putt-putt.

Putting seems kind of like kicking the extra point in football. You
know, the "real players" bang their bodies down the field, float long
spirals, and make impossible catches to gain 70 yards and punch the
ball into the end zone. After they get to pay dirt, a 5-foot-1 kicker with
no grass stains, mud, or blood on his uniform comes onto the field
and side-winds the ball through the uprights from 3 yards out of the
end-zone with a soccer cleat. It just doesn't seem that impressive.

But yes, even magnificent, godly golfers have to putt.

Recognizing the Importance of Putting Skills

Putting is the most important part of the game of golf when it
comes to scoring. You need precision, speed, nerve, and confidence, along with an ability to handle misses (they happen often.)
The challenge is to temper the enthusiasm for scoring with the
soft touch you need to be accurate.

Doing the math

Think about it in logical terms: You can pull out your giant Big Bobby
driver and sail the ball 300 yards, but that giant shot counts the
same on the scorecard as a lil' one-foot putt! So, simple math tells
you that putting is important. You need only one shot (assuming you
can handle that Big Bobby with some success) to hit your drive 300
yards, but if you don't have confidence in your putting, it may take
you three shots to end the hole. The numbers, in this case, don't lie.

Crunching another set of numbers, putting is important because it
requires the most precision of any shot you hit. You typically bang
your drives toward a fairway that measures about 40 or more
yards wide and a playing corridor sometimes 80 yards wide from
right boundary to left boundary. You have plenty of room for error
when you drive the ball, and no one really expects you to hit your
drive with laser precision. When you hit your approach shot, you
aim for the green, a target that can be as big as 10,000 square feet.
But when you putt, from no matter how long a distance, you aim at
a circle that measures 4¼ inches wide. Now that's pressure! The
margin for error in putting is comparatively tiny.

Getting in your opponent's head

Putting is just as important in a competitive sense. If your competitor in a match thinks of you as a good putter, it puts more pressure on her. She knows that she can't make a mistake on the green because you'll surely seize the moment and take her down.

Using superior putting to apply direct pressure on your opponent is an invaluable asset in competitive play. Say your ball is 30 feet from the hole, and your opponent's putt only spans 15 feet. She has the clear advantage, right? Well, that advantage may swing your way if you lag your long putt to inches from the hole for a certain two-putt while she waits to putt her 15-footer (for more on lag putting, see Chapter 9). Suddenly, she has something to think about. Should she try to make her 15-footer to win the hole? Should she be conservative and make sure she doesn't hit it too far by the hole, because a three-putt means she takes a loss? She watched your ball break two feet. Will her ball break that much? Even though you didn't sink your long putt, your proficiency has tightened her collar a bit and stretched her putt out. Conversely, if you miss your putt by six feet, your opponent's job becomes much easier. She knows that she can safely (and rather easily) two-putt from 15 feet and have a good opportunity to win the hole.

Ben Hogan on the emphasis of putting

Ben Hogan is still, long after his competitive era and passing, revered as the best pure ball-striker in the history of golf. Hogan's legendary appetite for practice in his quest for perfection has been emulated but never equaled, and his secret has been sought and speculated about.

It should therefore come as no surprise that the game's most dedicated ball-striker was outspoken in his disdain for the emphasis of putting on one's golf score. Many frustrated golfers may agree with Hogan, who felt a two-foot putt shouldn't have the same value as a brilliant 220-yard approach shot that puts the ball two feet from the hole!

Proponents of Hogan's beliefs have proposed some ideas for taking the emphasis off putting. Making the hole larger is one. Imagine if the hole were the circumference of, say, a bucket rather than its current water glass size? Or how about making putts worth only half a stroke rather than a full stroke? These suggestions may sound good, but we don't suggest you spend too much time fantasizing about them. The simple, current fact is that a two-foot putt carries the same weight as a huge drive, Mr. Hogan's objections aside, so get out there and practice. How often do you think the golf gods change the rules of the game anyway? Not often.

Putting Goals and Expectations

For every golf shot you hit, you should have both goals and expectations for the result in mind. Knowing the difference and how to push and prepare yourself for each shot allows you to start lowering your scores and your blood pressure. What do you want to accomplish with each putt? What's an acceptable result? A reasonable expectation?

Setting goals: Holing putts in two

If you want to lower your score to become a better player and have more fun, you need to avoid three- or four-putting a hole. You can hit good shots straight down the fairway and land the green in regulation, but if you take three strokes to jar the ball from a comparatively tiny distance, you'll forget your good shots instantly. This type of ending is positively criminal and will frustrate you endlessly.

Your initial *goal* — not your expectation — is to roll 36 or fewer putts in an 18-hole round of golf. That means hitting two or fewer putts on every green. Naturally, this goal becomes easy to achieve when you hit the ball close to the hole. But when you land it 40 feet away, two-putting is a major feat. Accomplishing your goal requires you to focus on the first putt every time — especially the long ones.

It can be too easy to approach a long putt and not think about the consequences of your stroke. You may think that you can't possibly make the long one, so you get lazy and your mind wanders. You make a halfhearted pass at it. On the opposite end of the spectrum, you may get too aggressive with the long putt, trying to make a heroic bomber. Be smart and careful with the first putt. If your goal is to roll no more than two putts per green, two-putting is a success and one-putting is a smashing success!

You may be thinking that the goal of two-putting every green doesn't sound terribly ambitious, but take a look at the PGA Tour professionals — the 200 or so finest players in the world. In 2003, John Huston led the Putting Average category with an average of 1.7 putts per green. 1.7 has won the category every year since 1986, with the exception of 2002, when Bob Heintz won the category with a 1.682 average.

So if the greatest players in the world can beat the goal of two-putting each green by just percentage points, you shouldn't hesitate to make it your goal to two-putt each green. Your scores will improve and stay consistently good.

Meeting your expectations

In principle, you can raise your expectations the more you practice — to a point. Be excited by good results, but try not to fret over missed putts. You can control your performance when it comes to two-foot putts, but you can only improve your performance with the 10-footers.

Sinking every two-footer

You should never miss one- or two-foot putts — your "money-making" putts. They provide wiggle room as you try to reach the goal of two-putting over the entire round. If you practice two-footers and focus on every putt during a round, you should make them every time. Sinking two-footers is at first a goal, and if you put any amount of time into your short game at all, it becomes a realistic expectation. Missing a short putt is a terrible way to waste a stroke.

Many club golfers and weekend golfers, in the interest of speedy play and sportsmanship, concede two-foot putts. Although conceding two-foot putts is fine in match, skins, or casual recreational play (gimmes are against the rules in stroke-play tournaments), it means you may never have the opportunity to practice and make them consistently for when you really need to.

Whenever possible, hole out all your putts. And practice two-footers, no matter how boring or remedial it may seem — especially if you often play with folks who treat them as gimmes on the course. Sometime, either in a stroke-play tournament or when your partners decide not to concede it to avoid losing a match, you'll need to make a two-footer. Short putts are as valuable as the longest drive, and you should never, ever miss them. (Check out Chapter 14 for ways to insert a bit of variety into your putting practice.)

A subtle gamesmanship trick your opponent may employ is to concede two-foot putts to you throughout the round, and then, when you need the putt and expect him to concede it, he makes you putt. This trick affects you in two ways. First, it unnerves you and perhaps annoys you that he doesn't concede it. Second, it forces you to make a two-foot putt when you haven't hit one all day and you haven't developed a rhythm for making them.

Looking at longer putts

You know you should make one- and two-foot putts all the time. But what's a reasonable expectation for longer putts? Consider that PGA Tour players make 10-foot putts 50 percent of the time. And though you may think tour players can make 3-footers all the time, the best players in the world make putts from three feet about 70 percent of the time. Surprised?

If you consider yourself to be an average player, you should be prepared to miss many long putts. If you're like most average Joes, your expectations are probably higher than reality allows. You may expect to make the longer putts as often — or more often — than the pros sink. But by having extremely high expectations, you put added pressure on yourself to make hard, long putts. Don't beat yourself up mentally, or you may find your scores increasing and your confidence falling as the pressure mounts.

Now, you don't want to throw strokes away. Missing a five-footer after you traverse 500 yards in three shots is disappointing, but you must be realistic. Statistically and realistically speaking, missing longer putts is a part of the game. When you miss, don't get angry and make a negative imprint on your self-image. If you beat yourself up for missing a putt, the next time you stand over a tough putt, you won't think you have a chance. You have a chance to make every putt; but even the greatest putters of all time didn't make them all.

The best putting rounds ever

What are the fewest putts ever struck in a PGA Tour round? 18. This amazing record has been accomplished six times:

- ✔ Sam Trahan in the final round of the 1979 IV Philadelphia Golf Classic at Whitemarsh Valley CC

- ✔ Mike McGee in the first round of the 1987 MCI Federal Express St. Jude Classic at Colonial CC

- ✔ Kenny Knox in the first round of the 1989 MCI Heritage Classic at Harbour Town Golf Links

- ✔ Andy North in the second round of the 1990 Anheuser-Busch Golf Classic at Kingsmill GC

- ✔ Jim McGovern in the second round of the 1992 Federal Express St. Jude Classic at TPC Southwind in Memphis

- ✔ Corey Pavin in the second round of the 2000 Bell Canadian Open at Glen Abbey GC near Toronto

The record for the fewest putts over a 9-hole span is seven! Stan Utley made the magic happen on the front-9 at Northview G&CC during the second round of the 2002 Air Canada Championship. Bill Nary, in 1952, rolled seven putts on the back during the third round of the 1952 El Paso Open at El Paso CC.

Turn a missed-putt negative into a positive: If you miss, make sure that you miss by a little. Keep the ball close enough to the hole to leave yourself a tap-in putt — giving yourself a shot at achieving your goal of hitting only 36 putts per round (see the section "Setting a goal: Holing your putt in two" earlier in this chapter).

Letting the misses go

Longer putts are difficult to make regularly, because despite your best efforts, sometimes putts just don't fall. And sometimes it just isn't your fault. You didn't miss-hit the putt. It just didn't go in. Many variables affect your putting, and you encounter factors that you may not be able to account for when you stroke a putt.

So sometimes you hit the absolute perfect putt, with a perfect grip, a perfect line, and the perfect speed, but when the ball approaches the hole, it takes an ungodly turn, hits the corner of the hole, or spins out. A miss isn't always your fault. In the following sections, we cover some of the factors that can knock even the most perfectly struck putt off course. Find some comfort here (and turn to Chapter 12 for information on the mental aspects of the short game).

Blowin' in the wind

Wind is difficult to factor into your putting game. Putting requires such precision that a stiff wind can affect a ball's path toward the hole. Although you know how the wind affects a long-iron shot, most players don't think about how the wind affects their putting.

But can you realistically factor in the wind when you line up your putt? Not likely. Wind mainly gusts and blows, and you can't depend on it. The only thing that you can do is safeguard yourself against an inadvertent penalty. If you address the ball by resting your putter behind the ball, and the wind blows your ball before the stroke, you incur a one-stroke penalty. In heavy winds, therefore, don't dawdle when you ground your putterhead behind the ball. Wait to ground your putterhead until the last possible moment — when you're truly ready to make the stroke.

Grinding it out on the green

Other course dwellers and the green itself provide some bumps in the road, literally, that you often can't factor in during putts:

 ✔ **Growing grass:** Although the slick and smooth surface of the green may seem constant and unchanging to you, you're still putting on grass, which is a living, growing organism. A crew mows the green before the day's play, and a green that no one has played on is much different than a green at 2 o'clock after 20 foursomes. The grass is cut so short that you can't see the growth, but it grows all the time.

✔ **Footprints:** Your fellow players should be polite and careful not to step in your line when you're on the green. But what about all the players who trotted the turf before you? You may not see all the footprints of all the golfers that have played before you, but their impressions are there!

✔ **The un-stepped-on zone:** When golfers walk on the green, read putts, talk, hit putts, walk to their next putt, and leave the green, they never (hopefully) step exactly right next to the hole. Even when players remove the ball from the hole, the closest they step is within 6 to 12 inches. So, after so many players have been on the green, the area within 6 to 12 inches of the hole ends up higher than the next 12 inches because people haven't stepped on it and pressed it down. And as you get away from the 6- to 12-inch area, the green begins to get lumpier.

✔ **Other imperfections:** Nature causes imperfections on the green. Players leave spike marks on the green. Balls leave ball marks on the green. And shoes carry loose impediments onto the green, like rocks and grass clippings.

Rolling with the Fundamentals

In putting, you practice fundamentals and incorporate personal preferences. Your putting style is the most personal of your golf swings, but players who execute the putting stroke according to the proven fundamentals experience better results. How you make yourself feel comfortable and confident enough to get the putterhead through the ball is a matter of preference.

More so than having technique, putting is all about having feel. Success comes with developing a feel for the weight of the putter, the speed of the green, and the roll of the ball. How do you develop feel? Practice, practice, and more practice.

Taking a stance

Where you stand in relation to the ball and the target line is a fundamental matter. To be a good putter, you must place your sight line directly over the ball and look down over your target line, as shown in Figures 7-1a and 7-2a (see the "Targeting a line" section later in this chapter for more on establishing your target line). With the putter, you stand closer to the ball than you do with any other club, because your putter is your shortest stick (unless you opt for a belly putter; see Chapter 3).

After you place your sight line directly over the ball and your target line, your stance is entirely up to you. Stand the way you feel comfortable. Unlike chipping and pitching (see Chapters 4 and 5), where you rarely see varying stances and styles, your putting stance is a preference. Just make sure that you move the putter-head smoothly back on the target line, through the ball, and down the target line without a hint of deceleration (see Figures 7-1b and 7-1c, and check out the "Swinging the flatstick" section later in this chapter).

With any type of golf swing, your legs and the way you stand give you a balanced foundation. Choose a stance that feels comfortable and natural to you when you putt. You may like your feet slightly open. Another player may stand with her feet straight. Simply stand in such a way that you can perform the fundamentals comfortably.

Getting a grip

Your grip pressure on your putter needs to be consistent and comfortable. You shouldn't squeeze the putter grip too tightly. You can sense the weight and position of the clubhead better if you don't squeeze it too tightly, and developing a feel for the putterhead is essential to keeping putts around the hole. You can grip the putter anyway you like, but keep the grip pressure light.

Removing your glove

If you watch professional golf on television, you see PGA Tour players removing their golf gloves before they putt. This act seems to have become fashionable among many recreational golfers, too. Perhaps players feel that removing their glove helps them have better feel when they putt.

If removing your glove makes you feel more confident, and you don't hold up play when you're next to putt, go ahead. But Jack Nicklaus, for one, never removed his glove to putt. He said he just didn't want to be bothered to take his glove on and off so many times during a round of golf. And Jack Nicklaus is considered one of the greatest clutch putters of all time.

Figure 7-1: Keep your sight line directly over the ball and form a triangle with your shoulders, arms, and grip.

From different stances, to the various types of putters on the market (see Chapter 3), to different putting grips, putting has become more and more individualized over the years. It used to be that most players had the same, or at least similar, standard putting grips and putter types.

Now the best players in the world make various putting grips fashionable when they play for big money on television. Some new-fangled putting grips are as simple as switching hand position for a cross-handed or "left-hand-low" grip (for righties). Bernhard Langer was one of the first to have people scratching their heads when he used one hand to clutch the putter grip and steady it against his other forearm. A good number of PGA Tour players now use a bizarre looking grip called "the claw," which makes one hand look like a lobster claw clutching the putter grip. To try it, place your lead hand on the putter as you normally do, but clutch the putter with your dominant hand as if your hand were a claw. Put the handle of the putter in the web between your thumb and first finger. The back of your hand will be flat, parallel to the ground and your target line.

Most of the grips the pros use are inspired through necessity — the necessity to adhere to the fundamentals of putting by quieting the wrists and keeping solid through impact (see the "Stiffening your wrists" section later in this chapter). If one of these grips helps you to putt solidly and in the subconscious — and you're not too self-conscious to use it — by all means, use it. As long as you adhere to the fundamentals, you can't hold a putter the wrong way.

Targeting a line

Every putt that you hit should be a straight putt. You wish, you say? We mean that you should stroke every putt straight down a target line, in the direction of the amount of break you need to play to make the putt roll into or near the hole (see the section "Reading the Break of the Greens" later in this chapter). You read the break of the green and determine the line the putt needs to go on and roll the ball straight on that line. You don't try to hook or bend a putt or put English on it. Choose your line. Keep it straight and simple (see Figure 7-2).

To hit a straight putt, imagine a straight line that goes from the back of the ball straight down your target line. The straight line should stretch to the hole or to a point you selected so the ball breaks to the hole. (Check out Chapter 15 for a straight-line putting drill.)

To increase your chance of success, pick a spot on the target line to aim for. The target isn't necessarily the hole; the target is the point you need to focus on in order to get your ball rolling down the proper target line and toward the hole. The spot may be a few feet in front of you, or it may be 10 feet in front of you. It depends on the length of your putt. Choose a spot somewhere between your ball and the hole on the target line.

Figure 7-2: Pick a target line, find a spot to aim at, and roll your ball straight down the line toward the target.

Imagine a bowling lane, which has a foul line and arrows that serve as aiming devices. Same concept (but without the curves or embarrassing gutter balls).

Swinging the flatstick

After you read the break of the green (see the section "Reading the Break of the Greens" later in this chapter), find your target line, pick a spot, and get your eyes over the line, you need to concentrate on swinging the putter back and forward along the line (see Figure 7-2), keeping the following fundamentals in mind:

✔ **Keep your putterhead on line through its entire movement.** The putter needs to travel straight back on the target line and then straight forward on the target line.

Keeping your legs, head, and shoulders still helps you swing the putter with your arms and hands.

✔ **Keep the putterhead square and aimed straight to the target.** The face of the blade should be perpendicular to the target (see Figure 7-3) and remain so throughout the stroke. The direction the blade faces shouldn't wobble; it should remain true to the arc of the putterhead.

Keeping your wrists solid and firm helps you maintain the direction of the putterface.

✔ **Never decelerate the putter during the swing.** This putting-scared style kills your putting stroke and your score. Accelerate an equal amount through the swing as you do with the backswing.

Putting is about rolling the ball, not hitting the ball. You want to be thinking about tumbling the ball end over end.

You could be anyone and go out on that putting green with Tiger Woods or Brad Faxon or the best putter in the world and putt 10-footers competitively. You don't have any chance to be competitive with them in any other part of the game. You can be 100 years old and frail as can be and still have enough strength to make the putter go back and through at the right speed to roll the ball. That's really all putting is about. You shouldn't do anything that takes away from the simple act of making the putter swing.

Figure 7-3: Keep your clubface square to the target line.

Playing in the subconscious is the best way to enjoy success, especially in putting. You practice and prepare in the conscious state, and you can turn it all off and go to the subconscious during your round.

Determining the proper speed

To determine the perfect speed for a ball to die at the hole, picture an area at a length within 12 to 17 inches beyond and around the hole where your target line should end. If you hit a putt at a speed that kills the ball in this area, the ball has the speed to roll over certain imperfections in the green and the brakes to submit to gravity and tumble into the hole without spinning out.

The old joke is very true: "Most short putts don't go in!" Your goal should be to get the ball just past the hole. If you leave the ball 12 inches past the hole, percentages dictate, even with the average player, that you'll make the 12-inch comeback putt more often than not. Leaving a putt short is a wasted effort. Give the ball a chance to go in! For more tips on straightening out the speed piece of the equation, see Chapter 9.

Staying low and level

When you swing the putter back and forward along the target line, keep the putter as low to the ground as you can without scraping the grass (see Figure 7-2b). It should feel more like you're letting the putter hang; you don't want to push it down. If you swing the blade close to the ground, you can stay level.

Awareness of the putterhead helps you keep the putter low throughout the stroke, and a light grip helps you get a sense for the size and the weight of the putterhead. Let the putterhead swing through the ball like the bottom of a pendulum on a grandfather clock. The pendulum swings as low as it physically can in the arc, and so too should your putterhead. Keeping the blade low helps you concentrate on *rolling* — not hitting — the putt.

You need to stay level. When you hit your driver, your shoulders should stay level when you turn. The same thing goes for putting. After you take your stance and put your eyes over the target line, you want to keep the putterhead close to the ground and level. Take it back as low to the ground as you can, using your level shoulders to propel the club, and follow through as low to the ground as you can.

Stilling your legs

Your legs should stay quiet throughout the putting stroke. Putting is about moving the putterhead at a specific speed to allow the ball to die within 12 inches of the hole. In order to do that, you need to feel the putterhead as you swing it. You don't need to make a bunch of shoulder and body turns or use any powerful leg action.

Stiffening your wrists

Another key to rolling the ball, bringing the putter back on line, sweeping the club low to the ground, and maintaining good speed is keeping your wrists firm and inactive during the putting stroke. You want your arms and hands working as one unit instead of independent of each other.

If your wrists get ahead of your arms as they guide the putter through the stroke, the direction of the putterhead or angle of the face can change.

Think of creating an upside down triangle with your body when you hold the putter and stand over the ball. Your shoulder line, parallel to the ground, is the base of the triangle, and your two arms, which lead to the putter, are the sides of the triangle. Your triangle should simply pivot as one unit as you take the putter back and through the ball. (See Figure 7-1 for the shape of this setup.)

Freezing your head and eyes

After you complete the putting stroke and send the ball toward the hole, keep your eyes focused on the spot the ball occupied (see Figure 7-1c). If you keep your eyes trained on the spot where the ball was, you're more likely to let the putter swing through to its completion and not interrupt it or swing it offline by looking up too early and decelerating.

When wrists ruled

If you watch old films, you'll see that golfers, like Bobby Jones and even up to the time of Billy Casper, were a lot "wristier" with their putting style. In the olden days, putters had more loft because the greens were much slower. The grass on the greens was longer because greenskeepers didn't cut the grass at the low level we enjoy today. When players putted, they used a flick of the wrist to get the ball airborne with enough "oomph" to get to the hole. It was much like chipping with a 7-iron to get the ball over longer grass and onto the green.

You don't face the same problems today. The greens you putt on are flat and fast and your putter has very little loft. Keep your wrists firm and inactive during the putting the stroke.

You don't need to watch the ball go into the hole or miss the hole — other than to satisfy your curiosity and excitement. Instead, try listening for the sound of the ball falling into the hole. What a wonderful sound to hear! Try it and see immediately how much more solidly you roll the ball.

Following through and holding your finish

After your putter strikes the ball, the followthrough is extremely important. You wonder, "What sense does it make to follow through when the ball has already left the putterface?" Letting the putterhead follow through and swing naturally ensures that you'll accelerate through the ball. The natural "fall" of the putterhead into the ball initiates the ball's forward roll along the target line. Any effort to slow the putterhead or stop it after the ball is gone causes the putterhead to wobble off-line, pulling or pushing the putt awry.

As the putterhead follows through toward the conclusion of the stroke, let it swing freely through and then hold your finish with the putterhead pointing toward the hole as if you're posing for a picture (see Figure 7-2b).

Mediocre and poor putters recoil their blade after the stroke. We've all done it. To recoil, you need to slow down your putter as it comes through the ball, and if you do that, your blade wanders off-line and hits the ball at the wrong speed.

You can't recoil without slowing down. Finish with the putterhead low to the ground on the target line and hold the finish — you become a better putter because you give the putterhead the opportunity to roll the ball end over end.

Reading the Break of the Greens

Reading the break of a green is an art and a gift. It all seems so simple — you look at the ground and decide which way the surface of the green tilts, and then you adjust the line of your putt accordingly.

Sometimes, however, the break and slope can be tricky to see. Sometimes you may face more than one break in a putt. Sometimes a nearby hill affects the break. Sometimes the green naturally breaks toward water. It takes patience and imagination to envision the path the ball may naturally take as it rolls along. We do have, however, a few ways that you can help yourself read the break — clues that help you forecast the way the ball will roll. (Check out Chapter 9 for more in-depth putting strategies, including ways to deal with particularly difficult breaks.)

Examining all angles

Don't hold up play, but do look at the putt from all angles. As you walk up to the green or while the other players putt, move discreetly around and look at your putt from behind the ball and from behind the hole back toward the ball. Look at the putt from the side. If you can, get down low and look at the ball from a worm's-eye view. (You can do this easily on raised greens or from bunkers.) The more information you can process, the better the result.

Closing your eyes

If you have trouble seeing the break, stand with your hands at your sides and close your eyes. You can stand at the hole and do this or stand behind your ball and do it. Closing your eyes causes your other senses to come alive to maintain your sense of balance. You feel yourself being pulled by gravity one way or another and your body naturally corrects that pull. Take these clues to heart.

Spilling a bucket of water

To help yourself read the break of a green, you can stand at the hole and imagine that you've spilled a huge bucket of water on top of the hole. Which way would all that water run after you fill up the hole and it overflows? Would it run off the front of the green? Would it stream to the back or off the side? Adjust your line accordingly. If you have trouble imagining, don't go for realism and dump water in . . . unless you think you can outrun the greenskeeper and the cops.

Looking into the hole

Looking down into the hole can provide a sloping clue. Because a plastic cup lines the actual hole after the greenskeeper cuts it, you can see the discrepancy in the earth that rings around the top of the cup if the hole sits on a rise or a hill. The side with more dirt is the lower side of the hole, and the side with less dirt is higher. Therefore, if you putt the ball toward the higher side, it rolls and slides down toward the lower side.

Watching other players' putts

The break of another player's putt isn't proprietary information. Pay attention to your playing partners and competitors when they putt and watch how their putts react to the break of the green. Sometimes you get lucky and someone has the exact same line as you. In the 2004 Masters, Phil Mickelson caught a break when Chris DiMarco's bunker shot rolled behind his ball, giving him a great view of the break of his winning putt. But even putts stroked from another angle can tell you something about the beak of the green.

Although it isn't against the rules of golf to stand directly behind or directly in front of another player (beyond the hole) on the line of his putt, players consider it bad form and inappropriate. The player may ask you to move so that you don't distract him. You should, if you want to look from directly on the line, wait until the ball leaves his putterhead to step into the line.

An ode to miniature golf

The clown's nose, the windmill, the waterfalls — ah, the joys of miniature golf. Also known as Putt-Putt Golf, miniature golf is considered child's play in the golf world. Although players attend the big-money championships of miniature golf, most golfers turn their noses up at 18 little par-1s or 2s with a snack bar at the end.

Some are very simple in design, and some are very elaborate, with wild landscaping, bridges, statues, and theme park features like pirate ships and cannons. Some have artificial turf, and some miniature golf courses, such as the "ladies putting course" at St. Andrews, are made of natural grass.

Arnold Palmer owned Putt-Putt golf franchises, and Walt Disney World and other big-name resorts have made miniature golf courses, or at least practice greens, a staple.

A trip to the miniature golf course can do you some good. You can use your own putter and your own ball — rather than a rubber red one — and in addition to getting a little putting practice in, you may even have fun and remember that fun is what the game is really about! (Just don't hit your ball down the hole on the 18th . . . it won't be your ball anymore, although you may win a free game!)

Part III
Short Game
Strategies

The 5th Wave   By Rich Tennant

"I'm practicing my short lobs. Now close the closet door."

In this part . . .

You need to do more than keep your eye on the ball to improve your short game. Part III reveals strategies that can take your performance to the next level. The pitch and run, the Texas wedge, the yips, and the flop aren't dance moves; they're short-game terms we explain in this part. And in case your head drifts into the clouds or your emotions plummet to the gutter, we give you tips on how to keep your mental game on point.

Chapter 8

Waging (and Wedging) a Ground Campaign

• •

In This Chapter

▶ Hitting short-game shots with a low trajectory

▶ Choking your club and punching your ball to the green

▶ Bumping and running to the flag

▶ Putting off the fringe

▶ Hanging onto the green for dear life

▶ Knowing when to yank the pin

• •

Is golf a game of vertical darts? Or is it more like lawn bowling over long distances? You most likely view and play the game somewhere between these two ends of the spectrum. You face times during a round when shots from both extremes are required and advisable. But as an overall philosophy, are you better off adopting a high-flying air attack or a low-to-the-earth ground campaign?

This chapter makes the case for going low to have lower scores. We explore the merits of playing the ball low and letting the ball roll to the hole rather than trying to dunk it in on the fly. We discuss the time-honored bump-and-run shot, as well as other tricks of the trade, such as choking down on your club and putting from the fringe. We also clue you in to ground-attack subtleties, such as what shots to hit in certain conditions and leaving the flag in for better results, that can improve your scores around the greens.

Gaining an Advantage by Keeping the Ball Low

For some reason, most golfers seem to enjoy hitting majestic, high shots that stick into the green. Maybe it's nature's backdrop as the ball flies through the sky or the thrill of seeing the ball land and stop close to the pin. Maybe players want to emulate a PGA Tour player's often-high trajectory. Truly, a great high shot is fun to watch, but television can distort reality.

Sometimes, hitting a high shot just isn't practical: You don't always face the obstacles that call for a flop shot (see Chapter 11), and sometimes, such as during heavy winds or when hard ground makes it tougher to use a more lofted club, trying to get a ball high in the air isn't advisable.

Charting your course

Keeping the ball low is an effective strategy that you can easily adopt. Big Ten college football coach Bo Schembechler, during his years at the University of Michigan, was famous for saying, "When you pass the ball, three things can happen . . . and two of them are bad." Bo liked completed passes, but he disdained the interceptions and incompletions and the risk that came with passing the football, so he embraced the safe, effective "three yards and a cloud of dust" philosophy that fans disliked due to its boring nature.

Want to take the risk out of your short game? Want to run the ball up the middle? The following circumstances encourage the ground game in golf:

  ✔ **You're close to the green:** You can judge how far a ball will roll much easier than you can judge how far it will fly. Therefore, if no impediments block your path to the hole, it makes sense to keep the ball low and get it rolling on the ground as soon as possible when you're close to the green. From 30 yards and closer, popping the ball high up in the air can only introduce problems. Instead, use the natural contour of the green to roll the ball to the hole.

  Hitting a chip shot or pitch shot at a low trajectory can help you become much more precise with your short shots. Imagine you have a baseball in your hand and a steel bucket sits 30 yards away. Do you think it would be easier to land the ball in the bucket through the air or to roll the ball so that it hits the bucket or stops near it? If given only one chance, which route would you rather take?

  ✔ **You have wind to deal with:** The higher you hit the ball, the more susceptible it is to the vagaries of the wind. The wind can blow your ball to the left or push it to the right when you hit it up high. If you hit your shot into the wind, breezes can knock

> a high ball down short of the target, and if the wind is at your back, a high ball may balloon over the green and into trouble.
>
> A low, firm shot can bore through the wind and hold its line much better than a high ball. Keeping the ball low in the wind is an easier, safer, and ultimately more effective shot.

Playing the ball low also gives you helpful options when you find your ball under a tree or behind branches that can block a high shot. Even if you can't reach the green, you can play a sensible, low-running lay-up shot to a suitable spot in the fairway. Practicing these types of shots helps you better understand the distance control involved around and away from the greens.

Choking down for a knockout knock-down

The dreaded C word . . . choking! But in golf, choking doesn't *always* mean the psychologically induced physical reaction to the pressure placed on the precision of a pitch shot! Oh, sure, you have plenty to get nervous about when you're in a tight match or trying to put the finishing touches on a career-best round. Golf is funny that way — it can get to you! But a good short game can help you achieve your goals in golf and set new ones. A *great* short game helps even more! Mastering the fundamentals means having a basic knowledge of how the short game works and an understanding of the options available to you.

Choking down . . . not choking . . . is a valuable fundamental for keeping a ball low to the ground. *Choking down* on a club simply means placing your hands lower on the grip than you normally do. You take your normal grip, but you position your hands halfway down the rubber or leather handle nearer to the exposed graphite or metal shaft of the club.

Reviewing the physics of choking down

The ability to play a variety of shots gives your game depth and versatility. And playing a variety of shots requires a variety of grips, stances, and swings. Hitting a *punch shot,* or *knock-down shot,* is one of those options. A ball you hit with a lower trajectory is a knock-down.

 A small physics lesson may help. The length of a club governs the arc and plane of a golf swing. Choking down shortens the club, shortens the arc, and makes the plane flatter, which makes the ball fly on a lower trajectory.

To achieve a low, controlled ball flight on some pitches and chips, you may put your hands low enough on the handle to almost reach the steel or the graphite of the shaft.

Choking down on the club also lets you stand very close to the target line, which allows you to look at the shot almost as if you're putting. And although you effectively shorten the club and reduce the distance the ball can travel, the lower trajectory can make up for that lost distance through control and feel.

Executing a successful choke-down shot

You choke down on a club when you want to hit a low-flying, hard, straight shot. These swings are often referred to as *punch shots* because of the abbreviated, controlled swing and the manner in which the ball seems to punch through the air. You don't have to use the word punch or think of it as a punch shot, however, because the word may cause you to tense up or swing the club in a violent, punch-like fashion.

Even a shot that requires abbreviated movements and causes a hard-driving ball, such as a punch shot, should come from a fluid, relaxed motion.

You can, if the situation dictates, punch a shot on a lower trajectory than normal with more lofted clubs. You may find that you like hitting a knockdown-style shot, for instance, if you find your ball at a distance from the green that puts you between clubs — too long for the pitching wedge but too short for the 9-iron. Choke down and hit a knock-down 9-iron.

Follow these steps to get your ball flying lower and straighter:

1. **Choke down on the handle of the club. Use your normal grip, but slide your hands farther down on the handle. The farther down your hands go, the shorter and lower the shot will fly.**

2. **Position the ball slightly back of center in your stance.**

3. **How far you take the club back depends on how far you want to hit it, but a three-quarter-length swing often does the trick.**

4. **Keep your swing speed consistent and hit down and through the ball on the target line.**

   Keep your hands ahead of the ball at impact to send the ball darting on a low path. Make sure you keep your hands and wrists firm to avoid any collapse (flipping) that could cause you to change the loft or direction of the clubface.

Some instructors teach that an abbreviated followthrough should follow the choked-down punch shot. The technique is sound, but only advanced players with a mastery of short-game fundamentals should attempt it. Typically, an abbreviated followthrough results in a natural deceleration at impact in an attempt to slow the club down in time to stop it quickly. Deceleration in any golf swing is a recipe for disaster: It almost always causes the ball to go offline or results in a poor swing. You don't want to inadvertently train yourself to decelerate your swing and ruin your short-game fundamentals. Work on your fundamentals before you experiment with an abbreviated followthrough.

Pitching and Running

The *pitch and run* shot, sometimes called a *bump and run,* is a good way to play the ball low around the greens and to keep it out of the wind on longer shots. The pitch and run acts just like its name suggests — you pitch the ball and it runs on the ground toward the hole. (See Chapter 5 for more on the pitching portion of the shot.)

Say you're standing 20 to 40 yards from the green and mulling over your options. A little wind is in the air, and you don't have bunkers or water hazards in your way; nothing but short grass lies between you and the hole. A pitch and run shot is an effective option, literally at your fingertips. A pitch and run stays low to the ground for only a short distance and then lands, bounces, and rolls the rest of the way to the hole.

Taking aim

With a pitch and run, you have a few more mental calculations to consider than you do when dropping a lob shot onto the green from the air. You must imagine the entire life of the shot before you hit it and then recreate your vision. It can be a fun and effective shot if you envision and line it up properly:

- ✔ **Decide on the shape and length of the "pitch" portion of the shot.** Decide how far you want the ball to fly before it starts rolling. Consider how hard you must hit the ball to get it to fly that far and pick a target to set up your target line (see Chapter 2 for more on the target line).

- ✔ **Figure out how far the ball has to roll after it touches down to reach the green or the hole.** You also have to take the roll into account when deciding on your backswing. You may have to hit the ball hard to get it to roll across the green. Take the thickness of the grass and other variables into account also.

✔ **Factor in the break and slope of the green.** Look at the green and predict what direction the ball will roll after it reaches the green. What's the break and slope of the green? Use this info to pick a target and target line. Essentially, you approach this aspect of the pitch and run as you do a putt, which we cover in Chapter 7.

Decide on a target line that will steer the ball in the proper direction. Stand behind your ball and envision this imaginary line from your ball to the spot you want the ball to initially land on. You now have a target line that you can use for aiming purposes. But to land your target, you have to grab a stick from your bag.

Selecting your club

A 7-iron is a perfect choice to hit the bump and run, but you can play a pitch and run shot with any iron you prefer — even a 3-iron! But a 7-iron is your best bet, because the face of the club is lofted enough to help the ball into the air and not lofted so much that it sends the ball too high. A 7-iron can get the ball easily off the turf and propel it forward.

Of course, you may face occasions when you want less loft and more distance, such as running a ball from outside 50 yards or trying to keep it under a tree branch. In these cases, a less lofted club, such as a 5-iron, may suit you. Practice with all your irons so you get comfortable with them and know how far each will send the ball and on what type of flight.

Getting in your stance

After you select your club, address the ball by turning your front toe to point 45 degrees between the target line and an imaginary line perpendicular to the target line. Open your shoulders an equal amount so that your body is open to and nearly facing the target. Keep the ball in the middle of your stance. Your stance is the same as it is for a standard pitch shot (see Chapter 5).

Taking your swing

The swing here is largely the one you make for a pitch shot (see Chapter 5); only the style of the shot differs. Design it in your head to land the ball front of the green and run up. Swing the club no further on your followthrough on the "hands of the clock" than when you took the club back. For instance, imagine that midnight is straight above your head and 6 o'clock is in between your feet where your club rests behind the ball. If you take the club back to 4 o'clock on the dial, follow through no farther than 7 o'clock, the corresponding number on the other side of the dial.

How far back you swing the club determines how far the ball flies, just as with a standard pitch. But in this case, you want to aim for the front of the green or just off the front of the green to give the ball enough room to run, so you want to take the club only far enough back to land the ball on the desired spot and let it bounce and run up to the hole.

Remember to take the club straight back on the target line and follow through along the target line. Don't decelerate the clubhead as it strikes through the ball. And keep your head down.

The best way to master the pitch and run is to spend time hitting the shot on the practice range or at a short game practice area. Try hitting the shot at varying lengths and with different clubs until you find an iron that you're comfortable with at different distances. Take pride in your ability to imagine these shots — you can enjoy consistent success with the shot after you get a feel for it. And in addition to being effective, pitch and runs are fun!

Discovering the Famed Texas Wedge

You may have heard the term *Texas wedge* bandied about by golfers before. And you may have wondered, "What the heck is a Texas wedge and why do they call it that?" The Texas wedge actually refers to the putter. You use the Texas wedge when you hit a shot from any spot off the green where you traditionally use a wedge. The slang refers more to a strategy and technique you can use as improvisation around the greens.

But why Texas? Because the plains of Texas are well known for their sweeping, whipping winds, which make keeping the ball low a necessity for golfers. And no club keeps the ball lower than a putter!

Using a putter from off the green can be a very effective strategy if the conditions and the situation warrant it:

- ✔ If the ground is firm, dry, and fast

- ✔ If the grass leading to the green is short

- ✔ If no bunker or other hazard lies between you and the hole or along the target line

- ✔ If the target line doesn't run too severely uphill, although moderate elevation is fine, provided you allow for it

- ✔ If strong winds make the shot a more attractive option than a pitch into the air

Playing this shot effectively requires imagination and practice on your part. Spend a little time around the practice green working it into your repertoire. After you become proficient at very long putts, you may be surprised at how much easier the short ones feel!

Don't be embarrassed to putt from off the green, and don't be swayed by players who tease your strategy by mocking it with the phrase "Texas wedge." Not everyone has this effective and unique shot in the bag, but we know that the best players in the world do.

Saddling up the Texas wedge in Scotland

Michael Patrick Shiels once played in Scotland with a man named Steve Forrest who was enduring the heat of a closely contested match. Standing 80 yards from the hole on the par-5 18th at Nairn, Forrest decided his most comfortable option was to use a putter to get the ball onto the green. His opponent had hit a wedge shot from a similar distance that bounced onto the green and stopped 30 feet away from the hole. Although his Scottish caddie protested mightily, Forrest insisted on pulling the putter from his bag. The caddie, realizing the result of the match was hanging in the balance, was so distraught that he looked away and covered his eyes, refusing to watch! What a sight he missed! Forrest gave the ball a full putt and it rolled all the way down the center of the fairway up onto the green and then curled gently toward the hole, stopping 10 feet from the flagstick. Forrest gave himself a great chance to birdie the hole and win! But alas, he and his opponent both two-putted and the match was halved, but his Texas-wedge tactic proved that with a little imagination, you have more than one way to skin a cat (or win a skin)!

Oh, and by the way: The next day, Forrest was so pleased with his long-putting prowess that he used only his putter to play the entire inward half of the New Course at St. Andrews as an experiment. He shot a 52.

Holding the Green

Keeping the ball on the green with your approach shot, whether you pitch or chip, is obviously your goal. And, after you practice your short game enough to get comfortable, sticking the green can become an expectation.

Sometimes, you have to be crafty to get the ball to stay on, or *hold,* the green. It may be more difficult in certain situations:

✔ Hard greens, from a lack of rain or maintenance practices, may cause the ball to bounce over.

✔ Fast, short-cut greens tend to run balls into the fringe.

✔ Crowned greens, which slope off every side from every angle, can be difficult to hold, especially if a greenskeeper or the weather makes them hard and/or fast.

✔ Greens with severe undulations or moguls can be tough to hold because of the angles the ball encounters when it hits the slopes and how it rolls afterward.

So how can you get your ball to stop on the green during these conditions? Get creative. Sometimes you may have to aim for a target away from the hole and visualize how the ball will roll after it hits that spot on the green.

Sometimes, with pitch shots especially, you may choose not to aim at the green at all. You may be better off landing the ball in front of the green and letting it roll on to the putting surface so it can run out of speed. Hitting the longer grass or a mound in front of the green can help to slow the ball down enough so that it trickles toward the hole and stops instead of skipping, sliding, rocketing, or rolling over the back of the green or off the side.

You may also consider hitting the ball high and dropping it down onto the green (see Chapter 11). A high, spinning ball falls in a vertical fashion and doesn't roll very far. Even a high pitch shot (see Chapter 5) struck with a light grip can land in a soft and deadened fashion and stop or check up before rolling out a bit or spinning back.

Pulling the Pin . . . or Leaving It In?

According to the rules of golf, when you play shots from off the green, you must decide whether you want to leave the flagstick in the hole, remove it, or have it tended by your caddie or playing partner. We outline the factors that go into making such a decision in the following sections.

From off the green

When your ball comes to rest off the green, including that closely mown area around the edge of the green called the *fringe* or the *collar,* you have the option of leaving the flagstick in the hole. Whether to pull or leave the pin is an age-old debate among golfers. When you have to play a short shot and you have flagstick options, what should you do?

The debate, as you may have guessed, features pros and cons for both approaches. The scenario goes something like this:

The pull-the-pin angle has its pros and cons:

- **Pros:** Taking the flagstick from the hole clears the pathway to the bottom from any obstruction. Without the pin in, the ball can fall freely into the hole.

- **Cons:** If you pull the pin, a ball moving too fast can roll right over the hole.

And the leave-it-in approach also has pluses and minuses:

- **Pros:** The advantage of leaving the pin in the hole is that your ball may hit the flagstick and fall in. In addition, if you hit your chip too aggressively, the ball may hit the flagstick and slow down. The flagstick can serve as a "backstop" for chip shots — especially downhill chip shots on fast greens, the type of shot that can run away from you in a hurry.

- **Cons:** Not taking the pin out can keep the ball from falling in, causing it to ricochet away from the cup. And if the green is speedy or downhill on the sides of the cup, your ball may roll quickly off the green.

And now we're back to the question at hand: pull the pin or leave it in? Everyone has an opinion on this matter. "The pin never helps a good shot" is one mantra, and some professionals say that they pull the pin when they want to make the shot and leave it in when they hope to get the ball close. Experts have conducted scientific research, but it ultimately proves inconclusive.

Ultimately, whether to pull the pin or leave it in is a matter of personal preference. But the following bits of advice may help you make your decision based on the situation you're in:

- ✔ You may consider leaving the flagstick in on slippery downhill chips and taking it out in uphill situations.

- ✔ Check the angle on which the hole is cut. If the hole is cut into the green at a severe angle, the flagstick may unevenly block one side of the hole.

   Without slowing up play, always check before you hit any short-game shot to be certain other players have properly inserted the flagstick into the cup so it doesn't lean to one side or impede the hole.

From on the green

According to the rules of golf, a ball played from on the green must not strike the flagstick. If it does, a two-stroke penalty, or loss of the hole in match play, is assessed.

When your ball is on the green and you can see the hole from where your ball lies, remove the flagstick. But if you're putting from far enough away that you can't clearly see the hole, your caddie or playing partner can to tend the flagstick by standing beside the hole and removing it after you stroke your putt and before it reaches the hole.

Good caddies, and hopefully fellow playing partners, know that when tending the flagstick during long putts, you should twist the pin and pull it from the bottom of the hole before the player strokes the putt. Sometimes the sand that builds up in the bottom of the cup can get wet or dry like paste and make the pin stick in the hole. You don't want this to happen when the ball is in motion, because if you can't remove the flagstick in time and the ball strikes it, the putter incurs a penalty. We have also heard of occasions when people tending the pin have attempted to remove it and pulled the entire plastic cup liner out of the hole, which impeded the ball from rolling into the hole (obviously) and forced the putter to take a costly two-stroke penalty.

"Now run up there!"

Michael Patrick Shiels was once paired with a novice player visiting from Switzerland named Alex at Emerald Dunes Golf Club near Palm Beach, Florida. He had spent time on a practice range but had never before set foot on an actual golf course. Poor Alex needed a sleeve of balls just to reach the first fairway. It began raining when we reached the first green, and Alex, who was ill prepared for any form of inclement weather, became thoroughly soaked from his round spectacles to the laces of his tennis shoes. Each time he sloshed back into the cart, he created a river on the seat that drained directly into my pockets. And return to the cart often he did, because the number of strokes he needed to complete the first hole was nearer to 20 than 5!

Slosh. Splat. Slosh. Splat.

With his eyeglasses steamed and spotted and his black curly hair matted, Alex joyfully struck earthbound balls all over the terrain and giggled his way to and fro. When he did reach the green, he was clueless as to where to step and stand and how to mark his ball. Trying to mark and line up our putts and stay out of each other's way looked more like a drunken square dance!

On the fourth hole, his ball was 60 yards from the green, so I advised him to pitch a controlled 7-iron shot and bump it up through the opening in front of the green to let it roll to the hole. As I watched from my seat in the cart, Alex did just that. He punched that 7-iron right on line. As the ball bounced about 15 yards short of the green, I urged it on by yelling, "Now run up there!"

Hearing me, Alex broke into a full sprint and ran up toward the green! I felt badly and tried not to laugh, because Alex was completely startled by my command and he took me literally, thinking I was impatiently yelling at him to "run up there!" When he got to the green, he was panting and peering back at me, wondering what to do next!

Chapter 9

Selecting Putting Strategies and Remedies

In This Chapter

▶ Targeting the hole

▶ Lagging for safety

▶ Controlling your speed

▶ Dealing with slick breaks

▶ Snipping the yips

*P*utting is a skill you perform with an innate sense of touch and feel. A sense of the speed and the break of the green is a gift that the best putters seem to be born with — a gift of skill mixed with steely nerves. But no great putter just walks onto a green and sinks every putt he looks at without carefully thinking over the situation, reviewing his options, considering the circumstances, and strategizing about how to sink it or get it close.

Of course, a great putter practices a great deal to become comfortable with his knowledge of the options and ability to assess the situation. Practice builds the confidence to implement whichever strategic approach is necessary.

In this chapter, we build on the putting mechanics we introduce in Chapter 7 by focusing on a number of putting strategies you can incorporate into your game. We suggest that you try these strategies out when you practice. If you get comfortable with them, continue to practice and become proficient enough to utilize them during play. When you play, concentrate on putting in the subconscious after you consider all your tried and tested strategies. You want your putting to become an effortless, Zen-like activity that happens through natural skill, not through mechanical technique. Practice your mechanics and technique well enough to shut off those thoughts. We also give you a hand if the wheels have fallen off your putting game by examining the causes and providing some possible corrections for the dreaded yips.

Becoming a Great Putter

You can always see something special in a great putter. And "great putter" can describe the piece of equipment you use to putt with and the person doing the putting.

On the inanimate side of coin, you can go out and spend hundreds of dollars on a great putter, but your flatstick is really only as great as you think it is. If you need to spend a lot of money to convince yourself that something is great, by all means, doll out the cash! (But check out Chapter 3 before you do, where we discuss the ins and outs of picking a putter.) But by the same token, if you really believe that the piece of metal you carry to the green — whether you have the latest and greatest in putting technology or your old, trusty-rusty putter from your youth — is a great putter, it will be! Heck, you can make putts with the leg of a table.

The key to becoming a great putter is confidence. If you believe that you're a great putter, you will be. Ask any good putter, and the confident Joe will tell you that he believes he has a chance to make any putt he looks at. You can spot good putters a mile away: They look over a putt with almost a grin on their face, as if they're working on the Sunday morning crossword puzzle. They approach their ball and line up over it like a gunslinger, cocked and ready to draw.

When the putt goes into the hole, they act humble and nonchalant; after all, they expect to make every putt. When they miss, the flatstick masters always have a ready-made, ego-protecting reason: The ball hit a stone or a spike mark. Sometimes you see them look at the hole as if it moved while the ball rolled toward it. Often, you hear them say things such as, "There's no way that putt can break that way" or "I hit a good putt, it just didn't go in." Your goal is to become as confident and witty as these rulers of the green.

Settling on a Style

Some golfers are so confident, or trick themselves into feeling so confident, that they convince themselves they can make any putt they look at, no matter the length or the severity of the break. Without reservation, like a gunslinger, they size up every putt, walk it off, read the break, figure the speed, and then, with squinty eyes and ice water in their veins, they fire at the hole.

Maybe your mindset doesn't boast the bravado required to putt like a gunslinger. But that doesn't mean you can't be effective. Your approach to becoming a good putter may be to stalk the hole like a predator and sneak up on it like a stealth cat. Yes, you guessed it: We're talking about lag putting, which can make you a formidable opponent on the greens.

Adopting, practicing, and perfecting either approach is a viable route to lowering your score. Your personality may steer you toward one mindset or the other, or experience on the golf course may lead you to prefer being bold or cautious.

In fact, you needn't even settle on one putting personality forever or on every putt. Maybe you like to feel cautious on long putts and adopt the gunslinger mentality on the shorter putts. Maybe on a given day you feel more confident with your putting, so you go for it more. If you don't have the confidence just yet, you may spend the round in a putt-lagging mindset. Conditions can also dictate the style of your putting. Are the greens dangerously fast enough to inspire caution? Are they flat and slow enough to encourage boldness? Whatever makes you comfortable and allows you to putt in the subconscious, go with it!

Make it or break it

So you've decided that the best way to get a putt close to the hole and win the showdown with your opponent is to try to make it. If you want to be a putting gunslinger, however, you need to heed a few factors to make certain you don't get yourself gunned down!

If you want to hit firmer, more aggressive putts, you should do so by simply lengthening your backstroke, not by swinging the putter harder or faster. Just like shooting an arrow from a bow, draw the string back more to make the arrow go farther. And be sure that your putterhead accelerates through the ball during and after contact.

You need to be aggressive if you want to knock down putts from all over the green, and throwing some muscle behind your putts can be tricky: Be careful not to make unusually firm, strong strokes that restrict your putterhead from moving smoothly along the target line. Here are some other drawbacks of ramming the ball home:

> ✔ Aggressively stroked, hard putts can speed right through the break. Speed may be the most important factor for a putt, but you can't become so concerned about the speed that you forget about the line. You can try to will the ball into the hole, but don't force it in.

✔ Faster, firmer putts are more likely to hit the hole and spin out (ride along the lip and, with centrifugal force, flip back up out of the hole) or hop over.

The only merit of firm, fast putting is that you never leave the putt short. But if you keep running putts three-feet beyond the hole, you're likely to three-putt more often.

Try to stop your putts within 17 inches (or less) beyond the hole. If you consistently leave yourself a one-foot comebacker, you can watch your scores lower and brag about your perfect speed control.

Learning from your putts

It sounds simple, but you have to spend as much time as you can trying to sink putts from as many different lengths and on as many different breaks as possible. Practice sinking long putts and short putts; spend time holing out straight putts; hit putts that break right-to-left or left-to right; and roll balls both uphill and downhill. By practicing every type of putt, you get comfortable with almost any mindset.

You get better and gain confidence with each putt you sink, but you also get better after you analyze the ones you miss:

✔ Did you misread the break? (See Chapter 7 and the "Conquering Speedy Breaks" section in this chapter.)

✔ Did you hit the putt too hard or too soft?

✔ Did you pull the putt or push it with an uneven or angled stroke? (See Chapter 15 for drills that help you with this problem.)

✔ How far past the hole did the ball go? Was it farther than you expected when you lined up the shot? Did you hit it too hard to sink it even if it hit the hole?

✔ Are you comfortable with the length of putt you left yourself?

✔ Did you hit the hole? Was the ball online? Was it fast enough to reach the hole?

✔ How did the ball react when it hit the hole? Was the speed too fast to allow the ball to tumble in? Did the ball hop over the hole or ride along the rim? Did you putt it too hard or did it just wander offline?

Going for pre-round precision

If you want to spend your round trying to make everything you look at, you should make certain you arrive early enough to spend time on the practice green. This make-it-or-break-it approach can pay off big, but the costs can also be huge. Hitting the practice green helps you

> ✔ **Get a feel for the conditions:** You need to get a sense for the speed of green, the type of grass you have to play on, and the grain (grainy Bermuda grass, for instance, leans one way or another — usually the blades lean toward the position of the sun), if the greens have any. Most of the time, the practice green represents the conditions you face on the greens during your round. Now's the time to get comfortable with the conditions and lay of the land.

> ✔ **Build some confidence:** Get used to the feeling of making putts. Frank Sinatra, the world's most vaunted performer during the 20th century, used to say that he felt a little nervous before his live performances. Even the Chairman of the Board felt uncertain about being "in voice" on a given evening! You don't want to step onto the first green of an important match feeling like Sinatra: wondering if your putting touch will show up that day. Hit some high notes before your performance. Work out the kinks and build up some confidence by sinking some on the practice green. Find your voice!

Lag it or flag it

Lag putting is a kinder, gentler technique with the flatstick than the more aggressive philosophy of make it or break it. The term *lag putt* provokes images of long putts that take their time drifting along a sweeping line toward the hole, where the ball eventually finishes with just enough speed to "die" at the hole.

A great lag putt is a beautiful thing; and, although a lag putt may occasionally stop just short of the hole, it should never run too far past. You should have a comeback putt of a comfortable, makeable length.

 Most lag putters create a mental circle around the hole to use as an aiming tool. For instance, if a player feels confident that she can always make a two-foot putt, she creates a circle that allows for two feet all around the hole. Instead of putting at the 4¼ inches of cup, she can aim at a 4-foot target. Sounds easier than jarring it, right? It is, and when you stop your ball in that imaginary circle, you virtually assure yourself of taking no more than two putts to complete the hole. (If you've practiced making two-footers consistently, that is. See Chapter 7 for more on the fundamentals of putting and Chapter 14 for a putting drill that can help you sink two-footers in your sleep.)

Revisiting the defensive label

Lag putting isn't necessarily as defensive a strategy as it may seem. Sure, on the long putts that have a lesser chance of going in, lagging to a safe area near the hole seems like a conservative strategy. And although it may test your hard-nosed reputation, it makes a lot of sense. But taking a conservative stroke doesn't mean that the lag putt doesn't have a chance to go in. If it does drop in, it trickles in softly in instead of ramming into the back of the cup.

Hitting shorter lag putts has its advantages, too. A soft, lagged putt rides the natural break of the green better than a burner. Lagged putts that finish close to the hole are more likely to tumble into the front or side of the cup, even if they veer a little bit off-line. If you think of the hole as the face of a clock, a lag putt can fall into the hole anywhere in between 3 o'clock and 9 o'clock, as opposed to an aggressive putt, where you probably have a window from 5 o'clock to 7 o'clock.

Taking the teeth out of long lag putts

You can make a long lag putt less daunting and give the ball a better chance of finishing near the hole by breaking the putt into two pieces:

1. **Take a look at your target line and walk along the line to the hole.**

   Make sure not to step in another player's line along the way.

2. **Determine the widest or highest spot on the target line between the ball and the hole where the ball will begin its turn toward the cup. Stand at that spot and look at the line.**

   You may even take a few practice strokes from that spot in order to get a feel for the break and the gravity.

3. **Go back to your ball. You have a new sense for the break, and you can easily visualize how the ball will roll over the course of the long lag putt.**

Watching Your Speed

Sometimes players concentrate too much on the target line they see for the putt and neglect to pay attention to the speed needed to get the ball close to the hole. The target line can easily vex you, especially if you have to putt on a highly contoured green with two or three tiers or swales and bumps. Standing over a ball and determining that the line of the putt has two breaks can be intimidating.

You may start thinking, "Where do I begin? The ball breaks right and then left and then right again!" Even a simple breaking putt, such as a right-to-left bender, can challenge your mind.

To simplify your challenge, read the break and then pick an intermediate spot between your ball and the hole to aim at. The spot can be a spike mark, a piece of sand, or perhaps a discolored spot on the green, but you should choose something that you can easily see.

After you determine a line, you need to clear your head so that you can pay attention to the speed. You've broken up the complicated putt into pieces, which helps you with the line and the speed. How fast do you need to hit the putt to get it to your initial spot, and what do you expect the putt to do after it hits that spot? In terms of speed, will the ball roll more quickly downhill or toward the break?

 If you can pick an initial target spot that sits close to where your ball lies, it makes quick putts much easier to handle. If you have to put some muscle behind the ball, you may want to pick a target farther from your ball that you can still clearly see. Picking a target allows you to concentrate on getting it close with the correct speed.

Conquering Speedy Breaks

Some courses have greens that feature severe slopes. Donald Ross-designed courses, for instance, are known for their undulating greens, which, depending on maintenance standards, can be very speedy. Sometimes, such as on crowned greens, you can easily see the breaks. But other times, such as when you play in the mountains or near bodies of water, you may have difficulty seeing the break.

 Uncertainty is a certain way to miss-hit a putt. Make sure, even if you have to convince yourself, that you make a good, informed decision on the break and stick with it. Use all your powers of analysis (see Chapter 7) to make a judgment on the line of the putt and the speed you need to get it close, and don't look back. Stroke the putt with conviction and confidence.

In some unfortunate incidences, you stare down a quick and hard-breaking putt. On some short, downhill putts, it seems like all you have to do is breathe on the ball and it will go rocketing past the hole. Science tells us that objects in motion tend to remain in motion, and a speedy green double-cut to run at 11 on the stimp-meter (which is a very fast condition, as determined by the USGA's stimpmeter, which measures green speeds), coupled with gravity, doesn't help matters much when you're on a downhill slope facing a pronounced right-to-left break.

You may be tempted to hit the ball as softly as you can in this situation or even in speedy downhill situations without much break. The danger in hitting the ball too softly is that you may, consciously or subconsciously, wind up decelerating the putterhead during the down-stroke, and deceleration can cause a jerky motion that pulls the club off-line or a stab that pushes or pulls the ball. Nerves can also take their toll on a hair-raising putt, causing the same types of mistakes.

You can take some of the speed, break, and fear-induced shakes out of a putt by hitting the ball off the toe of the putter. Line up for the putt with your putter behind the ball in its normal place. Slide the putterhead back toward your inseam until the far end of the blade, the *toe,* sits behind the center of the ball. Stroke the putt.

Because you strike the ball with less mass when the putterhead makes contact, you deaden the blow and take some speed off the putt. This crafty move also takes some of the break out of the putt and causes it to roll straighter. Try it on the practice green for yourself and see. Amaze your friends and opponents alike with this strategy!

Defeating the Yips and Other Putting Maladies

Golfers who suffer from a putting malady known as the *yips* are a pitiful sight. They may have a brilliant tee to green game, driving the ball long and straight with brilliant, confident approach shots onto the green. But with the putter in their hands, they suddenly become whimpering, simpering basket cases — unable to sink even the shortest of putts.

The yips, although prevalent from anywhere on the green and in any putting situation, are most evident during short putts. Imagine standing over a perfectly makeable two-foot putt and feeling completely unable to sink it. Now imagine hitting the putt with a stabby, jabby, fearful, timid stroke and watching the ball skid by the hole without even grazing the lip. You've yipped it.

The first words you may utter after a putt like this are, "I knew it!" Having the yips is an evil ailment that perpetuates itself by demolishing your confidence, leading to self-fulfilling putting prophecies. In the following sections, we outline some causes and solutions to common putting maladies. (And be sure to check out Chapter 12, where we provide a ton of tips on staying mentally strong, even when you face adversity.)

Cataloguing the causes

What causes the yips? If some pharmaceutical company could come up with a pill to guard against it, similar to a flu shot, every golfer would want it, because the yips can appear without warning and for no apparent reason. After you miss a few makeable putts and your confidence starts to falter, the yips spread like a quick virus and infect your entire stroke, destroying what confidence remains.

Anxiety

Your yips may be caused by anxiety over making a putt. If you look up too quickly to see the ball falling into the hole, you may not complete the stroke properly, pulling or pushing with your hands. Your hands may even shake and wobble.

Steering

Instead of letting the putterhead freely swing through the ball and propel it toward the hole, you may find yourself trying to steer the ball into the hole. Steering is typically a tension-filled attempt to guide the ball into the hole due to a lack of confidence in the putting stroke. Tension can cause you to push the putterhead toward the hole and mistakenly get your wrists or legs into the act.

Alignment

If you line up improperly before you hit the putt, and you misalign your putterhead, your body may subconsciously cause you to alter the swing path in mid-stroke in an attempt to make a correction. Attempting to correct the path of your putter in mid-stroke is immensely difficult and likely to result in a push or a pull, or the putterhead may cut across the ball and cause it to spin.

Wrist breakdown

A breakdown in your right wrist (if you're a right-handed player) can result in the yips. Often, a breakdown or flick of the wrist happens just before impact — a mechanical flaw that can send the putt off-line.

Over-analysis

You may get so caught up in the mechanics of your stroke that you paralyze your natural movement. You become so self-conscious of your body position, putting stroke, and movements that you can barely take the putter back in any simple, straight fashion along the target line. You may find yourself watching the putterhead go back and come through the ball or looking up to see how the ball rolls.

Lack o' confidence

Sweating over a putt, especially a shorty, is a sure way to miss it. Without confidence, you allow all manner of negative thoughts to enter your head and your play. What can you do to make the putt? Will it go in? Can you lose the hole or the match by missing it? What will your playing partner think of you missing such a short putt? How embarrassing!

Tacking some solutions

Pro golfers Johnny Miller, Tom Watson, and Mark O'Meara have suffered from the yips. But each of them found a way to overcome the yips enough to win again — at least temporarily. If you find yourself, as many golfers do at some point, suffering from the yips, don't panic. The condition doesn't need to last forever. How can you overcome a putting meltdown?

Fuggedaboudit

Because the major contributors to the yips are tension, anxiety, and a lack of confidence, one way to help rid yourself of the yips is to empty your mind. Play in the subconscious. Forget about the stroke, forget about the result, and forget about the circumstances. Just play, in the literal sense of the word.

If you walk up to a dartboard or pool table in a pub or a penny-pitching contest, you probably don't get all bogged down in your technique when you toss the dart or the penny. You may want to win the pool game, but you probably don't hang the balance of the world on your shot on the 8-ball. You just play casually, sipping a beer and shrugging it off if you miss. Try to put yourself into the same mindset when you putt. Just play. Let it happen. Let your athletic instincts take over. Trust the practice and effort you've put toward your game. Just step up and do it. Putt in the subconscious.

If you develop a consistent routine for all your putts, you'll feel more comfortable, and fewer thoughts will creep in to spoil your confidence.

Don't look now

Looking up or peeking to see if the ball goes into the hole is a sure way to miss a putt. Resist the temptation to watch the ball. Keep your head still over the ball and stare down at the empty spot the ball used to occupy long after you hit the putt. Listen to hear if the putt falls. You may also catch yourself, when afflicted with the yips, watching your putterhead go back away from the ball and come back through contact. Don't allow your eyes to follow the putterhead during the stroke.

To help focus on the ball, pick a small, noticeable mark on the ball to look at. Keep your eyes fixed on the brand name, printed logo, a single dimple, or on an identification mark throughout your stroke.

Maybe the best way to steady your eyes and to play in the subconscious is to stand over the putt, put your putterhead behind the ball, stare at a spot on the ball, and then stand perfectly still for five seconds. During these five seconds of still and calm, let the gaze of your eyes go out of focus. Your eyes still focus on the spot of the ball you were staring at, but everything else becomes fuzzy and soft. Go ahead and stroke the putt with your eyes and mind in this blurry, meditative state. You may be surprised by the result.

The theory of meditation is that you remove yourself from the stream of conscious thinking. This Zen-like method may cure you for good!

Check your alignment

Are you seeing too many angles when you stand over a putt? Have you checked to see if you may be lined up incorrectly? Your conscious alignment may be at war with your subconscious sense of straightness, and your putting stroke is caught in the middle as your body tries to issue a correction.

Pick a hole on a flat spot on the practice green and drop your ball a few feet from the hole. Stand behind the ball and line up the putt; use the printed brand name on the ball as a helper. Position the ball so that the name points straight at the hole. When you get over the ball with your putter, match the aiming line on the top of your putter to the line of the logo on the ball. Put the putterhead flush behind the ball on this line. Now take notice of your feet. Are they perpendicular to the line created by the logo? How about your shoulders? Finally, are you taking the putterhead straight back and straight through during the stroke?

If you struggle sensing a proper alignment, have a PGA professional, a friend, or another player on the putting green stand behind you and look at your alignment.

Take the hole out of your head

Take the hole out of the equation. Pick a spot on the practice green that has no hole. You can drop some balls and putt to a colored imperfection on the green or to a tee you stick in the ground. Removing the hole from the equation may take away any tension or concern you have about the result. It causes you to focus more on the stroke than on whether or not the ball goes into the hole.

"Let that sucker go"

Touring pro Brad Faxon is recognized as one of the finest putters on the PGA Tour. Faxon realizes that after the ball leaves the face of the putter, you can't do anything to affect the outcome. After you do all you can to read the break, line the putt up, judge the speed, and make a good stroke with a full followthrough, you can't do anything but watch and see whether the ball goes in or stays out. Either the putt falls or it doesn't.

Making the attempt is unavoidable, so instead of fretting over the putt and getting tense and nervous about the result, line up the putt and do as Faxon does: "Let that sucker go." Try it. Don't worry about the result. Putt in the subconscious and "let that sucker go!" You'll love the liberating feeling that helps you improve your putting.

Experiment

In your quest to defeat the yips, go to the practice green and try creating your own remedy. Here are a few drills to get you started:

- Hit some putts with your eyes closed.

- Hit some putts while looking at the hole.

- Try different putting grips, including a cross-handed grip or a claw-style grip (see Chapter 7).

- Hit putts making certain that you keep your wrists firm and that your arms, shoulders, and hands work as one solid triangle-shaped unit. (See Chapter 15 for more putting drills.)

- Ram some putts into the back of the hole with some speed.

- Lag some putts to the hole by hitting the middle of the ball with the bottom, leading edge of the putter blade.

  Don't hit real putts with this technique. You want to use this drill as a sort of shock therapy to get your mind off the yips. You can develop a better feel and awareness of the putterhead with this drill, and that feel helps you gain confidence.

- Hit some putts while gripping the putter with only your leading hand. Try neutralizing your other hand by sticking it into your pocket. If you find that you hit putts more solidly this way, it may be a clue that when your back hand is on the putter, your back wrist may be breaking down or flipping before impact.

Never panic when you have a case of the yips. The best way to fight the yips is to practice enough to putt in the subconscious.

Chapter 10

Taking an Unconventional Approach

In This Chapter

▶ Trying wood chips

▶ Facing putting predicaments

▶ Hitting (from) the road

▶ Going belly up

▶ Getting wet

▶ Swinging lefty (or righty)

Golf is such a *veddy veddy* staid and traditional game. Players wear collared shirts, tee off according to honor, compliment each other's shots, and shake hands at the end of a round. The game of golf is over 500 years old and built around time-honored traditions, musty as some of them may be.

From time to time, however, certain traditions give way to practicality. For instance, men used to play golf in wool jackets, overcoats, and ties, and women played in ankle-length skirts. Now, eegads, Tiger Woods won the U.S. Amateur Championship in a pair of shorts and now wears collarless, form-fitting shirts! Somewhere along the line, golfers realized that, despite its elegance, playing golf in stiff formalwear made the game more difficult than it had to be, and players broke with tradition and wore resort-wear in keeping with the dress code of the time.

Gene Sarazen, a Hall of Famer who won tournaments two generations ahead of Tiger Woods, including the Masters Tournament, invented the sand wedge out of necessity, after all, when he imagined he could improve his chances of escaping from deep bunkers with a lofted, heavy-bottomed club . . . and he was right! Bunker play immediately became a fairer challenge. Nowadays, the loft of the blade on Tiger's favorite short game club is 60 degrees — even more loft than a sand wedge. Clubmakers and players continue to improvise!

At the 2004 PGA Tour Championship, Ernie Els, showing a bit of temper, slammed his golf bag with an iron so hard that it made fellow competitor Woods wince. After he reached the green, Els learned that the seething swipe had bent his putter, so he was forced to play the last few greens by using a sand wedge in place of his putter.

On the golf course, you may find that, either by necessity or out of preference, you have to discard the traditional short-game shots. You may have to get creative, and you may want to be expressive. You have more than one way to skin a cat . . . or to win a skin!

Chipping with a 3-Wood

The object of chipping is to quickly get the ball rolling on the ground, keep the ball rolling on the ground, and have it roll into or near the hole. (See Chapter 4 for more on chipping.) One good way to accomplish these goals is by using your 3-wood.

Some players prefer to hit chip shots with a 7-iron, 8-iron, or 9-iron. But sometimes you may want to put a little more heft, and a little less loft, behind the ball than the blade of an iron offers. The traditional loft of the face of a 3-wood is about 15 degrees. The traditional loft of a 4-iron is about 24 degrees. Putter lofts are about 5 or 6 degrees and less. So chipping with a 3-wood propels the ball lower than an iron can (see Figure 10-1), but it gives the ball more immediate hop than a putter does. In addition, the heft of the head of a 3-wood gives more "oomph" when it strikes the ball, making the ball go farther with the minimal effort and touch you need in the short game.

When, exactly, does this situation arise? Well, the following conditions beg for you to grab your 3-wood out of the bag:

- ✔ **The ball rests on hard, firm, dry ground and short grass.** In this situation, you have less margin for error when you try to hit the ball with the blade of an iron. The more loft the club has, the more perfectly the clubhead or blade must strike the ball, and hitting a chip off a tight lie on hard, dry ground or shaved grass can be very tricky.

- ✔ **The green is above the ball, so you have to chip up.** If your ball comes to rest on hard ground, you may opt to use a putter to putt the ball onto the green instead of chipping it. But if the shot is uphill to the green or perhaps over a ridge, and striking a putter hard enough to get your ball up the hill and beyond the ridge feels a bit too unnatural, you have good chance to chip it hard enough with a 3-wood.

✔ **No bunkers or terribly long patches of grass block your way to the hole.** Either impediment quickly stops a ground-hugging 3-wood chip.

✔ **You have an opening to the green over which to chip and roll your ball.** Some greens have natural, unprotected pathways to the hole. Take advantage of these opportunities!

Figure 10-1: Using a low-lofted 3-wood to chip gets the ball rolling quicker and farther than irons can without as much effort.

The only disadvantage to chipping with your 3-wood is that because the shaft is so much longer than that of a short iron, you need to stand farther away from the target line than you normally do. Therefore, be sure to stand behind the ball before you take a swing and carefully line up the shot.

Otherwise, you use the 3-wood to chip in the very same way you use an iron — keeping a light grip and making certain the clubface goes straight back on the target line and comes straight through (see Chapter 4). The face of the wood is steeper and less lofted than that of an iron, so you can expect the ball to stay a great deal lower. The heft and size of the head makes the ball pop off the clubface with more energy, so temper your swing a bit (you discover just how much you need to tone the swing down through practice).

Chipping with a 3-wood is a valuable shot to have in your repertoire — if you practice it enough. You need to feel comfortable with this shot before you can use it effectively.

Putting from Bunkers

Sometimes, if the sand is hard and no lip of grass rises up between your ball and the green, you can consider the option of putting from a bunker rather than hitting a traditional bunker shot. Anytime you can put the putter in your hand, your chances of a good, precise shot improve, and putting from a bunker is no different. One old adage, often attributed to Arnold Palmer, is that "your worst putt is better than your best chip."

Assessing the situation is very important. The following conditions must exist if you want to consider putting from a bunker:

- ✔ Firm, hard, well-packed sand.

- ✔ The absence of a high lip of grass or landform between your ball and the green that could hamper the ball from rolling up and out of the bunker and onto the green.

- ✔ The absence of a hairy collar of grass between the bunker and your ball that could stop the ball or drag it down.

- ✔ The ball shouldn't have to roll over more than five feet or so of sand because, in most cases, it can be tougher to roll a ball over sand than over long grass.

- ✔ The hole should be fairly close to the bunker, so that the ball doesn't have to roll a long way to get to the hole after it rolls out of the bunker.

Putting from a bunker requires that you keep your head down, follow through with the putterhead, and have just the right amount of touch, feel, and imagination. Line up the shot just as you do a long putt: by examining the break of the green and choosing an appropriate target line (see Chapter 7). As with all putts, speed is also a very important part of the shot (see Chapter 9).

In addition to properly sizing up the situation and deciding if a putt from the bunker is the best course of action, spend time practicing the shot at some point before you try it. More and more golf courses or practice ranges with short game practice areas offer practice bunkers. When you practice hitting bunker shots, spend a little time dropping some balls in a part of the bunker you find suitable for putting. Bunkers on some golf courses have very soft, beach-like sand, but some regions, such as Texas and Georgia, have firmer, earthier sand. If you live and play in a region with firm, hard sand or play on courses that have this type of sand and bunkers without high lips and faces, this unconventional shot can be a common option for you. PGA Tour player Tom Purtzer, for instance, once putted successfully from a bunker during the Colonial National Invitational at Colonial Country Club in Fort Worth, Texas.

Also, if you're about to play a round on a golf course that has taken a good amount of rain, you may run into wet, hard, firm bunkers.

Putting without a Putter

Okay, we all lose our temper from time to time — especially on the golf course, where your play can get pretty frustrating. Sometimes the flatstick bears the brunt of the anger. Even PGA Tour players have broken putters over their knees or bent them on trees. Woody Austin, winner of the 2004 Buick Championship, once bent the shaft of his putter on his head after missing a crucial putt. Players who don't want to put their head through that kind of trauma normally toss their putters into trees or ponds.

Opening the rulebook

According to the rules, if your putter becomes damaged in the normal course of play, you can replace it. How exactly a putter can get broken during the course of play is a mystery, but imagine that your putterhead happens to fall off. In that case, you can have someone get you another putter, or you can use your cellular phone to call the golf shop and ask someone to run you out a putter on loan. In a tournament, you can send a friend, a spectator, or your caddie to run and get you a new putter. Depending on where you are on the golf course, that may not be very practical. You may remember Tiger Woods sending a PGA official to the trunk of his Buick after damaging his sand wedge on some rocks at the 2004 Deutsche Bank tournament when he lost his world No. 1 ranking.

More likely, you have, ah, "altered" your putter though some action other than the normal course of play and, according to the rules, you have to discontinue use of it without a replacement. Now you have a problem — what can you putt with to finish the round?

Making a decision

Assuming that your putter has met an unnatural end, you need to find a replacement. When you putt the ball on the green, you're not looking for loft. You want to roll the ball. So what club, other than the putter, can roll the ball into the hole? Some players left without a putter prefer to putt with a wedge. The advantage of using a wedge is that the shaft length is very similar, and that length allows you to use your normal putting stance and get your eyes over your line.

The trouble with using a wedge to putt is that you have to strike the middle of the ball with the very thin bottom leading edge of the blade. To do that, you have to have plenty of precision and confidence. And, try to accept it, if you break your putter in frustration or rage and have to putt with your wedge, your confidence can't be running very high in the first place!

Some guys on the PGA Tour, in this situation, choose to putt with their driver because, second to the putter, the driver is the least lofted club in the bag — the face is angled anywhere from 5 degrees to 10.5 degrees. Although the shaft of the driver is typically a great deal longer than that of your putter, the large face and small amount of loft make contacting the ball the easy part. The trickier part is standing so far from your target line, because standing the driver upright makes the large head of a driver awkward and decreases your sweet spot. Try choking down as much as you can on the driver, and keep the driver's head as close to the target line as possible when swinging the clubhead back and through the ball. Be aware, too, that the ball pops off the driver's face with more energy because of the mass of the clubface.

In any case, be sure to spend some time practicing putts with your driver or wedges just in case your putter goes awry and suffers your angry dismissal some day!

Playing from a Cart Path

You get free relief, normally, when your ball lies on an artificially surfaced road or cart path, according to the rules of golf. Sometimes, however, the free relief you receive, which must be no nearer to the hole than where the ball came to rest on the path, is at an undesirable position, perhaps in long, tangled grass or behind a tree. And sometimes you can't receive relief from a road, particularly one unpaved or deemed to be an integral part of the golf course, such the road along the 17th hole — known as the Road Hole — on the Old Course at St. Andrews in Scotland (see Chapter 20).

What shouldn't you do when you have to play a ball from a road or cart path? Here are two options that may spring into mind that you should leave unexplored:

- ✔ **Pulling out the putter:** The road at St. Andrews, for instance, is made up of many little pebbles. In this type of situation, putting makes the ball roll immediately, and if you roll a ball through pebbles, it faces a number of opportunities to waver and wobble off-line.

- ✔ **Getting some air:** Conversely, using a highly lofted club off the firm or rocky conditions of a road surface brings many different negative variables into play. Trying to use a wedge to hit a ball from a firm surface requires an almost impossible amount of precision, and the club is likely to bounce off the surface wildly and into the ball.

The best-case option when playing the ball on a road is to chip the ball with a 7-iron so that the club can clip the ball, loft it off the path, and get it to tumble over and roll out after it clears the road. (See Chapter 4 for more on chipping technique.)

The ball jumps much faster off a road surface, so be sure to account for that when you judge how far back to take your backswing. You become eager to see the outcome and nervous about how it will feel when the blade hits the road, so be sure to force yourself to keep your eye on the ball, accelerate through the shot, and follow through. Maintaining fundamentals increases your chances of making the best of a bad situation.

Bellying the Wedge

Sometimes you find your ball lying in a tough spot — perhaps up against a collar of long, thick grass on the edge of the green or, on a Pete Dye-designed course (see Chapter 20), up against a railroad tie. It may be to your advantage in these situations to hit the ball by bellying your wedge. Up against deep grass, when the club comes back toward the ball with a straight face, it catches on the tangled grass. Bellying the wedge can eliminate that hindrance.

To *belly* your wedge is to lay open the face of the club so much that you strike the ball with the only the leading edge (or *bounce*) of the bottom of the blade. Sort of like striking a billiard ball with a pool cue, only you use the thin bounce of your wedge. If you open up the wedge so much that the bounce (or *flange*) hits the ball, the club doesn't drag on the grass, and the leading edge hits the ball like a putter. Because the ball doesn't ride up the face of the wedge, it comes off with plenty of overspin and tumbles forward.

Open your stance as you do when making a standard chip shot (see Chapter 4). Grip the club normally after you open the face of the wedge. Take the clubhead back and bring it through the same distance; if you take the club back to 4 o'clock, follow through to 8 o'clock. Make sure you take the club along the target line and bring it through the ball and forward along the target line.

A bellied wedge is a nifty shot to have when you just need to nip the ball and send it forward. This shot takes real concentration and precision, so be certain to practice it before you try it on the golf course.

Splishing After You Splash

Finding your wayward golf ball in a greenside creek or pond is a bit of a mixed blessing. Oh, you can be happy about locating the ball and knowing for certain that you dunked it in the water hazard, but sometimes that ball is just close enough to the edge, sitting up so nicely — white and gleaming — that it tempts you to try to hit from the water (see Figure 10-2).

Playing from the water is sheer madness. The rules of golf offer you some very civilized options to keep you from soaking yourself with folly-filled swipes, and in every case we can imagine, you should take the penalty shot and avail yourself of the drop alternatives. (Depending on the hazard's shape and whether course officials mark it as lateral, red-lined, or yellow-lined, the drop options vary greatly and give you plenty of smart choices.) Live to fight another day.

But sometimes sensibility just isn't your cup of tea, and you want to let 'er rip by hitting a ball from the water.

If more than half the ball is below the water line, return to our previous suggestion: Forget about hitting the ball, take the penalty stroke, and drop. Always.

If you see a good portion of the ball above the water line, get ready to go wading. If you have a rain suit in your bag, put it on. You get wet hitting this shot. Take these steps to try to avoid aquatic doom:

1. **Open your stance and grip the club normally, keeping the ball in the middle of your stance if you can do so without sinking or stumbling into deeper water.**

2. **Swing the club back very steeply and try to hit the ball cleanly.**

   Unlike a bunker shot, you don't want to hit the water behind the ball. When the club makes contact with the water, the clubhead significantly slows down and the water tries to alter the swing path. Swing hard and do the best you can to get the club through the water. Be wary of rocks!

3. Try your best to follow through — and hope.

Completing your swing can be very difficult, because the water tries to bring your club to a screeching halt. But swing bravely and fully. Any hint of fear or deceleration won't allow you to punch your ball out of the water, which is the least you can hope for.

Figure 10-2: Make sure you can see at least half the ball on water shots; and don't be like Mike: Toss on a wet suit!

Hitting Lefty (or Righty)

If you miss the green often enough with your approach shots, especially on wooded courses, you eventually find your ball snuggled up against a tree or under a bush (see Figure 10-3). As if your shot isn't complicated enough already, you may find that your ball is snookered on the wrong side of the tree or bush, making your normal stance or a true swing at the ball impossible.

Figure 10-3: If you have a favorable lie and a clear path to shorter grass, you can flip the club over and take a shot from your opposite side.

You have options in this situation, and you should carefully consider them before you act:

- ✔ The first option, according to the rules of golf, is to declare the ball *unplayable,* which allows you, with one penalty stroke added, to move the ball one-club length from its current position or return the ball to the spot where you played it before it landed up against the tree or bush.

- ✔ Your other option is to attempt to hit the ball and advance it from where it lies.

Try not to allow your emotions to enter into your decision. You're disappointed and frustrated that your ball got into such trouble in the first place — don't let anger or impatience propel you into making a rash decision to take a wicked swipe at the ball. Although it may feel good to blow off some steam by taking a good chop at the ball, you have a good chance of compounding your problems by wasting a stroke: You may miss the ball or smack it into an even worse position.

You should also give yourself a bravado check. Feeling ironically heroic, you may plan to step up to the ball and show off your magic by making an astounding, par-saving trick shot. Again, the results of a foolhardy attempt can be embarrassing and damaging to your scorecard.

In this case, an old adage holds true: Discretion is the better part of valor. If you can't significantly advance the ball from its position, with little to no risk of whiffing or knocking the ball into another unplayable lie, take your medicine, invoke the unplayable lie option, take the one-stroke penalty, and drop the ball in the best possible spot the rules allow.

If, on the other hand, you've prepared yourself for a shot such as this by practicing, and you think the advantages of hitting a well-played left- or right-handed shot outweigh the risks, you can try playing a wrong-sided pitch. Understand that precision is difficult to achieve with a wrong-sided attempt and that a certain amount of luck is involved in the following methods.

Taking a backhand swing

Ever looked at life from a different direction? You may have to if your ball comes to rest against a tree or a hedge. In this case, you simply have to mimic the technique of an opposite-handed player. The forgiving loft of a 7-iron probably gives the best results if you have to try this switch-hitting swing off the back of the blade. So grab the club and head over to the unknown, and follow these steps as a roadmap to back to the fairway:

1. **Take a stance over the ball with a 7-iron as if you're a left- or right-handed player.**

2. **Reverse your hands on the club's handle so that you have the grip of a left- or right-handed player.**

   Just as when hitting a normal shot, grip the club lightly and stay aware of the clubface. The grip and the swing will obviously feel awkward, unless, that is, you give this shot a little practice from time to time.

3. **Swing the club as normally as possible and hit the ball with the back of the blade.**

4. **Make certain that you follow through as best you can.**

   Your goal is to propel the ball toward the green or the fairway and, at least, out of the trouble. Don't try to be a hero and jar it at the expense of missing the ball completely.

Flipping the blade

If you want to get a little bat on the ball and have the clubface make (almost) normal contact with the ball, you have to do a little flip-flop with your wedge or a short iron you feel comfortable with. Take out your club and run through the following steps:

1. **Take a stance over the ball with your wedge or short iron as if you're a left- or right-handed player.**

2. **Reverse your hands on the club handle so that your grip is that of a left- or right-handed player.**

3. **Flip the blade of the iron over and upside down so that when you take your swing, the true clubface, although it points toe-down, strikes the ball (refer to Figure 10-3).**

   Make sure that you adjust your aim to correspond to the new angle of the clubface.

4. **Swing the club as normally as possible and hit the ball with the clubface.**

5. **Make your best followthrough to propel the ball toward the green and, at least, out of trouble.**

Looking away

Many golfers try to heed the advice "keep your eye on the ball" or "keep your head down" when they find themselves eager to lift their head for a peek at the result. The shot we outline in this section makes peeking very difficult, because you actually face away from the hole. Craig Stadler and many other PGA Tour players have used this method in competition when they found their balls lodged against a tree, shrub, or fence. For a truly adventurous and effective trouble-escaping shot, follow these steps:

1. **Stand to the left of the ball if you're a righty or to the right of the ball if you're a lefty, facing away from the target.**

   It feels awkward at first to be looking away from the target, but try to relax and keep your body loose.

2. **Hold whatever club you deem appropriate extended down from your dominant hand, with the blade pointing towards your feet.**

   You aim the clubface toward the target. See where we're going with this yet?

3. **Put the blade of the club behind the ball, and turn your head back to properly aim the shot.**

4. **Pull the club up and extend it forward, and then swing it down along the target line as best you can. Follow through as far as your body position allows you to.**

5. **Try to resist the urge to turn too quickly to see the result.**

   Concentrate on following through and sending the ball out of trouble and toward the green.

Carrying an opposite-handed club in your bag

 If you play heavily wooded golf courses regularly, you may want to consider picking up a left- or right-handed 7-iron to carry in your bag to prepare for tough spots. If you practice enough with it, you can make fairly normal, successful shots out of awkward situations.

The rules of golf allow you to carry no more than 14 clubs in your bag, so you may have to take one out of play if you want to carry an opposite-handed club, especially if you carry a number of wedges. Which club can you do without? Is there a club in your standard set that you almost never use or are wary to hit because you don't have confidence with it? If you have the need, identify that problem club and pull it out in favor of an opposite-handed iron.

Rehearsing the Unconventional

Most of the time on the golf course when you need to improvise or conjure up some unconventional shot, you can point to a rare situation that you're unprepared for as the cause. So why not practice for some of the situations and ready yourself for the inevitable slings and arrows of outrageous fortune, as Billy Shakespeare would say? If nothing else, practicing rare types of shots varies your practice sessions and livens things up a bit from time to time.

Practically speaking, don't go hitting shots off a busy road. But, if you have a road or cart path on the course that you play regularly, you can make practicing off this road or path a regular part of your practice sessions. Hit a few 5-irons back into play so that if you're ever faced with the shot, you've been there before. People that play golf for a living practice like this. Tiger Woods prepares for almost any condition based on the course he has to play.

 Find an old iron similar to the ones you play or pick up an inexpensive or used club at a golf retail store so you can practice these shots without repeated damage to your regular clubs. Here are some unconventional shots you may want to try practicing to lighten the mood and prepare for rare situations:

✔ Playing from a road

✔ Playing from up against a fence or wall

✔ Playing from an inch of water

✔ Playing from behind a tree

✔ Playing from a "fried egg" lie in a bunker (a ball that lands deeply in the sand and partly buries itself; see Chapter 6)

✔ Putting from a bunker

✔ Chipping with a 3-wood

✔ Bellying a wedge

✔ Playing from hardpan-type ground or dried out grass

✔ Putting with a 3-wood

✔ Turning the club over to play from against a tree

✔ Hitting opposite-handed shots with the back of your iron to play from against a tree

✔ Playing from your knees when the ball is far below you in a bunker

Mastering the unconventional at The Masters

Each year, at The Masters tournament at Augusta National Golf Club in Georgia, the Tour professionals do something that they never ordinarily do on purpose: They hit their golf balls into the pond. Well, onto the pond, actually.

During the practice rounds before the Masters begins, gallery patrons surround the par-3 16th hole, where a pond fronts the green and runs along the left side. Aside from standing among the blooming azaleas and towering pines of the world's most exclusive golf club, the fans are in for a special treat.

After the players hit their shots to the green, with a little urging from the fans, they walk to the front of the tee, drop a few extra balls, and then use short irons to skip balls across the surface of the water and make them roll up the bank on the other side of the pond and onto the green. As the fans cheer with delight, one can only imagine the practice hours put in and the clubface mastery that touring professionals must possess in order to be able to hit these skip-shots!

Chapter 11

Flipping to Flop

In This Chapter

▶ Discovering the flop shot

▶ Flopping at the right time

▶ Figuring out the flop

▶ Leaving the risk in the bag

Second to a long drive, the flop shot is golf's sexiest, most head-turning shot; an odd phenomenon when you think about it, because the difference between a long drive and a flop shot is a massive amount of distance. A long drive may travel 350 yards, and a flop shot may amount to only a few. But both the long drive and the flop shot are dramatic in that players strike them with big, full swings and chorus-line finishes. You can easily see how a big, full swing and followthrough with a driver can result in a ball flying a long way, but you see the true complexity and magic of golf when a big swing with a lofted wedge results in a ball flying only a few feet!

Both shots, mind you, are towering, impressive, and majestic. PGA Tour players, especially Phil Mickelson, use the flop shot with remarkable success. When can you use the flop shot? How do you get it to flop? And, most importantly . . . should you attempt it? This chapter gives you all the answers.

Focusing On the Flop Shot

The *flop shot* sends a golf ball high into the air without much distance. Flopping the ball became en vogue with the advent of the 60-degree wedge and square grooves. With a highly lofted club, players can lay the clubface open, creating even more loft, and pop the ball almost straight up into the air. The ball comes down with backspin and sticks or draws back a tiny bit.

Backspin happens when the ball rides the face of the clubhead after it makes contact during the swing. The ball goes up the grooves on the clubface, the dimples catch, and it starts to revolve into a backspin. Because the clubhead moves softly as it cuts under the ball and through the grass with the flop, the ball doesn't "suck back" with much backspin when it hits the green, which is how a longer pitch shot with more clubhead speed behaves.

Choosing to Hit a Flop Shot

Because a flop shot flies through the air almost all the way to its target and doesn't fly very far, most good players utilize the flop shot around the green. Typically, you should attempt the shot when you need the ball to fly over an obstacle and stop quickly. You can use the flop to clear a bunker, the top of a hill, long grass, or water.

Here's a textbook scenario for when to play the flop shot: Say you miss the green with your approach shot, and you find your ball off the green to the right, lying in medium to long grass. When you assess the shot, you see that the green is elevated above the ball, and a bunker stands between your ball and the green. In addition, the hole is cut close to the edge of the green nearest to your ball, meaning that if you fly the ball very far over the top of the hill and onto the green, you leave yourself a long comeback putt. A chip shot flies too low and runs too long. A pitch shot flies longer but still may run out too much. A flop shot is the answer. The ball flies high for a short distance and doesn't roll very much after it lands.

Anytime you need to put the ball in the air but have only a short distance and little green to work with, the flop shot is a possible option.

Playing a Flop Shot

The fundamentals of hitting a flop shot are as follows:

Club: Use a highly lofted club, such as a 60-degree wedge.

Stance: Taking a basic pitch stance (see Chapter 5), move your target line a little bit to the left and open up your stance. Because you add more loft to the face and open the face angle, you can expect the ball to come out to the right (for righties). Lay open the face of the club at address to create even more loft. Hold the club lightly. Position the ball in the center of your stance. Put your weight a little more on your front leg.

Hand position: As in every golf shot, your lead hand must do just that at all times. Therefore, your hands should be slightly ahead of the ball through impact to maintain the open clubface swinging down the target line.

Swing: Swing the club steeply up and outside of the target line.

- ✔ **Take the clubhead back as far as you think you need to.** Use your feel. It seems nonsensical that you have to swing fully on this shot, but the angle of the clubface lofts the ball; it doesn't give the shot distance. You take the distance out of the shot with the loft and the opening of the face. The steeper you swing, the higher the ball flies with a minimal gain in distance.

- ✔ **Don't break your wrists through impact to keep the clubface open and lofted.** You can hit this shot with a lot of wrist movement and hand flipping, but you shouldn't expect success. If you look at the guys who hit the best flop shots, you can see that their clubface remains constant.

- ✔ **Be sure to follow through with a big, high finish.** The clubface should still open and lofted after impact.

You can make the ball pop even higher if you take the swing back outside the target line (meaning the clubhead doesn't go straight back on the line; it goes back on an angle away from you, as opposed to back around you, which would be inside the target line). This makes your swing steeper.

Deciding Against the Flop Shot

The flop shot is handy to have, but the only way to use it with success is to practice it. The average player often tries to use the flop shot after he sees it on television, but he doesn't really know how to play it, because he hasn't practiced with the proper technique. He tries the shot once or twice a round, and then he wonders why he shanks it or skulls the ball across the green.

It takes maximum practice time to master the flop shot to the point that you can rely on it. If you're an average, recreational player, or even an intermediate player who occasionally competes, consider how much time you really have to devote to practicing the flop shot and if you can better spend your time refining other areas of your game that have a more immediate impact on your short-game success.

Knowing the flop shot's dark side

Take time to ponder the downsides to playing the flop shot:

- ✔ The higher the ball goes up in the air, the more susceptible it is to the elements — especially the wind.

- ✔ To be effective, you have to strike the flop shot more precisely than a chip or pitch, because a mis-hit from close range with a full swing can be catastrophic.

- ✔ You have almost no margin of error when it comes to hitting the flop shot the proper distance. The ball travels so high and comes down so steeply that it almost has to land on top of the target, because it doesn't roll very much. If you want to hit a flop shot over a bunker out of long grass and have it end up right at the hole, you have to land the ball within a foot of the hole.

Sounds tough, right? It is. But if you spend enough time practicing and perfecting the shot, being able to land the ball near the hole consistently can help reduce your scores.

Considering your other options

You may be asking, "But if I don't play the flop shot, how can I get the ball close when I'm faced with a tight pin or a carry over a bunker or grassy hill?" The answer is simple.

If you want to improve your game, lower your handicap, and shoot better scores, when you're faced with this kind of shot — and most players without single-digit handicaps face extreme situations often — *don't get cute*. And a flop shot is getting cute. When you have to shoot to a tight pin or you face a delicate carry from just off the green, your expectation should be to get the ball on the green and two-putt. Your realistic goal isn't to stick it close to the hole and tap it in.

If you get the ball onto the green in one shot and two-putt, pat yourself on the back and move on! If you hit it on the green and hole out a putt, jump for joy. But don't try to get cute.

If you expect to pitch the ball over a bunker and onto the green from 25 yards and two-putt (which is realistic), you feel much better when you do, and you score much better in the long run. Conversely, if you stand over your ball and expect to flop the ball close to the hole and make the putt on a consistent basis, you feel disappointed more often than not. Even if you do pull off the flop shot and hit it to six feet, missing the short putt leaves you disappointed.

Play the percentages. Get the ball on the green safely with a shot you're comfortable with and two-putt. Make that your expectation and goal. After you become comfortable with the flop shot due to a good amount of practice, you can expect your scores to gradually lower as you use discretion by picking your spots to put it to effective use.

Chapter 12

Keeping Your Head in the Game

In This Chapter

▶ Overcoming on-course meltdowns

▶ Performing under pressure

▶ Being the ball (or at least seeing the ball)

▶ Talking to yourself

▶ Pairing a phrase with your swing

*Y*ogi Berra was talking about baseball when he famously said, "90 percent of the game is half mental." Had the beloved Yankee catcher been talking about golf, he may have said, "Half of the game is 100 percent mental." Maybe it's better to realize that 100 percent of the game is half mental . . . at least!

Your mind is undeniably a big part of your golf game — especially the short game. In golf, the mind can be overactive and distracted. You walk a fine line between being mentally engaged and being overly analytical. Although your goal should be to reach a point where you can play the game in the subconscious, you also have to be aware of your situation and the options available to you, not to mention the way playing conditions can affect your performance.

Taking all the factors and options into account at once can make you mad! But listen to the old contrary adages, both of which contain good advice: "Look before you leap" and "He who hesitates is lost!"

In this chapter, we explore the mental gluts that can destroy an otherwise poetic and effective short game and give you ways to combat your own mind.

Regrouping When the Wheels Come Off

It happens to all golfers. You have a nice, pleasant round cooking along when, suddenly, you're all thumbs. It seems to happen in an instant. You can't play golf effectively. You miss some short putts. You fumble around with your short irons or foozle pitch shots. You blade your chip shots over the green because of an ugly mis-hit or leave the ball short of the green with a chunky, fat shot. Your confidence abandons you faster than your enjoyment level, which is also quickly heading downhill.

Often, the more you try to pull yourself from this downward spiral, the further into the mire you slip. So relax and quit fighting it so hard. Recognize that these helpless, hapless spells of uselessness strike every amateur golfer (and even the pros). After you remind yourself that you're not alone:

- Don't panic
- Grin and bear it
- Live and laugh it off
- Be careful when your opponents make "double or nothing" offers
- Recognize that you've hit good shots before — and that you can hit them again

In this section, we cover some of the more common mental mishaps that occur on the course and the steps you can take to get your mind right.

Regaining your tempo

You can sense when you start to lose your tempo. Your golf swing feels quick and jerky rather than slow and fluid. You become aware of the fundamental disconnect between your upper and lower body and maybe between your hands and arms.

Don't make it a big deal. Keep it simple.

Talking tension

If you lose your tempo, you've lost your focus and, as it slips away, you get more fearful. With increasing fear comes a rising tension level. The more you think about it and the more you fight and struggle with your golf game, the higher your tension and anxiety levels rise. You stand over every shot and think: Can I hit this one correctly? Will I hit this putt too far past the hole? Don't leave this short of the green! I'm about to hit this shot in the bunker . . . again! Dear God, I made a seven on the last hole. Don't three-putt again! Could I possibly miss this one-foot putt? Why is this happening?

You need to get rid of your tension level. You need to get rid of your anxiety. You need your groove back!

Taking a deep breath

How can you regain your tempo? The more air you take into your system, the more you can relax. The more you relax, the faster you begin to regain your tempo. Try the following techniques:

- **Start breathing.** Take big, deep breaths that go all the way down to your diaphragm. The more oxygen that comes into your body, the more your heart rate begins to go down.

  Jean Van de Velde, for instance, would've benefited by stopping and spending a little time doing some deep breathing while he tried to put the finishing touches on what looked like a certain victory at the British Open Championship at Carnoustie in 1999. Van de Velde has gone down in history for squandering a comfortable lead. He suddenly found himself hanging on to make a seven on the final hole just to get into a playoff (which he lost). A bad bounce, and suddenly things can start happening fast. For Van de Velde, disaster ensued. Breathe deep and don't get caught up in the moment!

- **Fake a yawn.** Look at some of the greatest Olympic sprinters and track athletes. When they get ready to run, just before the 100-yard dash or the 400-meter hurdles, they seem relaxed because they start taking big yawns. You may think those athletes are about to fall asleep! The truth is that they become tense and want to get some air.

Overcoming paralysis of analysis

Golf games often go away during a round because players get too focused on the conscious part of the swing. You need to stay focused on playing in the subconscious. Smell the flowers, hear the music, and calm down. Don't over-think every situation. Don't over-examine your swing; trust it and the work you've put toward it on the range. Take aim at the target and let it go. *Play* golf.

The middle of a golf round is no time to fix a swing flaw or experiment with a new grip. Let it flow. Focus on the target. Talk with your playing partners. Do anything that stops you from overanalyzing your swing or breaking it down into small parts. Can you imagine the flood of swing thoughts and the number of mental checklist items you could clutter your mind with if you wanted to? It could take forever to play such a round, and what a mechanical, grueling affair it would be. Unless you round the links for a living, golf is still just a game.

Realizing that it ain't your fault

When it comes to putting, many factors are out of your control. You have too many variables to consider around the greens to always shoulder the blame. Remind yourself of this fact from time to time when the ball doesn't break as you read it and your frustration level starts rising.

First of all, the green beneath your feet is a living, growing organism. The grass grows — and changes all the time — as you play on it. And like any Saturday at any golf course, a number of foursomes have teed off in front of you (unless you're a part of the early-bird crew loaded with coffee and pancakes). One foursome takes as many as 140 steps on a green! (Feel free to use that little nugget of info to wow your playing partners.) If you play in the 10th foursome of the day, you putt on greens that have endured over 1,000 steps! Steps in your line, scuffed grass from someone who drags his feet, pitch marks, and general wear and tear concentrated around the hole prevent your ball from rolling on the pristine line you see in your head.

Did we forget to mention that mower lines, uneven grass, grass clippings, dew, fertilizer, pebbles, and sand can also contribute to even the best-stroked putts going off-line and missing the hole? How do you like your odds now?

The margin of error is very small when putting to a hole. Take your best read, concentrate on your smooth and controlled stroke, and give the ball your best roll. Sometimes, missing a putt just ain't your fault. (Check out Chapters 7 and 9 for a few more putting tips.)

Weathering the Heat of the Moment

From time to time, the shot you want to play may be simple, but the environment and situation you face may make it seem more difficult. Pitching a ball over a bunker and onto the green, for instance, may be something you normally pull off with no trouble. But pitching a ball over a bunker and onto a green when you're one-stroke ahead of a competitor on the last hole of a tournament or a 10-dollar match against a buddy makes the shot seem worlds more difficult.

Pressure and nervousness over the result of the shot can make you second-guess your strategy or stifle your technique. Suddenly, the pitch shot that seemed second nature on the third hole is life or death on the last hole.

Ken Venturi, who won the 1964 U.S. Open and went on to enjoy a long career as a CBS-TV golf analyst, often talked about the thrill of competition and how exciting it was to come down to the last hole with your heart beating and a chance to win. In your case, the situation may be the chance to shoot your best round ever. Or your opportunity to break 90 for the first time. Or you may want to impress your boss during a round. In any case, golfers find ways to deal with stress and nervousness in varied ways.

Accepting the fear

The more competitive you are, the more opportunities you face for fear to take over. Fear controls the mind. Fear causes you to top your drive off the first tee because you're not thinking about making a comfortable, fluid golf swing and just rolling with it. You think about who's watching your shot; you feel the eyes of all the people around.

The more competitive you are, the more you have to be able to manage your fear. If you're a 30 handicapper and you just play to hit and giggle and get exercise, you don't have any fear. You just want a walk in the park to enjoy the scenery. That's terrific, but because you're reading this book, you probably don't represent this type of player.

If you are or want to become competitive, however, you constantly try to get better. And the harder you try and the more you press, the more opportunities you face for fear to enter in.

Some sports psychologists, stress management experts, and hypnotists suggest that you make a conscious effort to recognize that you are, indeed, in a stressful situation. Tell yourself something like, "Heck yes, I'm nervous. What a tough spot. I need to get this ball over the bunker and onto the green to have any chance to win. I have good reason to be nervous. I should be nervous."

You recognize the situation for what it is and allow yourself to take your nervousness into account when you prepare for the shot. Knowing that you have to carry the bunker and get the ball onto the green, and that you have to do it with frayed nerves, is important information.

After you size up your situation, and perhaps even embrace it, you can put the fear aside and control it. Just as you recognize a patch of long grass, the wind, or airplane noise from above, recognize the drama and marginalize it just as you do the other factors.

Take some deep breaths. Shake your hands out. Roll your head around. Think happy thoughts. In the golf motion picture *Happy Gilmore,* Adam Sandler, playing the title role, mentally took himself to a happy place. Your "happy place" may be different from Happy's, but the idea isn't as silly as the movie makes it seem.

Ignoring the result

Forget about the outcome. Forget that a chip can set up a par-save, or that your putt is for birdie, or that if you hit the green you can two-putt for your best round ever. Forget that your opponent is watching and that you need this putt to tie the hole.

Zero in on the simple physics of the matter. The club goes back on the line . . . the club swings through . . . the ball goes toward the hole. The ball either goes in the hole or it doesn't. Simple as that.

If you want to be fatalistic about it, wouldn't you rather miss boldly than cowardly? You can live with making a confident swing and missing the shot or putt, but a weak, trembling, terror-provoked yip is a haunting indignity.

Practicing Visualization

Many psychologists say that the subconscious mind can't tell the difference between a real event and an imagined one. If you can clearly visualize a shot and its result, it may be easier to implement and achieve.

Taking the time to imagine your shots, whether you're in the boardroom dreaming of your round to come later that day or standing in front of the ball preparing for a shot you're about to hit, can help you emulate your vision — to literally live your dreams! Just follow these steps:

1. **Stand directly behind the ball, keeping it between yourself and the hole.**

2. **Envision the flight you want the ball to take.**

   Is it a pitch or a chip? Do you want the ball to fly high or hop low? Where do you want the ball to land? Will the ball roll a long way after it lands, or will it hit and stop quickly . . . or even immediately?

   Is it a putt? Will the ball break right, break left, or roll straight? Is the putt downhill or uphill? Have you watched the way the ball rolled when your playing partner or opponent putted from a similar line or distance? Do you want your ball to behave similarly?

   One sports psychologist advocates imagining that you can burn a fiery pathway to the hole with your eyes. Whatever colorful vision works for you and gives you confidence, use it!

3. **Whether you have to pitch, chip, or putt, see the ball roll into the hole.**

4. **Go ahead and hit the shot!**

Your execution may not always match your imagination, but you can certainly give yourself a better chance by imagining a good "flight plan." A good mental roadmap helps you steer the plane in the most efficient manner without getting lost.

Staying Positive with Self Talk

Ten feet isn't that far, is it? When you stand behind a 10-foot putt and look at the space between the ball and the hole, it really doesn't look that far. How many times out of 10 attempts do you think you can sink a 10-foot putt? Eight times? Six? Every time?

What's a reasonable expectation? Your mind may tell you that you can make a 10-footer all the time. Statistics, however, say that PGA Tour players — the guys who play golf every day, practice all day long, hit thousands of putts; the best players in the world — only make 10-footers half the time!

If PGA Tour players only make 10-foot putts half the time, why should you expect to make them 75 percent of the time? You're expecting an impossible level of consistency! So don't beat yourself up and tell yourself that you're a lousy putter when you miss a 10-footer. Have you ever made an expression of angst after lipping out a putt? Don't to that. You damage your ego — and your short game!

How close to the hole do you expect to chip the ball every time? Two feet? Four feet? Less? More? Remember the difference between a goal and an expectation (see Chapter 2). Just because you didn't chip the ball to within three feet of the hole doesn't mean you're a lousy player!

The minute you tell yourself you're a lousy putter or a crummy chipper as you walk off a green, you make a huge negative imprint on your psyche. Killing your confidence is a big mistake, because the next time you come up to a putt, you tell yourself that you can't make the putt because you missed the last one. You make yourself aware that you're a lousy putter, and that's what lousy putters do — miss putts.

Tiger Woods has many times, when describing a putt he missed, said, "I hit a good putt — it just didn't go in." Use similar positive self-talk to turn a positive into a negative.

Dispelling the Clouds of Doubt

No player likes having to hit the ball over a pond or a bunker and onto a green. Why not? Because players don't like the consequences of hitting the ball into the hazard or the bunker.

Say you have a 40-yard shot over a stream. You know you can hit the ball that far. After all, you just hit the ball 225 yards off the tee; therefore, you can certainly hit the ball 40 yards with just about any club in your bag! You can easily carry the ball 40 yards. No way you should dunk it in that stream.

But unless you practice that type of shot and feel comfortable with the club that you put in your hand, the shot can give you trouble. The minute you start having doubts about making proper contact with the ball and lofting it up and over the pond, you have a problem. Mis-hits happen when the mind starts wavering.

If, on the other hand, you remain confident and no doubt clouds your mind, you can execute the shot because you know you can, without a doubt. You can do it because you know you've hit this club before and you've hit this type of shot before. Let the clouds of doubt blow from your mind and see the sunny, clear skies of confidence. Get comfortable and free up your mind so that you can play subconsciously: target — swing — green. Instead of looking at the stream, find the spot on the green where you want to land your ball. The stream all but disappears.

Pacing Your Swing with a Phrase

Golf is a mental challenge, but you have to play in the subconscious to achieve success. To "lose" your mind, you may consider coming up with a little phrase, ditty, or song that can occupy your thoughts while you swing. Some PGA Tour players, such as Fuzzy Zoeller, whistle to relieve tension and maintain their tempo. Some golf teachers advocate mental catch phrases such as "super fluid" or "golden laddie" or even "hamburger," with the first syllable thought up on the back swing and the second syllable on the downswing: ham – burger.

Giving yourself some kind of magic phrase — something fun — can help you ease your mind into the subconscious when you swing the club. If you think about that little key word or ditty every time you hit a pitch, chip, or sand wedge shot, and it goes well four or five times, you feel pretty comfortable the next four or five times you try it. You can count on doing the same thing — with the key being the hypnotic phrase, a phrase you can rely on under pressure, becoming part of your routine.

The myth of "keep your head down"

How can you be target oriented and not be overcome with anticipation about the result? Golfers blame many bad shots on "looking up," meaning that a player is so eager to see the result of the shot that he or she fails to complete the swing, which results in a mis-hit.

As a cure or a precaution, people often remind themselves or others to "keep your head down." Not good advice. Seriously.

Try swinging a golf club with your head down. Touch your chin to your chest and see what happens to your shoulders. You notice that this posture is very uncomfortable. The more you keep your head down, the more you restrict your swing. Technically, keeping your head down is improper form.

The phrase "keeping your head down" isn't about literally keeping your head down; it should remind you to keep your head still and follow though, making sure to finish the shot before you look up to see the result.

You have to swing the golf club. And to swing the golf club, you can't be rigid. Keeping your head down makes you rigid.

Part IV

Short Cuts to the Short Game

The 5th Wave By Rich Tennant

"The only thing that will improve Greg's performance around the greens is a prescription for Prozac."

In this part . . .

Time to put your knowledge — and your commitment — to the test. Knowledge is power, but talk is cheap. Part IV details the less-than-obvious things you can do to improve your short game. Stretching and warming up, practicing on and off the golf course, challenging your friends to competitive contests, and watching the golf stars on television are among the short cuts to an improved short game.

Chapter 13

Warming Up to the Short Game

In This Chapter

▶ Stretching before you stripe it

▶ Turning practice habits into playing habits

▶ Knowing the difference between practice and pre-game

▶ Incorporating a pre-round warm-up

*R*ace car drivers rev their engines before putting the car in gear, and race horses get a good trot before entering the starting gate. Baseball pitchers get an opportunity to throw warm-up pitches before each inning, and basketball players always have a shoot-around before tip-off. The same needs and opportunities exist in golf — especially when it comes to the precision you need for the short game. Like a symphony orchestra before a performance, you need a little time before every golf round to sharpen your touch and hone your instrument.

When you arrive at the course, the putting green, or the edge of your backyard to practice, you should remember that 50 percent of your score comes from 50 yards and in; therefore, you should devote 50 percent of your practice time to improving your short game. If you do that without fail, you can become a better player.

The best players in the world don't go into "their office" for an eight- or nine-hour day for nothing: They want to practice all aspects of their game, but they need to spend a lot of time on the aspects that make up 50 percent of their score. That work ethic and dedication is what makes them what they are — stars! You, however, can't devote an eight-hour block to practice. But you can divvy up your practice time in the same manner. And if you do, you get better and your scores start to drop.

In this chapter, you discover the difference between practice and pre-round preparation, and you find out how to effectively and properly do both.

Limbering Up Before You Play or Practice

Before you hit the driving range, practice green, or the course for a round, you need to stretch your golf muscles. You use these muscles throughout your practice session (in the short game and in the full swing) and, if you plan to play, the subsequent golf round. In the following sections, we cover a number of warm up exercises for each of your golf muscles. If you devote at least five minutes to warming up without even hitting a ball, you'll be ready to start swinging. You can knock out all these warm-ups in five minutes.

Loosening the legs

Your legs (including your ankles and feet) are very important to your golf swing. Your legs give you foundation, balance, and power. When you get out of your cart, before you walk over to the practice tee or green, stretch your hamstrings, which are the most powerful muscles in your legs and the ones most featured in the swing.

Simply put your heel on back of the cart, and slowly lean forward to grab your toe (or as close as possible) with the opposite hand, keeping your leg straight (see Figure 13-1). You should feel your hamstring on the back of your leg stretching. Hold still when you grab your toe, count to five, and repeat a few times with both legs. If you don't have a golf cart, a bench or raised landscaped area like a flower box does the trick. This exercise also stretches your ankles.

Working the upper arms and shoulders

You also need to stretch the muscles in your shoulders and upper arms, including your rotator cuffs. Stretching out your shoulders and your arms is easy, but you should perform the stretch deliberately and with patience and care.

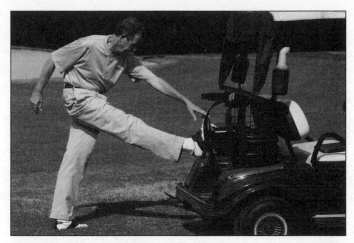

Figure 13-1: Using your cart or a bench as a spotter, do your best cheerleader imitation by reaching for your toes to stretch out the hamstrings.

First, take a club (or two) — a wedge works nicely — and hold it by the grip. Using a club or two gives this activity some weight for resistance. Now work those rotator cuffs:

1. **With your off-hand at your side, gently begin to swing your arm with the club alongside your body, forward and back, without bending your elbow.**

2. **When you're comfortable, swing your arm forward, keeping it relatively straight, all the way above your head and back behind you, making a large circle (see Figure 13-2).**

   You may find it difficult to go backwards and around, so try going forward and around.

3. **Stretch with each arm until your shoulders feel loose.**

The next exercise stretches your shoulders and your back. Take out the shortest club in your bag — your putter or sand wedge — and follow these steps:

1. **Point the grip end of the club into the palm of one of your outstretched hands and the blade of the club into your other palm, with your arms extended straight out in front of you.**

   The shaft of the club should be at arms' length in front of you, parallel to the ground.

Figure 13-2: Make a circle with a club to stretch out your rotator cuffs.

2. **Keeping opposing pressure to hold the club in place, bring your left arm up and over your right until your arms are crossed and you feel pressure on your shoulders and back, as shown in Figure 13-3.**

   Hold the position for five to ten seconds.

3. **Perform the same movement in a counter-clockwise fashion.**

   Again, hold the position for five to ten seconds.

4. **Repeat Steps 2 and 3 a few more times.**

Figure 13-3: Rotate your arms in front of you, using the pressure of a golf club to stretch your shoulders and back.

Don't feel ready yet? Here's another shoulder, arm, and back stretch:

1. **Hold your shortest club between your palms at arms' length in front of your body, applying pressure on the ends of the grip and blade.**

2. **Keeping your left arm firm and straight, with a little resistance, push the club with your right hand toward the left side of your body, rotating the back of your shoulder blades, as shown in Figure 13-4.**

   This stretches out your biceps and shoulders. Hold the finish for five to ten seconds.

3. **Do this pushing exercise a few times in both directions.**

Figure 13-4: Push one of your arms away from your body with your shortest club to apply pressure to the shoulders and biceps.

Bending over backwards

Your back needs to be loose for the twisting that the proper golf swing requires. In the "Working the upper arms and shoulders" section earlier in the chapter, we cover a stretch that works your shoulders and back. This section covers an exercise that focuses on the back and torso. Grab a longer club (your driver or 3-iron; see Figure 13-5) and follow along:

1. **Put the club behind your back and across your body and thread it through the crooks of your bent elbows (see Figure 13-5a).**

2. **Assume your golf stance as if you're standing over the ball.**

   Keep some flex in your knees, with a straight spine and your butt stuck a bit out.

3. **Mimic your backswing with your upper body by making a level turn back. Hold it.**

   Feel that motion and that weight on your back hip. Your belt buckle should point directly to your right (for righties), as shown in Figure 13-5a. Hold the position for 10 seconds or so.

4. **Turn back the other way, up off your back side and onto your front, into your followthrough as you normally finish your swing.**

   Hold that position for about 10 seconds.

5. **Repeat the exercise slowly, holding at both ends.**

Figure 13-5: Mimic your normal swing to stretch the back and torso.

You can also slide the club up behind your shoulders, grasping each end, as shown in Figure 13-5b. Repeat the swing motions, again holding the position for 10 seconds or so at the end of the backswing and your finish.

Readying your wrists and forearms

Your wrists and forearms play a key role in the golf swing — especially in the short game — and shouldn't be overlooked in favor of the larger muscles. Here's a quick stretch: Hold your right arm straight out in front of you and arch your palm outward as if you're signaling someone to "stop!" (See Figure 13-6.) With your left hand, reach over and grab the tips of your fingers, pulling them back toward you. This stretches your wrist, and you should feel a stretch of the muscles in your forearm. Hold it for five to ten seconds, release, and pull again. Do this with both hands.

Figure 13-6: Make a stop sign with your hand and pull back your fingers to stretch the wrist and forearm muscles.

Practicing Like You Play

No one outside of Vijay Singh likes to practice. The very word conjures up images of drudgery. Some golfers even refer to the practice range as "the rock pile."

For improvement, however, practice is unavoidable. When you can't get to the golf course, and the practice tee is your only option, try to make the best of the situation. And the way to really make the best of it is to practice like you play — that is, make your practice session as important and varied as an experience on the golf course can be.

You won't improve your game if you stomp out there and pound away ball after ball with a driver. Golf practice isn't a purely quantitative endeavor. Quantity doesn't equal quality. Vijay Singh may hit hundreds of balls a day, but he hits every ball like he's standing on the 18th hole with a chance to win a tournament.

Think of a football coach. He may have his team hit blocking sleds or run drills from time to time, but the most vital part of any football practice is the scrimmage in which the team tries its plays out against a mock opposing team. The scrimmage is designed to simulate the real game situation as closely as possible. You can do the same in golf.

You should conduct goal-oriented, organized practice sessions. Before you begin your session, break down your practice time so that your routine mimics an actual round — instead of falling into the grip-it-and-rip-it pattern — so you can practice the specific aspects of your game that need work. Say you have one hour to practice. That means you spend the first 5 minutes stretching out (as we cover in the "Limbering Up Before You Play or Practice" section earlier in this chapter). After you stretch out, you can start hitting short shots and putts for 30 minutes. Spend the final 25 minutes hitting range balls with your longer irons and drivers. Set the schedule in your head and stick to it!

When you plan to practice, set a method for yourself, but try varying it every time. Don't get stale, because practice gets boring.

Making the short game at home on the range

Variety rules the range. Use the entire practice range — and your entire range of shots. Check out the following list to organize your time:

- **Start with the short irons and work your way up.** If you haven't been driving the ball real well lately or you've been watching John Daly play, your first thought upon hitting the range may be to reach for your driver. But don't spend all your allotted time on the range on your driver. You may hit around 14 drives in a round, so your skill with the club is important. But you have to prepare to hit *all* your irons, too.

    Work your way up to the driver by practicing your technique with short irons. Working through the clubs gives your short game the attention it deserves. Plus, nothing says that you can't take a break from the big stick after you have it going. Hit a few 9-irons. Find a specific target. Hit a few fades and a few draws, and then go back to the driver.

- **Vary your targets.** It doesn't matter where you position yourself on the range or in the hitting bays, because you don't have to smack every practice shot straight out into the field from your spot on the range. Although the tee markers, mats, and sidewalls tend to point players straight out, you should avoid mechanical, rote ball striking.

Sure, go ahead and hit some shots straight out, especially at the beginning of the session when you want to get a feel for the ball and find your alignment. But after you get comfortable, hit three shots to the right. Aim 40 yards to the left and hit some balls. Pick out a target — a tree, flag, or green — on the left and then pick out some aiming points on the right.

✔ **Vary your shot selection.** You don't need to swing for the fences all the time. Take your practice time to work on your bump-and-runs to improve your scores around the greens; your knockdowns for windy weather; or shots between your club distances (we cover the fundamentals of these shots in Chapter 8).

One routine you need to avoid during your practice session is grabbing ball after ball and whacking them without a target. Many players just hit ball after ball. They hit a bad shot and, sometimes while that ball is still in the air, they grab another. These firing squad players don't have a routine to focus on. They go to the golf course to play with no plans for practice or improvement. If you get into a routine of practicing the way you play, you become a far better player. And if you practice like you want to join the firing squad, your play won't be pretty.

Practicing with the wind

If you have the luxury of hitting balls on a large range with many options, always practice into the wind. It makes you extend your swing a little bit more, because you naturally sense the need for more followthrough and power. It makes you hit more driving, low shots that don't balloon up into the air. Having a good followthrough is important on every shot after you get on the golf course, no matter which way the wind is blowing when you approach a shot.

Hitting shots downwind is the next-best option, because it allows you to try to hit straight shots and get pure feedback as to whether you hit them straight.

A right-to-left wind can be beneficial as well. Sometimes you're stuck with it, but if you can avoid it, you never want to practice into a left-to-right wind if you're a right-handed player (and vice-versa for lefties). You have a harder time controlling the ball in a left-to-right wind. The easiest mistake to make is a slice. Most people cut the ball and make it fade a little, and if you face a left-to-right wind, you have to fight to get the ball straight, which can mess up your swing.

Go at each ball as if you're standing on the tee or in the fairway in the middle of a round and you need to come up with an accurate shot. Pick your alignment and pick your target, and know what you want to do with every shot. Get your mind set before every swing like you do before a shot on the golf course and turn off your conscious mind. Hit each shot and watch it finish before dragging another ball over and preparing for the next swipe.

Spending time on the green

Variety is also the keyword when working around the greens. If you putt first to start practice one day, try chipping first in your next session. Vary the types of shots you hit during a practice session and the location from where you hit them.

Chip some balls in one direction, and then walk over and chip a few from another spot in another direction (see Chapter 4 for chipping instruction). Don't make the same putt over and over; save that drill for a putting-specific practice session (we cover putting mechanics in Chapter 7 and drills in Chapters 14 and 15). Move around the hole and vary the lengths. Hit some bunker shots in the middle to spice things up (see Chapter 6 for instructional info). Choose a different target, flag, or hole to hit pitches to.

You can try to make every one of your practice shots, and we could tell you to grind over every one as if you're facing your final shot to win the U.S. Open, but you can't realistically expect that from yourself. Try to remain focused and result oriented, but don't be afraid to experiment with your swing and stance until you're comfortable and confident. Try hitting shots lower, higher, longer, and shorter. Play while you practice. For some drills to help you remain focused, turn to Chapter 15.

On the golf course, you get a different look on every hole and on every shot, so you should practice with that in mind. You never get the same shot. It never happens. So don't keep hitting the same chip over and over. After you successfully master a chip shot from a specific lie, move on to another lie or distance from the hole and go about practicing that one until you feel comfortable with it.

Preparing before a Round

You should never confuse practice with warming up. Practicing golf and getting ready to play a round of golf are two decidedly different activities. Practice is what it is: practicing specific areas of your game to increase your skill and technique.

Getting ready to play a round involves preparing yourself mentally and physically for the round. You don't want to head to the practice range and say, "I can't hook a 5-iron. I want to try to figure out how to hook a 5-iron, because not being able to is bugging the heck out of me," and then keep hitting 5-iron after 5-iron to try to work the problem out. Doing that before a round sends you to the first tee frustrated and unprepared.

In the sections that follow, we provide a perfect pre-game preparation for a round of golf and some suggestions for an abbreviated routine if you don't have the time for a full warm-up.

Utilizing the perfect pre-round warm-up

Give yourself at least 40 minutes before your tee time to prepare your mind and body if you can. Arrive at the golf course with plenty of time to unload your clubs, change your shoes, pay your fees, and greet your fellow players, and leave yourself 40 minutes to warm up.

To the putting green!

Where else would you expect a book on the short game to start? Get a feel for the club in your hand. Do a few stretches (see the section "Limbering Up Before You Play or Practice" earlier in this chapter). Hit a few putts and get a feel for the speed of the green. Focus on rolling the ball, staying quiet and relaxed, and not worrying about the outcome. Do this for five minutes, and after you're comfortable, hit six or seven two-foot putts in a row into the hole. Stroke them nicely into the hole without even thinking about it. Get accustomed to the sound of the balls landing in the bottom of the cup.

After you have a feel for the green, pull out your favorite chipping club, whether you prefer a 7- or 9-iron or one of your wedges, and hit some chip shots from off the green for five minutes. Hit the shots to different parts of the green with the same relaxed, quiet attitude you had when you hit your putts. Get a feel for the blade making contact with the ball and the speed of the green. Chapter 4 can show you how to hit effective chip shots.

On to the practice range!

Put your flatstick away and head to the practice range; but before you hit a ball, do five minutes of the full stretching exercises we describe earlier in this chapter under "Limbering Up Before You Play or Practice."

After you finish your stretches, begin your practice range preparation by hitting six or seven wedge shots with a soft, loose, smooth, rhythmic swing. If you normally hit a wedge 100 yards, you should shoot for 60 yards now. These shots, like the putts and chips you start with, are for feel and comfort — to loosen up your swing muscles. You can pick a target, but you should just concentrate on ramping up little by little to a full swing. Do this for about five minutes.

Now you have about 20 minutes left before your starting time. Take out your favorite club. Everybody has one. It may be a 7-iron, or it may be a 5-iron. For most golfers, the favorite club is a 6-, 7-, or 8-iron. You call it your "money club," and every time you pull it out, you love it and you're comfortable with it.

Take that club, pick a target, and hit some balls to the target. Man is that ball flight pretty! Your swing feels best when you hit this club, so you instill a great deal of positive impact and, at the same time, you get loose.

You don't want to do anything that could negatively impact your mood or psyche, such as trying to fix a problem club at the last minute. You can be nervous, and you may not even hit your favorite club very well. It may be due to the big match or tournament. Chances are, however, that you'll hit your favorite club pretty well. The object of this part of your pre-game warm-up is to hit nice shots and feel comfortable. Confidence is extremely important to a successful short game, and nothing builds confidence quite like hitting good shots.

You've now used up another five minutes. About 15 minutes to go before your starting time. You typically strike your first shot on your first hole with a driver. Whether the driver is your worst club or best club, take out the "big dog," because how you hit it determines how well you start your round, and this is, after all, a dress rehearsal. The final thing you should do at the range is to take the beautiful, feel-good swing that you've grooved and bang out about three or four drives. Don't worry if you hit a few bad ones. Concentrate on what you want to do and focus. Play in the subconscious and swing away just as you did with your favorite club. Do your best to gain confidence and end with a good shot.

Back to the putting green!

With 10 minutes left before your tee time, get in your cart or walk back over to the putting green. You should be on the tee five minutes before your time, so you have a few moments to spare.

You're loose, warmed up, and feeling good. Hit a few 10-foot putts. Get a good read with a couple of balls and really concentrate on trying to make them. Take the balls to the other side of the hole and give yourself a different break and green speed.

Finally, hit a couple two-footers and make sure you bang them into the hole with confidence.

Now, go to the tee — you're ready to roll!

Warming up under the gun

If you come running to the golf course late and you have to race to the tee, you need to change your strategy to find a way to prepare yourself. How can you best use the 10 minutes you have left?

If you're running late, take the few minutes to just slow down. Stop and relax. Forget about hitting any balls. Depending on your time situation, practice the following exercises:

- ✔ **If you have 10 minutes:** Take five of the minutes to stretch and get loose (see the section "Limbering Up Before You Play or Practice" earlier in this chapter). Warm up right next to the putting green so you can take your putter and calmly hit a few 10-foot putts after you finish. Follow those with a series of two-footers. Stretching and putting help you get loose and calm down, which is far better than racing out to the range not fully stretched because you have to hit balls.

- ✔ **If you have 5 minutes:** If you're really running late, just work on the stretching exercises. Forget the putting. The key is to get rid of as much of the real-life baggage — stress, frustration, and anger — as you can.

If you're running late to the first tee, don't hit driver. Hit something comfortable that you don't feel you have to overpower. Don't be concerned about anything but making a nice, soft swing and getting the ball safely in play. Your body will warm up and get loose as you move along.

Chapter 14

The Games People Play

In This Chapter

▶ Practicing as you play

▶ Improving by competing

▶ Playing games alone

▶ Arriving late for a round

*B*en Hogan is credited with saying that "for every day you miss practicing, it will take you one day longer to be good." But practice, practice, practice is like work, work, work. Who needs it? All work and no play makes you a dull golfer! Hitting mindless chip shot after chip shot and robotic pitches while your bored brain wonders — "Do I have dry cleaning to pick up?" — does you no good.

One way to keep your head in the game when you practice is to banish the term "drill" by creating exciting scenarios and playing games with yourself and others. Not only do the practice games in this chapter keep your mind engaged, but they also simulate the real challenges your short game faces on the golf course while sharpening your short-game skills. After all, how scary can a four-foot putt on the golf course be when you know you've cavalierly converted scores of eight-footers on the practice green?

Whether you want to hone your skills alone or enjoy the company of a fellow short-game wizard, the practice drills we disguise as challenge games in this chapter can get you started in your love affair with practice.

Pitching for Dollars

Pitching for Dollars is a one-on-one, closest-to-the-pin contest that can make you more aggressive with your pitch shots (see Chapter 5 for more on pitching). Hitting chips and pitches to a flagstick without competition often results in a lack of focus. Remember, you want to practice like you play. Putting $1 on each swing and a competitor's ball on the green simulates competition and builds confidence.

The more individual battles you edge your opponent out in, the more dollars you earn; therefore, this game also teaches you not to let up on your opponent when you're ahead and not to give up when you're down. Some folks say that the best way to get a shot close to the hole is to try to sink it, and this game provides you plenty of incentive to hole shots.

Here's the deal: You and a friend grab a small bucket of practice balls (40) and meet at the chipping green. Upon arrival, follow these steps:

1. **Pick a grassy spot about 20 paces off the green and divide the balls between the two of you.**

2. **Taking turns, pitch the balls to the hole one at a time.**

3. **After you each pitch one, keep track of whose ball stops closer to the hole.**

   Whoever's pitch is closer to the hole goes up 1 point. Wager $1 for each point — and $5 for holing a shot — and keep a running tally of the score.

4. **Keep the game going until you pitch all the balls.**

5. **Loser pays up!**

   Of course, you don't have to play for money. Try substituting a hot dog in the clubhouse or a drink after the session for the winner. Anything that keeps you competitive and driving to win!

After you hit and retrieve the first 20 balls, and you figure the totals, try a different club. If you used a pitching wedge for the first round, try crafting less-lofted shots with an 8-iron in the second round. This helps you develop a strong sense of distance, feel, and touch — the key to shots around the greens!

Or you can create certain types of golf shots for subsequent rounds by

- Pitching from a bad lie
- Placing the ball in heavy rough
- Pitching over a bunker
- Blasting out of the sand
- Rehearsing other on-course conditions, such as chipping balls from behind a tree or hitting balls over a branch.

"Horse-ing" Around

Consistency wins this game — and rounds on the golf course. Being able to sink five-footers under pressure isn't a talent; it's a gift . . . and a skill that you can improve through a game such as *Horse*.

Saddle up for a game of Horse by following these steps:

1. **You and an opponent take one golf ball each to the practice green.**

2. **Just as in the basketball version of Horse (which can be shortened to "Pig" if you're short on time), one player picks a spot around the hole and attempts to sink a putt from there.**

   • **If player one sinks it:** His opponent must sink it too. If the opponent fails to duplicate the putt, he picks up an H, the first letter of H-o-r-s-e. If player two sinks it, player one conjures up another challenge.

   • **If player one misses it:** Player two chooses a putt of his own design and attempts to make it.

3. **The first player to get stuck with all five letters spelling "Horse" loses.**

 Just as in the basketball game, your first temptation may be to choose wild, long, downhill, or side-hill putts with swinging breaks in them. These tough putts are fun and useful to practice, so keep your opponent guessing by mixing in the occasional cross-country slider. But making your opponent sink a straight-in five-footer right after you make yours is a sure way to give him fits, too. (For more on putting fundamentals, head to Chapter 7.)

Bingo, Bango, Bongo (Jingles)

Bingo, Bango, Bongo is a short game competition that you can play on the golf course during a round. Also known as *Jingles,* the game works best with a foursome. Bingo, Bango, Bongo is great fun because players of varying strength and age can compete due to the game's focus on the short game. Now you have a fun way to see how your short game stacks up against others.

The fun begins at the first tee by following these steps:

1. **Starting at the tee, each player plays a ball.**

You must remember to execute your shots according to the etiquette of golf, which dictates that the player farthest from the hole plays first.

2. **Three points are awarded on each hole:**

   - One point for the *first on* (the first ball on the green).

   - One point for the *closest to* (the closest ball to the hole).

   - One point for the *first in* (the first ball in the hole).

3. **If a player captures all three points on any hole, her point total is doubled to six.**

Although getting the ball on the green and close to the hole is obviously the goal, strategy should enter in from time to time. For instance, if a player has no chance of reaching the green to win the first-on point, she may carefully lay up her ball into a good position from which to chip for the closest-to point.

The game sounds simple, but it can become a dramatic and complex strategic match. In the following list, we outline a few sample scenarios to help explain the game:

✔ **First on:** Assume that all four players hit their drives on a par-4 and Johnny rests the farthest from the hole at 170 yards out. Johnny has the first chance to win the first-on point — if he hits the green! If he misses the green, the next farthest player to the hole has a chance to win the point for first on, and so forth.

✔ **Closest to:** You also have incentive to get the ball not only onto the green but also close to the hole, because you can gain a point for that. Johnny misses the green by five yards to the right with his second shot. Maggie, who stands at 160 yards out, plays next. She hits the green, so Maggie wins the first-on point. The other two players, Harrison and Julie, hit the green in turn with their shots. All three players who hit the green are various distances from the hole, but Johnny still has to play up. If he can get the ball closer to the hole than anyone on the green, he wins the closest-to point. The point is awarded to whoever lands closest to the pin after all players are on the green, no matter how many shots it takes, as long as the players hit in turn.

✔ **First in:** After all four players land the green, the putter decides the first-in point. Johnny wins the closest-to point by hitting his chip shot to within five feet of the hole. Harrison's ball is farthest from the hole — 20 feet away — so he gets the first chance to putt. If he holes it, he wins the first-in point.

Bingo, Bango, Bongo requires golfers to play in turn, based on who is *away,* which is the traditional manner of play in standard, competitive golf. But many golfers, in the interest of speedy play, subscribe to playing *ready golf* — meaning any ready player can hit. If you want to play Bingo, Bango, Bongo, each player, in the interest of maintaining speedy play, should always be ready to hit in turn and be aware of where the other players are at all times.

Snake

Throughout the ages, the sinister snake has symbolized evil. On the golf course, nothing is more evil, more heartbreaking, and more maddening than a three-putt. You play *Snake* on the golf course to punish the three-putt.

Snake sharpens your putting by forcing you to pay closer attention to your first putt. Many players hit their first putts during a round carelessly and without real purpose. Snake teaches you to be more precise with your putts — not running them too far by or leaving them woefully short — because the punishment for a three-putt means more than just another stroke on your scorecard. It means hearing it from your partners.

Holing out all your putts is a good habit to get into. Although you may find it sporting to concede small putts to each other in the interest of speedy play, you encounter times, particularly when you play in stroke-play tournaments, when you need to make two-footers. The slightest lack of attention to a two-foot tap-in can result in a hideous miss, as you find out playing Snake.

Follow these steps and the game of Snake is on:

1. **Purchase a rubber snake at any toy store — the uglier the snake, the better.**

2. **As soon as the round of golf begins, pull the reptile from your golf bag.**

3. **The first player to three-putt takes possession of the snake, and the other players hang it from his golf bag or cart.**

   Be sure to putt in turn based on who's away — more than one player may three-putt on a given green.

4. **The three-putter suffers the indignity of carrying the snake until another player three-putts.**

5. **The player who carries the snake when the round ends loses the match.**

You concede no gimmies or inside the leather putts in Snake. *Gimmies* are putts so short that the players, based on the presumption that they can't miss the putt, concede them in a friendly match. *Inside the leather* means that if a putt is shorter than the length of your putter (a throwback to when grips were made of leather, not rubber), you count it as a gimmie putt. Because of the pressure the Snake game induces, you must hole all putts, no matter how short.

 Snake provides some natural opportunities to tease your opponents mercilessly. But be warned: You may be on the receiving end of some ribbing as well. Three-putts resulting from missing little tap-ins that players normally concede during friendly rounds can be embarrassing and frustrating. Go easy on the needle, unless you can handle the other players applying it to your backside!

Eight in a Row

Do you believe that you can make eight 8-foot putts in a row? You may be able to.

Eight in a Row is a fantastic putting game that you can play all by yourself. The immediate improvement of your putting may astound you after you play the game. Putting consistently is a huge confidence builder. The knowledge that you can hole eight 8-footers in a row in practice takes the teeth out of a knee-knocking four-footer on the golf course.

Take these steps toward putting success:

1. **Pull eight balls from your golf bag.**

2. **Find a fairly flat hole on a practice green and pull the little flag from the hole.**

3. **Set yourself up two feet from the hole, and try to make all eight putts consecutively.**

   Repeat from the beginning until you make all eight putts.

4. **Back up one foot, and try to make all the three-foot putts consecutively.**

   • If you miss one, begin again until you make all eight putts consecutively.

   • If you fail to make all the three-footers again, go back to two feet and start over.

5. **Repeat the process, moving back one foot every time you make eight consecutive putts.**

6. **Keep going until you stand eight feet from the hole.**

   Don't be startled when you find yourself repeatedly draining eight-footers.

7. **After you master the flat putt, try the same game on a side-hill, uphill, or downhill putt.**

Making a bunch of two-foot putts consecutively isn't difficult. It may seem easy, as may the three-footers, after you get into a rhythm. But this game tests your focus and attention span. If you allow your mind to wander, you quickly find out how easy it is to miss a three-footer.

You also find that the pressure increases as you go back. After you take the time and energy to hole eight consecutive putts from two, three, and four feet, that eighth putt from the five-foot range is important. After all, who wants to go back to two feet and start all over again? (For more helpful putting drills, check out Chapter 15.)

First to Make Five

Arriving late at the golf course with only a limited time to warm up on the practice green? The best way to roll as many putts as possible is to join forces with another player. Instead of taking four or five balls to the practice green and chasing them around, pick a partner and grab one ball each.

After you each have a ball in hand, follow these steps to quickly get up to speed:

1. **Choose two holes on the practice green cut about 10 to 15 feet apart.**

2. **Position yourself to the side of one hole while your partner stands at the other.**

   Keep your ball between your feet and the hole closest to you.

3. **At the same time, or in a quickly alternating fashion, putt to the opposite hole.**

4. **When the ball arrives at or in your hole, rake it up and putt it to the other hole.**

5. **The first player to sink five putts wins. You can switch sides to continue the game.**

The practice prowess of Se Ri Pak

At the age of 14, a high school track star named Se Ri Pak took up golf. Six years later, in 1998, Pak was named the LPGA Rookie of the Year! By the end of her 2003 season, she became a virtual lock for the LPGA Hall of Fame, having won 21 times, including four LPGA major championships.

Talk about the fast track. Pak was an overnight success, right? How did she do it? "I really love golf. I love to play, so I spend most of my time at the golf course. I always like to spend time on my game," she said before the 2002 U.S. Women's Open.

You can relate, right? Yeah, you can relate . . . if, like her, spending time at the golf course means nine-hour practice sessions. Se Ri, on her "off days," practices all aspects of her game, including a myriad of short-game shots, over a nine-hour session (with a one-hour lunch break).

But how can she possibly keep her mind engaged while she hits practice shots for nine hours? She squints with confusion when asked the question. "It's my job," she finally answers.

Although the name *First to Make Five* implies a race, don't hurry yourself. The speed of this game isn't important. You can hit putt after putt in rapid fashion, but concentrate on making good strokes and trying to hole your putts. Think of the alternating putts as baseball innings.

Because you don't have to retrieve your putts (a fresh ball your opponent putts instantly arrives at your feet), you can roll countless putts and build a solid, repeating, confident stroke in a short time. After you and your practice partner find a rhythm, you don't have to move your feet to keep putting — you begin to read the break and the speed so well that the 10- to 15-foot putt seems easy, so you start to putt without fear. Your only goal is to consistently make that putt.

Subconsciously, when you go onto the golf course, you find yourself confidently attempting 15-foot putts because you know the speed and develop a hunger for sinking them.

Chapter 15

Tricks and Treats: Techniques and Tools to Improve Your Game

In This Chapter

▶ Drilling on the driving range

▶ Building your own sand-play trainer

▶ Putting aids for the practice green and carpet

▶ Working at home

In the 1984 motion picture *The Karate Kid,* Mr. Miyagi teaches his pupil Daniel the fundamental secrets of martial arts by putting the boy through his paces. Miyagi has him do chores, such as sanding the deck, painting the fence, and waxing the car, which frustrates Daniel until he finds out how the chores apply to Karate — they actually strengthen his techniques for fighting! You don't have to get so menial in your training, but you can utilize some simple devices that can help you train — on and off the golf course.

Before you run out on a buying binge (or *another* buying binge) — grabbing all the trinkets that you can find in retail golf shops, magazines, or on television infomercials — check out our recommendations in this chapter. You have to buy some of these devices, but you can make many of them yourself. One trip to a hardware store to buy a rubber band, a chalk line, two 2 x 4s, and a dowel, and you can build yourself five short-game training devices for less than $20.

Another step to take before you shell out your hard-earned cash for the latest gadget is to pay a visit to a PGA professional at your club or your course. See what he or she uses to teach. The devices golf professionals use to teach likely are time-honored and tested and focus on the key, fundamental points.

In this chapter, we give you some easy tricks to try to improve your short game. The treat is the fun you have on the golf course when you begin to notice the results!

Riding the Range

Going to the practice range doesn't have to be like "going to the rock pile." You can make the experience useful and fun by experimenting with different ways to practice. Use some of the following tricks to make practice more like play.

Standing up for balance

Good balance aids your golf game because it helps you swing smoothly and evenly — you have a better chance of taking the club back along the target line and through the ball with good tempo and rhythm. Rather than a choppy or forced feeling, you want an even, fluid swing — and good balance helps you do just that. Hitting shots or taking swings with your feet placed together improves your balance and gives you a good sense of the physics involved in the golf swing (see Figure 15-1).

Figure 15-1: Hit some balls with your feet together to get a feel for balance and the physics of the golf swing.

It may feel a bit awkward at first, but you can discover a lot about the turn of your body and the release of your hands by swinging with your feet together. Hitting shots with a condensed base gives you a good sense for the weight and power of the clubhead and how it shoots the ball virtually on its own without the aid of your body.

When you have time on the practice range, hit 10 or 15 balls with your feet squarely together. Try using a pitching wedge and position the ball back in your stance, off your back foot (see Figure 15-1). Swing along the target line, keeping your hands ahead of the ball at all times. Stand closer to your line than on most other shots. You're not looking for distance here; you just want to make good contact without falling over.

Becoming a one-armed bandit

A brilliant way to develop your sense for the swing and for ball striking is to hit golf shots with one hand. Here's how:

1. **Stand over the ball at the practice range and take your normal stance with a wedge or a 9-iron.**

2. **Remove your dominant hand from the club and leave it to dangle at your side.**

   You don't need it for this drill.

3. **Start by hitting some one-handed chip shots.**

   Hitting these little chips helps you develop a feel for getting the club on the ball and lets you see how the ball comes off the clubface.

4. **Work your way up to three-quarter-swing pitch shots, using only your non-dominant hand.**

   Your confidence with one arm begins to improve, and your shots become stronger and fly farther.

   If you find that your dangling arm gets in the way of your swing, try stuffing your hand into your pocket before you make the swing.

It may seem difficult to hit one-handed shots, but hitting them without your dominant hand guiding the swing helps your short game in a number of ways:

✔ It proves to you that, in the short game and in the full golf swing, the non-dominant hand truly is the leader, and the dominant hand serves only as a guide. You discover after a few swings that you can hit the ball a long way and in an effective fashion with your non-dominant hand. This psychologically frees up your mind and your sense of the swing, helping you rely on the non-dominant hand and arm. (See Chapter 2 for the importance of letting your non-dominant hand lead the way.)

✔ You're forced to practice pulling your non-dominant hand and arm through the shot and letting that arm truly "captain" the swing, because it has no "first mate" to help.

✔ You develop a greater awareness of the face of the club. Using only one hand heightens the sensation of feel with that one hand.

Tuning your swing with music

More often these days, players, especially the young ones, show up on the practice range wearing stereo headphones. They hit practice balls while they listen to music. And the youngsters aren't the only ones. PGA Tour player Vijay Singh has admitted that he has a little ditty he thinks of and sings in his head when he swings a golf club. A former Canadian professional, Richard Zokol, wore headphones when he played sometimes. No rule prohibits it. But is it a good idea? We think so.

Playing in the subconcious

If you listen to music while you hit golf shots, you play in the subconscious. The activity trains you to play the game from a mentally suspended state. Think about it. When you're driving a car down the road and listening to music on the radio, do you consciously think about every move you make while you drive? Keep my foot on the gas pedal . . . check the rear view mirror . . . turn on my right turn signal . . . check the right lane . . . turn the steering wheel to the right . . . merge to the right to change lanes . . . move my foot to the brake to decrease my speed.

No. You don't drive that way. Although driving demands concentration and attention to ensure safety, more often than not, it just kind of happens without much thought. You use your instincts and force of habit to drive mile after mile.

The biggest advantage to practicing or playing while listening to music is that it trains you to hit golf shots in the subconscious. If you listen to the music, you don't think about the literal components of your swing: Is my face square . . . take the club back slowly . . . gotta keep my elbow tucked . . . okay, pause at the top and shift my weight to the left side . . . and don't decelerate. These types of thoughts can paralyze you.

It may seem like a mystical phrase, but *playing in the subconscious* improves your short game. You want to get to the point where you can grab the club and just swing it naturally, instead of stepping over the ball with a series of running thoughts. (See Chapter 2 for more on the power of the subconscious.)

Talking about tempo

Music can also help one of the most important characteristics of the golf swing: your tempo. Your ideal tempo as you swing is really a matter of preference. Tempo isn't a fundamental set in stone. Some may think of tempo as smooth and rhythmic, conjuring up images of Fred Astaire and Ginger Rogers. Good tempo to others may be more like the Jitterbug.

You can have a fast swing as long as you make it consistent. We don't recommend it, but you can have it. Lanny Wadkins was pretty fast. Nick Price has a quicker speed than most. The bottom line is that you can have as fast a swing as you like, but the fundamentals — including where the clubhead is at impact and maintaining balance — must be there. Nick Price looks much faster than Tom Watson, but when Price finishes the shot, he's completely in balance.

Tempo is a "what's right for you" part of the golf game. Hard rock is terrible for a slow, rhythmic swing. Another guy would benefit from hard rock, because it makes him feel like his fast swing has rhythm and balance. Probably the best choice for music, if you have no preference, is a waltz. In Chapter 12, we cover tips for regaining your tempo.

Practicing in the Sand and on the Green

Not all practice takes place on the driving range. Really. Anytime you're at a facility that has a practice bunker, short-game area, or practice green, take advantage of the situation to try some of the following tricks.

Bunker board

Hitting sand shots is dry and dirty work. Who wants to spend time in a bunker? Well, you do if you want to lower your golf scores by improving your bunker game. But another, less obvious advantage to swinging a mean sand wedge is confidence. If you're confident about how you play a bunker shot, that confidence spills over to shots outside of the bunker, like flop shots over bunkers and short shots out of high rough. Confidence breeds success, which equals lower scores and a lower handicap.

But instead of just dropping practice balls into a bunker and thrashing about, approach bunker practice with a plan. One way to teach yourself to handle bunker shots is to practice with a bunker board.

The goal of the bunker board exercise is to train yourself to hit through the sand positioned under the ball and splash it out at the right depth. The setup is simple: Buy a wooden 2-x-4 board at the lumberyard or hardware store and take it to the course with you. Place the board in a practice bunker along your target line and perpendicular to your feet. Put two to three inches of sand on top of the board, and carefully leave the ends of the board uncovered so you don't hit the end when you swing. Put a golf ball on the middle of the board.

Set up for a bunker shot with your sand wedge and hit the ball from its position on the sand above the board, trying not to hit down on the board. As we explain in Chapter 6, if you take more than two inches of sand on your bunker shots, you hit too many heavy, short shots. If you splash the club through the inch or two of sand you put on the board, you shouldn't hit it. A proper shot may skim the board with the wedge, but that's about it.

The board prevents you from digging in any further than the two inches of sand. The club should glide through the sand and reveal the board lying underneath (see Figure 15-2). If you do hit the board, you feel it. If you hit the board, you're digging too low. The presence of the board helps you, consciously at first and then subconsciously, not to dig the club too deep and leave your shots in the bunker or short of the green.

Figure 15-2: Pick the ball cleanly out of the few inches of sand to sweep the board dry.

Conversely, if you bring the clubface in too high, you hit the shot *thin* — which means you hit the top of the ball and send a line drive — and the ball may stay in the bunker or bound across the green, possibly into another bunker!

Chalk talk

After you line up a putt and determine the target line that can sink the putt or get it near the hole, your task is to swing the putter back and bring it forward along the target line.

When the ball doesn't go where you expect it to, you're left to wonder what went wrong. Did it leave the target line? Did your putter wobble off the target line? One way to get immediate feedback as to why your putts go astray is to make the target line visible.

Go to a hardware or home improvement store and buy a powder chalk line normally used for carpentry work. The device contains a string loaded with blue or white chalk, and when you lay the string down on the ground and snap the line, it creates a straight chalk line on the surface of the green (see Figure 15-3).

Take the chalk line and go out to the practice green at your golf course, to your carpet at home, or to the office. Pick a flat area and a line that you want to roll the golf ball on — which may or may not end at a hole. Pull out the chalky string and snap it down on the ground. Let the green or the carpet pick up the chalk so that when you remove the string, it leaves an exact line on the ground.

Put the golf ball on the chalk line and stand over the putt. You have an immediate visual feel for your putting line as you stand with your eyes directly over the ball and the putting line. Now you don't just focus on the ball and a hole — you literally see the line.

Hit putts down the line and into the hole. Notice the blade on the takeaway:

✔ Does the blade stay on the line as you take it back?

✔ Does the blade stay on the line during the followthrough?

✔ Does the ball roll nicely along the line toward the hole or toward the end of the line?

✔ When does the ball leave the line?

You can look for a number of possible reasons why a ball leaves the target line when putting:

✔ **The blade doesn't go straight back along the target line.** This means you have to somehow correct the path of the putterhead in mid-stroke, which causes an unnatural, forced flow to the putt.

✔ **The blade doesn't come straight forward and through the ball along the target line.** Anticipation of the shot or anxiety about the result can cause you to let your eyes wander toward the hole or hurry the putterhead through the ball. A push or a pull can result, sending the ball right or left of the target line.

✔ **You decelerate the blade at impact.** The putterhead veers off the target line as it slows instead of moving confidently, like a pendulum, through the ball.

Figure 15-3: Make like a carpenter and snap a chalk line to help you with your putting.

Trench warfare

Need more than just an imaginary target line or a chalk line to keep your putterhead on target during the stroke? Try a little practice in the trench to groove a repeating putting stroke that goes straight back and straight through the ball every time.

Buy an extra 2-x-4 board when you buy the one to use as a bunker board (see the section "Bunker board" earlier in this chapter), or buy two if you haven't yet bought the other. Take both boards to the practice green (or the carpet in your home or office). Lay the boards down flat, parallel to each other and pointing at the target, as shown in Figure 15-4. Leave just enough room between the boards for your putterhead to swing parallel to the boards. They should be far enough apart so your putter has room to swing freely, but they need to be close enough that you get immediate feedback if your putter sways and bangs into either or both of the boards.

Figure 15-4: Employ two wooden boards to help you keep your putterhead on-line throughout the stroke.

Stand over the boards with your putter in the trench. Swing your putterhead down the putting line, and try to do it without banging the toe or the heel of the putter into the 2-x-4 boards. This helps you train your putting stroke.

Repeatedly swinging the putter between the boards helps you clearly see the backward and forward path of the putterhead, and it also trains you to pivot at your shoulder, using your arms and hands to take the putterhead straight back and straight through the ball. Do this drill often enough and you'll start taking your putter back and forth with your eyes closed. Awareness of the putter helps you putt with great precision.

You can put a ball in the trench and putt it out of the opening if you like, and you can combine the trench drill with the chalk line drill we discuss in the previous section to really groove a straight and steady putting stroke (see Figure 15-4). You don't need the ball or the chalk line, however, because you can use the boards alone to discover the nature of your swing.

Dowel drill

Accurate putting starts with rolling the golf ball straight to your target. Being one degree off can cause the putt to be several inches off. The dowel drill is a good way to get a feel for hitting through the ball on the intended line. On your trip to the hardware store to buy tools for the other drills in this chapter, buy an inch-wide dowel. A *dowel* is a piece of solid wood shaped like a rod or a cylinder. Have the dowel cut to about eight inches long.

Put the dowel on the practice green (or your carpet) and choose a putting line; place the dowel perpendicular to the line. Put your putterhead flush behind the dowel. Make your stroke and hit the dowel. The rolling dowel should resemble the rolling golf ball.

When you hit the dowel, you want to hit it flush with the blade (see Figure 15-5). The rolling dowel gives you immediate feedback on the movement of your putterhead when it hits the ball. If you hit it on the money, the dowel rolls straight, end-over-end. But if you hit it with an errant stroke, you don't get the intended roll:

- If the heel of your putter comes in first, even at the slightest percentage angle, and your putter doesn't hit the dowel flush, you push the dowel instead of rolling it down the line.
- If the toe comes through first, you pull the dowel off-line.

If the misdirected dowel veers right or left, your putterhead isn't coming squarely through the ball on the target line. You can try to correct the path of your putter on your own or try the drills we cover in the "Chalk talk" and "Trench warfare" sections earlier in this chapter to straighten the swing path of your putter.

Figure 15-5: You can use a dowel to help you roll your putts on-line with a proper putting stroke.

Improving at Home

The phrase "don't try this at home" doesn't apply to improving your short game. Anytime you can get a little practice in or do some drills to improve your technique, do it! Some of the following tricks and drills can help you at home when your golf course is under winter's snow or when you just can't get out of the office.

Stretching your putting skill

The following stretching exercise is designed to help you build your sense for letting your putterhead fall through the ball, swing to completion, and hold at the finish — as great putting strokes do. It trains your muscles — and your mind — to make sure that your putterhead extends forward along the target line after the ball leaves the face.

Get a strong, six-inch rubber band. Take one end and put it around the thin leg of a table or any piece of furniture — something heavy and stable that won't move with minimal pressure. Put your putter-head through the space in the middle of the band. Take your putting stance, with your putter on the left side of the table leg for righties and on the right side for lefties. Stretch the blade and rubber band forward, as if you're putting away from the table toward an imaginary hole, and hold the finish, as shown in Figure 15-6.

The band tries to pull your putter back, but keep stretching out the band. Stop after you complete a normal followthrough. Hold the finish, and then stretch it out again. Maintain a nice soft grip. You don't want to break the rubber band; you just want to stretch it out. All you want to do is train your muscles.

 You'll also see that trying to use your wrists to pull the putter forward doesn't work as well as keeping your wrists firm and having them work in concert with your arms and shoulders. Wristy putting isn't solid, and it complicates matters, as you can tell by trying to pull the putter forward with your wrists. Your hands, arms, and wrists should pull the rubber band as one triangular unit, which is what they should do during a real putting stroke.

Now take the rubber band off and go hit some real putts on a practice green or on your carpet. Without the rubber band, you feel so much freer to accelerate through the ball, which is what you want to do on every putt you hit. Keep the same light grip, and let the muscles you've trained do the dirty work.

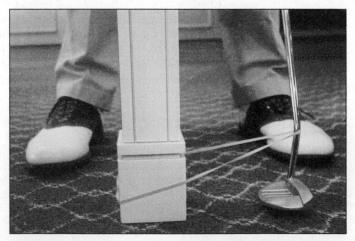

Figure 15-6: Train your muscles to accelerate through your putts by practicing with a strong rubber band and a piece of furniture.

Weighing in on weights

In any golf shop or in most sporting goods stores, you can buy a small, lead, donut-shaped weight. You typically use a donut to add weight to a golf club for loosening up and swinging. But in this case, you should take the club home with the weight.

You can sit in your chair watching television or be in any room in the house to perform this drill. Drop the donut weight around the shaft of your club so that it falls all the way down and stops at the *hosel* (where the shaft connects to the blade). If you push the donut against the hosel, the rubber coating around the weight sticks and holds the donut in place. With your forearm on the chair's armrest, grip the club with your non-dominant hand first.

With the club extended out in front of you, slowly lift the club up to a 90-degree angle, using just your wrist, and then slowly, using your wrist and forearm for resistance, lower the club back down so it points directly outward. Repeat — from flat to a 90-degree angle and back.

Now, instead of going up and down, use your grip and wrist to maneuver the club from side to side — to the right and back to the middle and to the left and back to the middle — on a flat plane. Repeat.

This drill builds up your forearm and wrist strength, which helps you swing the club firmly and fully on pitch shots and approach shots. Strong wrists and arms are also useful when hitting full wedge shots from long grass and tangled rough, or when you need to pitch a ball a long way. Building these muscles also benefits your mental game, because while you build up your wrist and forearm strength, you can see the face of the club and increase your conscious and subconscious awareness of the clubface. You train your hand into the grip, and you see the face of the club . . . all while you watch the news or read a magazine.

 If you're a righty, do more lifting with your left hand and arm than you do with the right. If you're a lefty, concentrate on your right side. The non-dominant arm is the one that provides the power and direction of the club. The non-dominant arm is the "captain," and the dominant arm is the "first mate."

Asking your mirror, mirror

Awareness of the clubface is vital when you try to swing the club along the target line (see Chapter 2 for more on the target line).

Overall awareness of your alignment and the position of your body are also important. Are you actually aiming where you think you're aiming? Are you swinging your clubhead along the target line? Are your shoulders aligned parallel to the target line?

Your PGA professional, or even a friend, can check your swing on the practice range, but you're on your own during a round, so you need to be able to sense good alignment and have an awareness of the proper positioning of your body. As with many aspects of self-awareness and introspection, you need to look no further than the mirror for answers!

Stand in front of a floor-length mirror with one of your short irons. Without looking into the mirror, take your golf stance — the position you take for chipping or putting — as if you're aiming to hit a ball into the mirror. After you get comfortable, look at yourself in the mirror. Now take your stance with your chest facing the mirror, as if you're hitting a ball to the side. Get set and then look up at the mirror. In both cases:

- ✔ **Look at the way you're standing.** Are your feet open to the target line?

- ✔ **Look at the face angle of the blade on the club.** Is it square to the target line?

- ✔ **Look at the angle of the shaft.** Do you have the club properly positioned in a vertical fashion in the middle of your stance, with, perhaps, a slight forward lean?

- ✔ **Look at where your head is over the ball.** Can you see down the target line?

- ✔ **Look at how far apart your feet are.** Are they shoulder-width?

- ✔ **Look at where your hands fall.** Are they close to your body and gripping the club lightly?

Looking at yourself in the mirror gives you immediate pieces of important feedback. Seeing is believing . . . and recognizing where your body is as opposed to where you think it is helps train your mind and muscles. You can even compare what you see in the mirror to the descriptions and figures we include in Part II. Use mirrors as much as you can.

Chapter 16

Learning from the Stars

● ●

In This Chapter

▶ Feeling it like Seve Ballesteros

▶ Beaching it like Gary Player

▶ Discovering your soft side like John Daly

▶ Improvising like Lee Trevino

▶ Rolling it like Ben Crenshaw

▶ Closing the door like Annika Sorenstam

▶ Not yanking your putts like Johnny Miller

● ●

They make it look easy! PGA Tour and LPGA players compete for big bucks while you catch their act from your living room recliner or from a horizontal position between afternoon snoozes on the couch. Maybe you spent the morning before the telecast chili-dipping pitch shots, blading wedges, and skulling bunker shots in your own weekend golf match. Now you tune in to a golf telecast showing the virtuoso performances of masterful professionals.

Watching the stars display such precision is both an agony and a joy. Fred Couples hits a short iron that stops the ball stone dead next to the hole — a kick-in! Annika Sorenstam scares the hole with a chip shot. Tiger Woods cans yet another clutch eight-footer. You marvel, but you can't help but ask yourself, "Why can't I do that?"

The good news is, you can. It may not be with the astonishing regularity of pros, but it can be with enough frequency to make you score better and enjoy playing more. Golf is one of the only sports where an amateur can hit a shot just as well as the best of the best. You may not be able to hit a drive as long as Hammerin' Hank Kuehne — he averages 321.4 yards! — but you can hole the same putts or hit the same pitch, chip, or bunker shot as any PGA Tour player in history. Lightning you can capture in your own bottle!

One way to emulate the great players is to closely watch their techniques. You can learn to play and think like the stars. This chapter identifies a few of the greats and their specific strengths and gives you to pointers to recreate their magic.

Feeling like Seve Ballesteros

Seve Ballesteros was a dashing young Spaniard when he splashed onto the scene as a teenager and began playing professionally in 1974. By the time his full-time playing career started to wind down, Seve had become the first player to pass the $3 million mark on the European Tour and won 87 titles worldwide, including three British Open Championships and two Masters titles. He also successfully captained the European team in the 1987 Ryder Cup Matches.

Ballesteros began teaching himself to play golf at age seven by hitting balls at the beach on the Bay of Santander in Spain with a single club — a cut-down 3-iron his brother gave him. The result of hitting shots of all length, trajectory, and shape with that single club was Seve's great sense of touch and feel. He was forced to use his hands and imagination to hit the shots he needed. "Golf, in my opinion, was invented to develop the skill and the intelligence and the feel of the human being," said Ballesteros at the Ford Championship at Doral in 2004.

His intelligence and feel served him well when he turned profes-sional, and those attributes gave him a reputation as a magician. Seve began wowing the world at the 1976 British Open at Royal Birkdale, where he hit a crafty chip shot on the 18th hole that dis-sected two bunkers and settled one yard from the cup. He finished in second place, but he was only 19 at the time!

Seve did capture the 1979 British Open, where he managed to fash-ion an approach shot in the final round from the parking lot along the 16th hole to set up a birdie. When Ballesteros outran Tom Kite to win the 1983 Masters, Kite, a brilliant wedge player in his own right, said, "When he gets it going, it's almost as if Seve is driving a Ferrari and the rest of us are in Chevrolets."

His decisive birdie putt to win the 1984 British Open at St. Andrews was thrilling, as was an amazing bunker shot he struck with a 3-wood on the way to beating Fuzzy Zoeller at the Ryder Cup one year ear-lier (see Chapter 10 for tips on executing unconventional shots).

Ben Crenshaw said of the Spaniard, "Seve plays shots I don't even see in my dreams!" Be like Seve Ballesteros:

   ✔ **Imagine** different types of shots in different situations.
   ✔ **Develop touch and feel** by hitting different shots with the same club.

> ✔ **Feel** the clubhead making contact with the ball.
>
> ✔ **Practice** trouble shots from treacherous positions.

Escaping (Not Sleeping in) Bunkers like Gary Player

A poor, 18-year-old South African golfer a long way from home, Gary Player spent long nights sleeping in the bunkers of Scottish golf courses when he turned pro in 1953. Player went on to win 163 tournaments worldwide over six decades, including nine majors. He was only the third man in history to win the career grand slam: The Masters, U.S. Open, British Open, and PGA Championships. (Gene Sarazen, the first man to do so, actually invented the sand wedge!)

Few ever imagined that the 5'7", 146-pound Player could enjoy such success, but he made up for any deficiencies with a sterling short game — especially from the bunkers. He aggressively attacked bunker shots because he had no fear of playing from the sand and was confident that he could get up and down from anywhere.

Player believed that the harder he practiced, the luckier he became. Close examination of Player's technique, and attention to the times he has talked about it over the years, reveals that, unlike many others, Player doesn't "blast" the ball out of the sand; instead, he focuses on accelerating his clubhead through the sand and lifting the ball into the air. To keep from swaying, he puts his weight on his front side and keeps his head still throughout the shot. His swing is smooth and his finish high.

Player, a member of the World Golf Hall of Fame, has delivered elegant bunker shots under pressure for over half a century. Be like Gary Player:

> ✔ **Practice,** practice, practice.
>
> ✔ **Accelerate** — don't think "blast" — through the sand. Think "splash!"
>
> ✔ **Be still** and keep your weight on your front side to avoid swaying.
>
> ✔ **Confidence** in your bunker play makes you fearless when hitting approach shots, because, like Player, you know you can make the best of being in a bunker.

Living Hard and Playing Soft like John Daly

He's been called a redneck and a drunk . . . endured the shakes in the middle of a tournament . . . been through rehab . . . been married four times . . . been forced off an airplane for misbehavior . . . broken his putter in anger . . . scored an 18 on a hole during a PGA Tour event . . . fought with a spectator . . . been disqualified . . . been suspended . . . been fired . . . lost millions gambling in casinos . . . six-putted from eight feet . . . driven an RV from tournament to tournament and sold merchandise out of the back . . . recorded an album . . . lost and gained large amounts of weight . . . thrown his putter into a water hazard . . . and despite, and maybe for, these antics, golf fans unabashedly love him. No player relates to the common man more than John Daly (that is, if the common man can hit a golf ball 350 yards with a world-class short game).

John Daly, who turned professional in 1987, has won nine tournaments worldwide, including the 1991 PGA Championship at Crooked Stick in Indianapolis and the 1995 British Open at St. Andrews. He also shot a course record 62 at TPC at The Canyons in the 2001 Las Vegas Invitational.

Everyone knows John Daly as a big-hitter — in 2003, his average drive on the PGA Tour was 314 yards! But Big John's driving accuracy, however, was only 49.7 percent. Enter the short game: "Any time you win a tournament, you win with your short game. Whether it is chipping or putting, you win tournaments with your short game," said Daly. "I won the British Open with my short game. I won the PGA Championship with my short game. You can't win tournaments if you don't have the short game going."

Daly won the 2004 Buick Invitational at Torrey Pines in San Diego by hitting a masterful bunker shot on the first playoff hole. "I'd been chipping and putting so good, I really didn't worry when I missed a green. I felt confident I could get it up and down."

Daly is a big, hardened man with soft hands. Be like John Daly:

- ✔ **Enjoy belting big drives,** but take pride in the magic and beauty of an impressive short game, too.

- ✔ **Keep a light touch with soft hands,** because Big John may "grip it and rip it" with the driver, but he keeps a very light grip when chipping or pitching. Make certain you don't squeeze the handle when you play a short-game shot.

✔ **Get prenuptial agreements** each time you marry; otherwise, like John, you'll be singing "All My Ex's Wear Rolexes."

✔ **Limit** your booze intake the night before and during a golf round.

Scrambling like Lee Trevino

Lee Trevino is an entirely self-taught golfer. Unlike many silver-spoon professionals raised at golf clubs, Trevino honed his skills at Hardy's Driving Range in Dallas and served a stint in the Marines before he turned professional in 1960. Learning to play golf in Texas winds on hardscrabble conditions made Trevino one of the toughest shot-shapers in the history of golf. Trevino doesn't believe a player can have a "natural touch." He believes touch is something you create by hitting millions of golf balls.

Trevino won the Vardon Trophy for the lowest scoring average on Tour five times. He won 29 times on the PGA Tour, including two U.S. Opens, two PGA Championships, and two British Opens.

Trevino used his short game to demand victory in his second consecutive British Open win in 1972 at Muirfield Village in Scotland. Trevino closed out the third round with five straight birdies, including putts of 15 and 30 feet, a holed bunker shot, and a chip-in. "If I played golf with my wife, I'd try to beat the daylights out of her," Trevino once said. The "Merry Mex," in the midst of a final round temper tantrum, chipped-in from behind the 17th green with a 9-iron for a tournament-saving par. The unlikely shot stunned his opponent, Tony Jacklin, who seemed sure to overtake Trevino, into three-putting from 18 feet for bogey. "God is a Mexican" was Trevino's only explanation.

Trevino was so competitive that, when he arrived early at a PGA Tour stop, he went into the clubhouse, sought out the club champion, and asked him to play for money. Be like Lee Trevino:

✔ **Practice** in all types of conditions, including heavy wind.

✔ **Expect to hole** every single shot you hit. Trevino made his goal and expectation the same: to be a gunslinger and shoot for the pin on every shot. When your short game's that good, fire up those six-guns.

✔ **Never give up** on a hole — even when it looks grim and your temper starts to get the best of you.

✔ **Be tough.** Trevino survived a lightning strike on the golf course at the 1975 Western Open in Chicago.

Putting like Ben Crenshaw

Ben Crenshaw putted his way into the World Golf Hall of Fame, named his autobiography *A Feel for the Game,* and released a video called *The Art of Putting.* Known as Gentle Ben, the Texan has won 19 times on the PGA Tour and captained the 1999 Ryder Cup team to its first win since 1993 when Justin Leonard hit that famous, riot-inducing 45-foot putt on the 17th hole. He won two Masters titles on Augusta National's demanding, complex, and slippery greens.

With a trusty putter named "Little Ben" he's owned since he was a teenager, Crenshaw addresses the ball slightly forward in his stance and, with his hands a bit ahead of the ball, rotates very slowly from his shoulders to produce a wristless, soft putt that dies at the hole.

Crenshaw's love for putting is evident. When asked about the greens at The Country Club in Brookline, MA before the 1999 Ryder Cup, he said, "I think they're beautiful. They're beautifully shaped. They're sufficiently undulating with some puzzling rolls in them. You've got to know where and where not to put the ball. They're beautiful greens — a good test of putting." Be like Ben Crenshaw:

- **Study** the subtle breaks, hills, dips, and valleys of every green from different angles.

- **Play** the ball in the front of your stance and, with your hands forward, make a smooth, slow putting stroke.

- **Practice** hitting putts that die at the hole and not short of it.

- **Fall in love** with a putter . . . and be loyal to it!

- **Respect** the traditions of golf. Learn the rules and the history.

- **Believe** in fate and your own "magic."

Finishing like Annika Sorenstam

Annika Sorenstam was born in Sweden in 1970, started playing golf at the age of 12, and became an LPGA player in 1994. Less than 10 years later, the 5'6", blue-eyed blonde had qualified for the LPGA Tour and World Golf Hall of Fames. In 2002, she won 11 LPGA Tournaments in one season — a feat only one person, Mickey Wright in 1964, had ever accomplished.

So prolific was Annika that in 2003 she even played in a PGA Tour event — the Colonial National Invitational — against an all-male field! Later that season she played in the Skins Game against Fred Couples, Phil Mickelson, and Mark O'Meara. She holed a 39-yard bunker shot for an eagle to win $175,000 on the first day — the most money ever won on the first day of the Skins Game. At the end of the 2004 season, she owned 59 victories on the LPGA Tour.

To enjoy such consistent success no matter the circumstances, a player must own a world-class short game. Annika: check. One of the most noticeable features of Annika's short game is the way she finishes her pitches, chips, bunker shots, and putts. At the end of her stroke, long after the ball has gone, she keeps the clubhead frozen at the finish. Her tempo is even and smooth, as if she swings the club without even hitting a ball. Annika looks up to watch the ball go to the hole, but only after the ball is well gone and she fully completes her stroke. Her concentration allows her to be consistent and relaxed during any type of shot. Be like Annika:

- ✔ **Hold the club still** at the top of your followthrough or at the end of your putting stroke.

- ✔ **Only look up** to see where the ball goes after you fully complete the stroke.

- ✔ **Listen** for the putt to go in instead of hurrying to watch it.

- ✔ **Only lower the club** after the ball comes to a complete stop.

Yipping like Johnny Miller

Johnny Miller is best known now as a controversial television golf analyst who pulls no punches, but the man was once the game's golden boy, anointed by critics as "the next Nicklaus."

Miller turned professional in 1969 and won 25 times on the PGA Tour. People will always remember his playing career for two things: the 63 he shot in the final round to win the 1973 U.S. Open at Oakmont and the yips that effectively ended his competitive career. Miller last won at Pebble Beach in 1994 when he was 46 years old, but he jabbed and stabbed his way to that win while holding his breath over every little putt.

Miller made his debut on the Champions (senior) Tour in 1997 (he's only played two tournaments on the senior circuit). During that three-round debut in his home state of Utah, Miller led the field in the statistical categories of fairways hit and greens in regulation, but he still only finished T-44, 14 shots behind the winner. Never was an indictment of poor putting more evident.

Jack Nicklaus' suspect short game

With 73 PGA Tour victories, including 18 major championships, two U.S. Amateur titles, and 10 Champions Tour wins, Jack Nicklaus is the most prolific winner in golf history. He is one of only five men in history to achieve the career grand slam, and he won all the tournaments by making more putts when he needed them than anyone . . . ever.

When asked what he would change if he could start his career over, Nicklaus said, "I would have spent a little more time on the short game. I never worried too much about my short game because I usually made all of my short putts. If you are not making short putts and you are missing greens and having to chip, you are making bogey every time. You can't put pressure on your putter, you've got to put pressure on your golf game."

Granted, Nicklaus was so good in his golden years that he rarely missed greens, and therefore he rarely even hit pitches, chip shots, or bunker shots. But not paying attention to his short game eventually caught up with the Golden Bear.

"I hit a lot of nice shots, but my short game has been pathetic," said Nicklaus at the 2003 U.S. Senior Open. At the beginning of the 2004 season, Nicklaus admitted, "My first year on the Senior Tour I realized that my short game wasn't very good. I came back with a very different way of practicing. I'm putting for a least half-an-hour before a round, then chipping, and then, if I have time, I go to the driving range."

Don't yip putts like Johnny Miller:

- ✔ **Practice** regularly. Turn to Chapter 9 to find out more about the yips and how to banish them!
- ✔ **Be confident** when you hit your putts.
- ✔ **Putt in the sub-conscious** without fretting over the result.
- ✔ **Listen** for the ball to fall into the hole instead of watching it.
- ✔ **Stroke** putts instead of hitting them. You want to roll the ball, not skip it.

Part V
The Part of Tens

The 5th Wave   By Rich Tennant

WAYNE SHOULD HAVE KNOWN THE OTHER DAY NOT TO BREAK COURSE ETIQUETTE WITH A THREESOME FROM NEW JERSEY.

In this part . . .

Everyone loves a top-10 list. Part V gives you lots to love. You discover 10 secrets of short game success. You relive 10 memorable short game triumphs, and we show you how to take your clubs home or to the office to practice recreating these triumphs. And after the work is done, you join us on a worldwide tour of 10 of the great short game golf courses.

Chapter 17

Ten Simple Secrets of Short-Shot Success

In This Chapter

▶ Knowing when to turn your mind on and off

▶ Adhering to the short-game fundamentals

▶ Playing with realistic expectations

▶ Using the green to your advantage

Can the magical complexity and strategic subtlety of golf's most vexing aspect really be whittled down to 10 secrets? Sure. Why not? The secret to success, and especially to improvement, is to simplify the short game, and what could be more simple and chic than a list of 10 short-game tips?

Play in the Subconscious

Don't allow negative self-talk to cloud your mind and ruin your self-esteem. You can't be too concerned about the result or mechanics of the stroke. You want to visualize the shot and the target line, prepare yourself, and then get your mind out of the way and let your body make the shot, concentrating only on your target. Allow your athletic instincts, feel, and touch to take over. You didn't spend all that time practicing for nothing. Let your preparation do the talking and the swinging. Check out Chapter 2 for more on playing out of the mind.

Be Aware of the Clubface

The face of the club, when aimed properly, sends the ball directly toward the target at impact; therefore, you need to aim the clubface at the target and swing the clubhead along the target line. You must have a sense of where you aim the clubface throughout the swing. Light grip pressure allows you to feel the weight of the club-head, which improves your distance and direction control on short shots. Chapter 2 goes into more clubface detail.

Swing Along the Target Line

As when drawing a bow straight back to shoot an arrow, you should take the clubhead back along the target line and then forward along the line to completion. No matter how far back you draw the club, how hard the clubhead strikes the ball, or how high you follow through, you must keep your swing straight along the target line and directed at your intended target.

Maintain Consistent Speed

Deceleration is death. No matter what your swing speed is, you have to maintain it through the ball. Whether you swing your club from "nine-o'clock" to "three o'clock" or use a longer swing and finish, you must do so with acceleration through the ball. Make sure you have the confidence and the right club to make a full swing, because decelerating can only result in flubbed and shanked balls or dying putts.

Salute the Lead Hand as the Captain

Your lead hand is the "captain" of the swing, and your back hand is resigned to "first mate." Grip your club with the fingers of your lead hand and let your back hand add support. You should swing the club with your lead hand and guide the club along the target line with the back. If you need reinforcement about why this hierar-chy is important, try hitting some one-handed shots on the practice tee. You can easily see how much more powerful the shots you hit with your lead hand are.

Let the Ball Get in the Way

You should execute your pitch shot, chip shot, bunker shot, or putt the same way every time — whether you're taking a practice swing or actually striking the ball. Swing "through" the shot, not "at" the ball, to hit authoritative, confident shots that always have a chance to go into the hole.

Follow Through

Swinging through the ball and holding your finish is a pivotal example of "form follows function." Whether you end with a big "chorus line" finish or simply hold your putter at the end of your stroke, all good, consistent short game players, and golfers in general, follow through and hold their finish. A golf shot isn't finished when the club strikes the ball.

Following through is important in the form of most sports. Think of a free throw shooter in basketball, a fly fisherman, or the throwing arm of a quarterback. Those motions would be awkward and inefficient if the athletes halted and abbreviated them. The same goes for pitches, chips, and putts.

But the ball is gone after the clubhead hits it! Why follow through? You follow through to make certain you don't decelerate at impact. Deceleration stunts the swing and sends the ball offline or an improper distance. Swing freely and fully and follow through to a big, high finish.

Keep Realistic Expectations

Your mission, with every shot within 75 yards of the hole, is to get the ball onto the green. Yes, you want to get the ball close to the hole — the closer the better — but getting the ball onto the green, anywhere onto the green, in one shot is the most important goal. Eventually, depending on the circumstances, it can be an expectation.

After you reach the green, your realistic expectation is to hit only two putts to get the ball into the hole. The best way to minimize your green time to two putts is to have a realistic expectation of how close to the hole you can get the first putt. Remember — even a professional golfer can only expect to make a 10-footer half the time. Give your first putt a chance to go into the hole, but be satisfied when it stops close enough to leave you an easy tap-in for the second putt. Leaving your first putt a foot to two feet from the hole is a reasonable expectation.

Sometimes you miss two-foot putts. It's just the nature of the beast. You don't putt in a vacuum. Too many variables can keep a putt from going into the hole, even if your aim is perfect and your stroke stays on the target line. Flip to Chapters 7 and 9 for more putting tips and strategies.

Roll the Ball on the Ground

Rolling the ball is more effective for stopping the ball close to the hole than flying it through the air. Think of your chip shots and pitch shots as long putts and treat them as such. Pick a spot on the green to chip the ball to and read the "putt" from there. A ball rolling on the green has a much better chance to go in the hole than one that flies vertically at the hole. Just think of how much easier Bozo's Grand Prize Game would have been if kids could have rolled balls into holes instead of tossing them through the air. Think bowling, not basketball.

For most chip shots, the ball should be in the air for 20 percent of the distance and rolling on the ground for 80 percent. You should assume that pitch shots that need to carry a bunker or longer grass need to be in the air for 40 percent of the shot and rolling on the ground for 60 percent. Bunker shots may fly as much as 80 percent, but the longer the ball is in the air, the more precise the shot must be — and therefore, the more difficult it becomes.

Putts, of course, should be all roll. For tips on chipping, pitching, bunker shots, and putting, head to Part II.

Recognize that Every Putt is Straight

No matter how the green breaks — left-to-right, right-to-left, or even a double-breaker — your aim and stroke should always be on a straight line. Pick a target that allows for the break, and roll the ball in a straight line to that spot. Let the green do all the work and take the ball to the hole, using as much *"borrow"* as you've given it; don't vary your stroke to steer the ball toward the hole. (*Borrow* is an English term referring to how much aim you need to take away from the hole in order for the ball to curve into the hole. Use it with your friends to sound especially imperious and worldly.)

The same goes for hitting a chip shot to the hole. Don't vary your swing; pick a spot that allows for the break and chip straight down the target line to that spot. For some helpful putting drills, check out Chapter 15.

Chapter 18

Ten Ways You Can Practice Off the Course

In This Chapter

▶ Improving your game at home

▶ Taking your game on the road

▶ Getting a mental and physical workout

▶ Keeping your game tidy

▶ Varying your sporting repertoire

Golf is a passion. Don't leave it behind just because you leave the golf course. If you eat, breathe, and sleep short game, you come to the course better prepared to show off your skills. This chapter highlights 10 activities you can do away from the course — in your office, bedroom, or while you wait in line at the grocery store.

Putt on Your Carpet

Carpet putting is a time-honored tradition. The invention of the speakerphone made it even easier for business executives to take conference calls while secretly stroking putts across the office carpet. The invention of the cube to replace offices was a blow to office-carpet putters everywhere, but the exercise still has value if you can find the time and place.

Be certain that the carpet you putt on is short and speedy. Shag carpet is too thick and long, and linoleum, in most cases, is unrealistically fast. A good industrial-grade office carpet or Astroturf-type rug works fine.

Many retail golf shops sell electric putting cups. These devices shoot your golf ball back to you after you putt it into a slot. Electric putting cups drive the family dog crazy, but they can be fun and useful. Retail golf shops also sell non-mechanical carpet-putting targets.

But you don't have to shell out cash to carpet putt. You can lay a glass on its side and putt into the opening or lay an ashtray on the ground. You needn't even putt into something as long as you have a target. (Take a look at Chapter 15 for some putting practice techniques you can use indoors.)

Whatever you choose as your target, don't place the item against the wall, because when you miss, you want to see how far the ball rolls past the target.

Carpet putting is a great way to beat the midday blues and stay connected to the game. You can also have fun betting against your fellow office workers after crafting a putting course through the hallways of the company. Just be sure none of the holes pass the management offices!

Watch Golf on Television

What? The idiot box is good for something other than soap operas and reality shows? You don't really need another reason to spend some time as a couch potato, but watching golf on television can definitely improve your short game.

Most golfers watch golf on a Saturday afternoon sacked out on the couch after they play a morning round. The combination of fatigue, a post-round beer, the air conditioning, and the hushed, reverent tones of golf broadcasters is a recipe for dozing. Face it: Golf on TV can be an effective sleeping pill. So sit up, avoid the nap, and pay attention.

PGA and LPGA Tour players have spent thousands of hours honing their short-game skills, and you can take advantage of all their hard work through the following observations:

✔ **Examine their pre-shot routines.** Notice how they examine the break of a putt from all angles. Do they approach each shot the same way every time? Do they stand behind the ball to examine where it lies and visualize the target line? Do they settle in over the shot quietly so they can play in the subconscious?

✔ **Pay attention to their grip and stance.** Do they squeeze the club? How do they set up for different types of shots? Where are their bodies facing in relation to the ball and the target line? Should you set up that way? Do you set up that way? Chapter 2 outlines some short game certainties — fundamentals — that you should begin with, just as these players begin every shot with their grip and stance.

✔ **Check out the swings.** Pay attention to the tempo. Their swings are fluid, smooth, and rhythmic — not hurried. (In Chapter 13, we help you warm up before each round to improve your flexibility and swing fluidity.)

Notice how they finish their swings to completion — a common trait among professional golfers on almost every shot. They don't decelerate. They finish bunker shots with their hands high, and they hold their finish on putts. (Chapter 5 talks about the importance of completing each shot in terms of pitching — but the concept of following through is important on every golf shot.)

Stand up and emulate what you see with a wedge or carpet putt while you watch. Playing a round of golf after you watch on TV can also be fun. The players you view make the game look easy with their effortless, languid swings and precise shots. The nice tempo you watch may rub off on you. (Check out Chapter 16 for some ideas on which Tour professionals to watch and what to take away from them.)

Get Attached to Your Wedge

Developing a good feel for your short-game tools is one of the biggest success factors for improving your score. You develop feel through practice. But what can you do off the course to enhance feel?

You can take one of your short irons in the house after you play or practice. While you watch television, enjoy a mint julep on the porch, attend your daughter's soccer game, or just go about your daily routine, hold the club in your fingers and try to feel the club at all times. You don't have to swing the club; you just want to feel its weight.

Your wedge is a short club, so you can easily maneuver it. Carrying a driver into a phone booth or taxi or onto the Staten Island Ferry may be awkward. And a 3-iron in a public restroom stall could create an incident, so if you plan to become attached to a golf club, your wedge is the best choice for a new appendage.

Keep the club in your non-dominant hand as much as possible. You want that hand always to be the leader. You need to develop a good sense of feel in your leading hand.

What particularly can you do with the wedge that you carry with you so often?

- ✔ Feel the club swing through your fingers.

- ✔ Feel the grip and how it lays in your hand.

- ✔ Sense the weight of the clubhead and how it reacts to the slightest swinging.

- ✔ Practice full swings when you have the space and overhead to do so safely.

- ✔ Grip the club at the top of the handle between two fingers and see how it acts like a pendulum with only the slightest prompting.

- ✔ Practice your grip and observe how your fingers lay against the handle and each other. Be aware of where the clubface is.

Get to know your golf club. It becomes an appendage or a fashion accessory as people get used to seeing you with it.

Chip into the Drapes

Stuck in a hotel room or your living room on a rainy day? Do what Lee Trevino reportedly used to do: Hit little chip shots into the drapes.

Thin lace curtains cause security to knock at your door or make your spouse furious, but most hotels have heavy drapes designed to keep the sunlight out — and your pitch shots in. You're on your own when it comes to the missus. You needn't bang the ball, anyway. You just want to develop muscle memory and get a little "bat on the ball." It never hurts to develop continuing awareness of the clubface and how the ball reacts to it.

Bulk Up

You don't have to resemble a certain California governor, but strengthening exercises can help your short game and your golf game in general. Here are some exercises to get you going:

- ✔ Hold your wedge by the handle, extended in front of you in one hand, and slowly lift the clubhead up and down 90 degrees, using only your wrist. (Check out Chapter 15 for a weighted variation of this drill.)

- ✔ Hold the club the same as in the first exercise and lift it repeatedly, this time bending from the elbow.

✔ Put two golf balls next to each other in the palm and fingers of one hand and roll them so that they switch places.

✔ Grab a sheet of newspaper at the end with one hand and crumble it up into a ball. Sounds easy, huh? Try it over and over while you watch golf on television. Your wrist and forearm start to tire and you start to improve your strength (and you will no longer be a golf girly man).

✔ Use a club to stretch out your muscles and limber up (check out Michael K. getting his stretch on in Chapters 13 and 15).

Visualize Good Shots

Psychologists say that the subconscious mind can't distinguish between an actual event and an imagined one. If that's the case, you can get in plenty of swing reps while you sit seat-belted on a flight and stuck on the tarmac for a few hours before the captain tells you that the plane can't make the trip but the airline has rescheduled the flight for three hours and one missed connection later . . . but we digress.

You may have heard of the story of an American prisoner in Vietnam who passed the horrible days by playing rounds of golf at his favorite club, taking the time to visualize each shot, each swing, in real time. And you may remember the television commercial that had Annika Sorenstam lying on a recliner with her eyes closed, listening to a tape recorder that, over and over, played the sound of a putt falling into the hole. In the golf film *Caddyshack,* Ty Webb urges Danny Noonan, who is about to hit a shot with a blindfold on, to visualize success and "be the ball."

 In your spare moments, play all the shots on your favorite course virtually in your mind and shoot your best score ever. After you get a good visual and gain some confidence, go and do it in real time! It also helps to visualize a good shot right before you strike the ball in order to train your mind to make the swing you need to produce the shot.

Review Your Scorecard

If you didn't tear up the scorecard from your last round in disgust or leave it stuck to the golf cart steering wheel, open it up at home or at your office and review your round. Don't just check out the scores; review the specific shots you remember that caused the scores. Ask yourself the following questions:

✔ How many putts did you hit on each hole? How many two-putt greens? How many three-putt greens?

✔ How many of your strokes came from short-game shots around the green?

✔ How many bunkers were you in, and how well did you manage to escape from them?

Where can you eliminate some of the strokes you took? What part of your game needs the most practice? Your scorecard has all the answers . . . whether you like them or not!

Get into the habit of marking the number of putts you hit on your scorecard to make this process easier. You can also come up with a marking system to indicate bunker shots or chip shots to keep tabs on your short game for a more detailed analysis of where your game needs practice.

Clean Up Your Act

Cleaning your golf clubs and golf shoes does more than make you look tidy and fashionable. Oh, you can still adhere to the "look good, play good" theory (and if you're playing badly, you should at least look good!), but clean clubs and shoes actually help your performance.

Check out this list for helpful cleaning tips:

✔ Use a brush to scrub out the mud and dirt from between the grooves of your wedges and other irons. The grooves are put into the club to help control the spin of the ball on impact, and if the grooves are filled with dirt, the desired result gets muddied. Warm soapy water and a towel do the trick, although some golf shops sell special brushes and polish.

✔ Don't forget to wash your grips. You should also consider changing them twice a season, depending on frequency of use. Slippery grips can easily defeat a good golf swing.

✔ As for your shoes, clean their bottoms as well as their tops. Remove mud and grass clinging to the spikes, and replace the spikes regularly for better traction and stability.

Ben Hogan studied the bottoms of his shoes to see which spikes wore down more than the others, and then he adjusted his balance accordingly. This task is more difficult with the new soft rubber spikes, but the least you can do is keep them clean and sharp.

Play Other Sports and Games

Being active in non-golf games helps your overall hand-eye coordination and precision. Some are more useful than others, but almost any activity can have a positive impact on the skill and endurance you need for golf. Check out the following activities:

- ✔ **Other major sports:** Basketball, Soccer, Softball, and Tennis.
- ✔ **Recreational sports:** Billiards, Bocce Ball, Bowling, Curling, Darts, Frisbee/Disc Golf, Horseshoes, Shooting, and Shuffleboard.
- ✔ **Leisure activities:** Dancing, video games, and walking.

These activities provide excellent hand-eye coordination practice, and some of them even have movements similar to the golf swing. Besides, all golf all the time can burn you out. Even Tiger Woods has other hobbies (such as his *own* video game)!

Read This Book When Necessary

Re-reading parts of *Golf's Short Game For Dummies* helps remind you of the important points and key phrases that escape you during the heat of battle on the golf course. Making notes and taking them to the practice range isn't such a nerdy thing to do . . . although you can keep them secretly to yourself if you're embarrassed to show your crib notes. If your buddies give you a hard time about the notes, give them a hard time with your improved short game. You may even see them show up with notes after they buy your lunch enough times.

The best way to improve your short game is to practice and play, but doing your homework better prepares you for your 18-hole tests and makes your practice sessions more meaningful.

Chapter 19

Ten of the Greatest Short Shots Ever

In This Chapter

▶ Canning clutch shots for majors

▶ Holing out or a million bucks

▶ Heart-stopping Ryder Cup clinchers

▶ Defining a career with the flatstick

Golf fans have witnessed magical and creative short-game play by some of the world's greatest players under high-pressure situations. Sure, a big drive is impressive, but not as impressive as seeing the ball stick close to the flagstick or dive into the hole. We hope you enjoy the following fine examples of great short shots and take inspiration from them!

Tway at the PGA

The 1986 PGA Championship at Inverness Club came down to the short games of the final two challengers.

In one corner, Bob Tway of Oklahoma, who'd been a full-fledged PGA Tour member for only two seasons but had already won four times that year.

And in the other corner, Australian Greg Norman, also known as "the Shark," the flashy golf "superhero" of the time. He had five tournament wins at the time — one of them the British Open Championship just a month earlier.

It looked to be Norman's championship to lose after he opened with rounds of 65 and 68. Tway was nine strokes behind the Shark at the midway point, managing pedestrian rounds of 72 and 70 — but he made the cut.

On Saturday, Tway set a PGA Championship third-round record by shooting 64 on the Donald Ross-designed course. Norman continued to play brilliantly, shooting 69, and he still led Tway by four shots at the beginning of Sunday's fourth and final round.

By the time Norman and Tway reached the famed, par-4 final hole at Inverness, they were knotted. Strangely, because the 18th is a short hole, both Norman and Tway missed the small, pushed up green with their second shots. Norman had a clear chip to the hole. Tway, however, found himself looking up from under his visor at the bottom of a high-lipped, deep sand bunker 22 feet from the hole on the short side of the pin. Tway was ranked 96th on the Tour "sand-save" list and seemed to be half swallowed in this devious trap.

With the eyes of the world watching, Tway expertly swiped the ball from the cushion of sand and, having cleared the lip, landed the ball on the green and rolled it right into the hole for birdie! Tway himself seemed startled, and he lifted his arms into a V of victory.

When Norman, understandably rattled by this most unlikely occurrence, failed to hole his chip shot, Tway won his first and only major championship to this day.

Turn to Chapter 6 to find out how you can deliver like Tway did when faced with the same sand situation.

Mize at the Masters

What? A local boy, who was once a scoring volunteer at Augusta National Golf Club, had a chance to win the 1987 Masters? It was novel enough that 28-year-old Larry Mize birdied the last hole to scramble his way into a sudden death playoff, but he now had to outplay two of the world's finest and most intimidating players — the flamboyant Spaniard Seve Ballesteros and Australian Great Greg Norman. Surely Mize, who had only one minor Tour win under his belt, was lagging superfluous on this stage? Surely his shirt that afternoon, colored with varying shades of purple, would be a pitiful clash with the winner's traditional green jacket?

Minutes later, the sight of a lonely Ballesteros, with his head lowered, walking back up the hill along the left side of the abandoned 10th hole toward the clubhouse was telling. Ballesteros, himself a short-game wizard, had been eliminated on the first playoff hole. Mize now had to grab the shark by the tail.

It seemed like Norman was about to sink his teeth into a coveted green jacket when Mize sliced his second shot, a 5-iron approach, to the right of the 11th green — safely away from the water, but far from the hole, especially considering Norman had hit the green in two shots. Norman could two-putt for par and Mize needed to get up and down from the side of a slippery green to make par.

In the late-afternoon sunlight, with part of the green shaded, Mize used a sand wedge to strike the ball from a tight lie on the turf. The ball flew softly from the clubface, and the look on Mize's face was hopeful as he watched it bounce near the crest of the green, kick forward, and begin to roll toward the hole. Were it not such a nice evening, lightning would have literally struck. Instead, it was a figurative dagger that struck Norman in the heart at the electric moment when Mize's ball tracked toward the cup and fell into the hole.

Mize was incredulous, his arms lifted above his head, basking in one of the greatest shots in the history of the Masters. Norman was unable to hole his long putt, and Mize claimed his first and only major title. Norman called it the toughest loss he'd ever endured, and it came eight months after Bob Tway broke his heart at the PGA with a winning bunker shot (see the previous section). "Larry's shot was tougher than Bob's," said Norman at the post-tournament press conference.

Before Mize, no player had ever pitched or chipped in to win the Masters.

Turn to Chapter 5 to find out how to play the pitch like Mize did — whether you ever get the chance to win the Masters or not!

Hail Hale!

Hale Irwin had already won two U.S. Open titles (his first at Winged Foot Country Club in 1974), but 11 years had passed since he won it at Inverness Club in 1979. He had another chance as the final round approached at Medinah Country Club outside Chicago in 1990. This time Irwin, who was 45 years old, gamely worked his way up the leader board during the final round. He opened the championship with nice rounds of 69 and 70, but a third round 74 spoiled the party, and he admitted later that he was merely hoping to play well enough the final day to finish high enough to qualify for the next year's U.S. Open.

Irwin made solid putt after solid putt in that final round, and the birdies added up as he was suddenly in reach of Mike Donald, who opened the tournament with rounds of 67, 70, and 72.

Nobody can confidently say that they expected Irwin's putt to roll in, including Irwin himself, but he started a 45-foot birdie putt rolling on the final hole, and it tracked all the way across the green and dove into the cup! Irwin, known as one of the least expressive players on the PGA Tour, broke out of his time-honored robotic shell and, in full sprint, ran around Medinah's 18th green with his putter in one hand while high-fiving the spectators with his other. Irwin played college football at the University of Colorado, and he looked more like a football player than a golfer at that moment. If he'd picked the ball from the hole, he may have spiked it!

Irwin's "putt heard round the world" forced a tie when Donald closed with a 71. The U.S. Open employs an 18-hole playoff held on Monday. The next day, when Irwin and Donald were still tied after another 18 holes, Irwin sunk a 15-foot birdie putt to finish off Donald on the first sudden death hole.

The unlikely victory, which was undoubtedly aided by luck, made Irwin the oldest man ever to win the U.S. Open. His spontaneous, unbridled joy provoked by sinking that putt forever changed how golf fans perceive Irwin.

Turn to Chapter 9 for the scoop on how to lag long putts near, and maybe into, the hole! If you succeed, you can run around the green giving your own high-fives.

Rocca Rocks the British Open

Playing a chip shot to the final green, Constantino Rocca blew a chance to win the 124th British Open in 1995 at the Old Course at St. Andrews in Scotland (see Chapter 20). Seconds later, Rocca used his normal short-game magic to give himself a chance to win it.

Rocca needed a birdie on the par-4 home hole to tie John Daly and force a playoff. He drove his tee ball close to the green and was left with a good chance to chip the ball close to the hole and putt for birdie. But in one of the most stunning foozles in the history of golf's oldest championship, Rocca topped the ball just yards in front of him into the collection area in front of the green known as the "Valley of Sin." The mis-hit was a classic example of looking up, likely caused by nervousness or loss of focus under pressure.

But what Rocca pulled off next was the exact opposite failing in the clutch. The spectators and the worldwide television audience were heartbroken and embarrassed for Rocca and presumed he was now playing for second place. But Rocca used a putter from off the front of the green and rolled the ball out of the Valley of Sin, across the green, and into the hole for what was, essentially, a game-tying, 65-foot birdie putt! After watching the ball go in, Rocca fell to the ground and pounded the turf with his fists while weeping for joy. He later admitted he only wanted to two-putt.

Can you imagine that range of emotion — from ultimate failure to astonishing redemption in the span of two swings of a club — happening at the birthplace of golf?

A four-hole playoff ensued between Rocca and Daly, and the tables turned yet again. Rocca three-putted the first playoff hole, and Daly rolled in a 40-foot birdie putt on the second hole. When Rocca hit a shot into the penal "Road Hole Bunker" on the third playoff hole, all hope was basically lost. But most people who remember the tournament recall Rocca's dramatics on the final hole of regulation, when never was the nerve-wracking pathos and importance of the short game more evidently displayed.

To become as versatile as Rocca needed to be, turn to Chapter 4 for your chipping needs, Chapter 9 to put some strategy into your putting game, and Chapter 10 to get some tips on putting from off the green and avoiding the foozle Rocca made.

The Million-Dollar Ace

Imagine making one swing of your pitching wedge and winning $1 million on the spot. That's exactly what happened to Lee Trevino, on national television, at the 2002 Million-Dollar Par-Three-Shootout at Treetops Resort.

Trevino was 61-years-old when he stepped up to the 6th tee on the Threetops Course at Treetops Resort in Gaylord, Michigan. Threetops is a 9-hole collection of dramatic par-3s. (See Chapter 20 for more great short-game courses.)

The big money contest, which offered a million dollars to any player who could make a hole-in-one, was shown on ESPN and pitted Trevino, Paul Azinger, Raymond Floyd, and Phil Mickelson against each other.

The 6th hole, known as "High Five," is 138 yards with a 90-foot vertical drop that makes club selection tricky. Trevino selected his pitching wedge, and he thought he hit it too stiff when the ball left the clubface. The ball flew directly over the flag and landed on the fringe with backspin that pulled it 20 feet back — and right into the hole!

The hole-in-one was Trevino's fifth ace in competition, but it was certainly his richest! He gave half of the $1 million to his favorite charity: St. Jude's Children's Hospital in Memphis.

Amazingly, one year earlier, Hale Irwin competed in the Million-Dollar Shootout and decided to play a few practice holes. His ball went in for an ace on the 9th hole at Threetops, but because he hit the shot in a practice round, he didn't collect a cool million! (Are you noticing how the same players are showing up throughout this chapter? Not a coincidence. A good short game always wins out.)

Turn to Chapter 3 to consider club selection options.

Watson Plunders Pebble

Arnold Palmer took Ben Hogan's crown as the King of the Golf World. Palmer eventually seceded to Jack Nicklaus. And when Tom Watson came on the scene in the late 1970s, critics and fans alike expected him to force Nicklaus to abdicate. But Nicklaus and Watson fought some heart-thumping duels, including the 1982 U.S. Open at Pebble Beach Golf Links in Monterey, California.

Watson attended college at nearby Stanford University and had played golf at Pebble Beach many times, but Nicklaus had his own history at Pebble — the Golden Bear won the U.S. Open there 10 years earlier. Watson had major credentials by this time as well, having won two Masters Tournaments and five British Open Championships — but never the U.S. Open. A turf war ensued.

Watson, Nicklaus, and Bill Rogers were tied for the lead at the beginning of the final round, but Rogers derailed and Nicklaus and Watson remained tied at the turn — Nicklaus having tempered three bogeys with five straight birdies.

Watson used his flatstick to grab a two-stroke lead by making birdie putts of 20 feet on the 10th and 11th holes, but, true to form, Nicklaus wasn't going down easily. He birdied the 15th hole and made par the rest of the way, ending his round tied with Watson.

Nicklaus was on the 18th green while Watson played the par-3 17th, where his 2-iron shot drifted left and fell into the heaviest of green-side rough. Watson didn't have much room to operate — the grass was thick and tangled, and although the hole was close to the grass, the ocean-side green sloped away from Watson. Sound like a challenge?

Watson's caddie, the late Bruce Edwards, implored his boss to "get it close." Watson, with bravado, told him that he wanted to sink the shot.

Using a sand wedge, Watson managed not only to extricate the ball from its fescue prison, but also to hit it in such a way that the ball popped up, landed softly, and rolled on-line right into the hole! Watson made his birdie, and he sunk a 22-foot birdie putt on the last hole for good measure to win his first and only U.S. Open.

What an example of grace and courage under pressure! You can display such bravado if you put in practice time. Turn to Chapter 13 for effective practice advice and scheduling tips.

Leonard Lets Loose

For the modern age of golf, the Ryder Cup is the game's most high-pressure event. Samuel Ryder created the matches in the 1927 as a goodwill exhibition to showcase the best American golfers against the best of Great Britain. So dominant were the Americans over the early years, however, that the opposing team was widened to include Ireland and then widened even further to include players from throughout Europe. As the matches became more competitive, the "goodwill" aspect was clouded over with gamesmanship, and fiery matches started to draw fanfare every two years. The 1991 contest, known as "The War at the Shore," won by the Americans at Kiawah Island's Ocean Course (see Chapter 20), goes down as one of the fiercest battles.

The 1990s were a contentious decade for Ryder Cup matches. The Europeans, captained by Seve Ballesteros, retained the cup in the 1997 edition in Spain by a single point, so when the matches were held near Boston at The Country Club in 1999, the Americans, captained by Ben Crenshaw, were eager to retake the Cup. The original dominators hadn't held the cup since they lost it at Oak Hills in 1995, also by a point.

The contest didn't go well for the Yanks initially. The Americans were down 10 points to 6 after the first two days of *four-ball* (best score between two partners) and *foursomes* (alternate shot) matches, and captain Ben Crenshaw, along with former President George H.W. Bush, gave the team an emotional pep talk the night before the final day's singles matches.

The roused Americans stormed to a singles record of 8-3-1 to win back the cup. The U.S. assured victory on the 17th green during a match between American Justin Leonard and Spain's Jose Maria Olazabal. Leonard, one of the shortest drivers of the ball on the PGA Tour, relies on his short game for success. He holed a 45-foot putt to ensure at least a half-point gain against his opponent — enough for an overall total that would clinch the cup. The look on Leonard's face as he watched the putt was priceless. As the ball rolled closer and closer to the hole, breaking properly and tracking in, Leonard's expression changed from stoic to curious to hopeful to surprised to ecstatic. If that putt hadn't fallen, it surely would've rolled about eight feet past the hole.

The moment has gone down in history not only for the pivotal cross-country putt Leonard holed to win, but also for the unbridled celebration that took place when the putt fell. The American players, their wives, and some spectators — along with television crews — spilled onto the green and danced with glee, stepping into the putting line of Olazabal, who, it was forgotten, still had a long putt to halve the hole.

Turn to Chapter 7 for a review of the putting fundamentals that can give you a chance to hole the occasional game-winner!

Lanny Lands the Cup

When Virginia-native Lanny Wadkins played on the 1983 Ryder Cup team, the competition hadn't yet become the media event and spectacle that it is today. America hadn't lost the competition since 1957 at Lindrick in Yorkshire and only twice in history before that! (The Great Britain and Ireland team managed a half in 1969, thanks in large part to the sportsmanship of Jack Nicklaus, who conceded a putt to Tony Jacklin. The U.S. retained the cup with a tie.)

The 1983 Ryder Cup competition, held at PGA National Resort in Palm Beach Gardens, Florida, was a surprise to the Americans and a foreshadowing of the renewed competition to come. The European team played hard and gave the Americans a real scare. So close was the competition that the result hinged on the final day singles match between Wadkins and Spain's Jose Maria Canizares.

Wadkins, with eerie lightning punctuating the scene, nearly holed a wedge shot over water to beat Canizares and clinch a tie for the cup. Some players can reach the hole, a soft par-5, in two shots, but Wadkins was left to hit his third shot with a pitching wedge to a green guarded by water along the right side. The circumstances turned what could be considered an easy shot for a PGA Tour player into a cheek-squeezer!

Wadkins delivered. The shot stopped 18 inches from the hole. U.S. captain Jack Nicklaus was so relieved by the shot that he kissed the divot left by the ball!

The United States retained the Cup by one point — their slimmest outright win ever at the time — thanks to the wedge of Wadkins.

One Small Shot for Mankind

School kids, space fans, and history buffs know that Alan Shepard was the first American in space. Golfers know that Shepard was also the first man to play golf in space — on the moon!

Shepard, at 47 years old, talked his way into the command of the Apollo 14 moon mission that launched on January 31, 1971.

Shepard and astronaut Ed Mitchell spent 33-and-a-half hours trudging around on the moon, shifting in deep lunar dust and conducting research. When they finished their work, Shepard surprised everyone by pulling out two golf balls and a folded, collapsible golf club he specially made for the occasion and stashed in his suit.

The club had the loft of a 6-iron. Because of the bulkiness of his space suit, Shepard had to take one-handed swipes at the balls, which he dropped in the lunar dust.

The half-swing pitch shots he hit were essentially bunker shots, except, due to low gravity, they flew as far as 200 yards. Shepard later said he'd hoped low gravity would have allowed him to hit the ball 1,500 yards!

Payne's Putts at Pinehurst

Payne Stewart's 1999 U.S. Open victory, only months before his tragic death in an airplane accident, will always be remembered for the 15-foot winning par putt he sank on the last hole and his exuberant display of raw emotion when the putt fell. In fact, Pinehurst

Resort in North Carolina erected a life-sized statue of Stewart, with his fist thrust into the drizzly air as he stands on one leg, behind the 18th green of its #2 course, where his victory took place. (See Chapter 20 for more great short-game courses.)

It may be hard to believe, but that putt made Stewart the first person in the then 99 years of the Championship to win with a substantial putt on the final hole of regulation play.

Stewart was 42 years old at the time, and the putt gave him a one-stroke victory over Phil Mickelson, who wore a pager because his wife Amy, back home in Arizona, was due to deliver their first child at any time (how's that for a Hollywood script?). As Mickelson offered congratulations, Stewart grabbed him by the face and comforted him with the assurance, "There's nothing like being a father."

Most remember Stewart's dramatic, 15-foot putt on the final hole and the emotional events that resulted, but he also canned a 25-footer for par on the 16th hole that put him in position to win with his par on the 18th.

Chapter 20

Ten Great Short Game Golf Courses

• •

In This Chapter

▶ Infamous putting challenges

▶ Pot-bunkered paradise (or purgatory)

▶ Par-3 and picturesque

• •

*A*dvances in modern technology, when applied to golf equipment, are making some course designs too short. Because golf balls fly farther and big drivers loaded with spring-like faces launch balls like never before, many classic golf courses have hired designers to renovate the landscape. When land or space is available, designers are building new tees to make the holes longer.

However, equipment promising all the distance in the world doesn't help the short game, which remains the most elegant and important aspect of golf.

The golf courses we highlight in this chapter are exciting not because of their length, which they may or may not have, but for the short-game aspects of their intriguing designs. Challenges abound at these 10 great short game golf courses.

Many of these courses host televised tournaments, including R&A, PGA, LPGA, and Champions Tour events. If you want to pick up some short-game strategy or just catch some exciting action, tune in when you see these courses on the dial (or, better yet, attend the tournament). And if you have the time and resources, get out there and test your short game on these courses!

The Old Course at St. Andrews: Fife, Scotland

The birthplace of golf, where the game was invented over 500 years ago, is a cherished antique that golfers all over the globe make a pilgrimage to. Every six years or so (including in 2005), the Old Course hosts the British Open Championship — the oldest golf championship on record. The Old Course is a *links course,* which technically means that it rests on sandy soil that links the town to the sea. Its seaside location means that the wind blows more often than not. Crafty Scots realized that wind is bad for a golf ball flying through the air, so they started perfecting low-running pitches and chips.

The Old Course, which was designed more by nature than man, offers plenty of opportunity to be imaginative with pitch and run shots. The short grass and open fronts to greens even encourage you to use a putter from as far as 20 paces off the green. The Old Course is full of aptly named areas, with the "Valley of Sin" in front of the 18th green perhaps the most famous.

Players must beware of the menacing, deep, sod-faced bunkers that suck in wayward shots. Every bunker on the golf course is named with monikers such as the "Principal's Nose" and the "Hell Bunker." So severe are these bunkers, which were originally dug by sheep looking for escape from the wind, that players sometimes resign themselves to playing shots out sideways rather than toward the hole just to escape their dark depths and have a fighting chance at a respectable score.

The Old Course also has giant double greens that serve two holes at once, so players often face cross-country putts.

Pinehurst #2: Pinehurst, North Carolina

Donald Ross designed Pinehurst #2, which is part of the famed, eight-course Pinehurst Resort. Ross, a Scotsman, was prolific in his effort to build Scottish-style golf courses in the United States in the early 1900s.

The Pinehurst Resort, which opened in 1895 amid the timberland of the North Carolina sand hills, retains much of its old-fashioned charm — especially its old-fashioned design. #2 looms large because of its undulating, crowned greens and strategically placed bunkers. Putts misdirected with too much bravado can roll right off the green and into a bunker.

Pinehurst #2, considered to be the ultimate Ross masterpiece, hosted the 1999 U.S. Open and was named host course for the national open in 2005.

Stadium Course, TPC at Sawgrass: Ponte Vedra Beach, Florida

The Tournament Players Club at Sawgrass is the home of The Players Championship — each year the richest tournament on the PGA Tour. And boy do the players earn their money that week! So frustrated were PGA Tour players after the first Players Championship that the winner, Jerry Pate, threw then PGA Tour commissioner Deane Beman into the pond next to the 18th green during the trophy presentation.

Golf course architect Pete Dye took Florida swampland between Jacksonville and Saint Augustine and created 18 snarling holes that seem to rise from the wetlands just enough to allow the passage of play. Wooden bulkheads hold back the swamp on most holes.

The 132-yard, par-3 17th hole is one of the most famous in golf, because its green literally rests on an island — a small patch of land in the middle of an alligator-filled pond that claims thousands of mis-hit golf balls each year.

Dye also punctuated his TPC course with waste bunkers that line one side or another on most every hole. The greens are undulated and speedy, and most of them are perched on severe slopes with thatched rough, meaning players who miss the green often have awkward stances and bad lies. The course also has quirky moguls and chocolate drop mounds to play from, beside and behind the greens, that Dye inserted to make the flat land more punishing. You can't find anything subtle about the TPC at Sawgrass Stadium Course — you have to play do-or-die target golf.

Ballybunion Old Course: County Kerry, Ireland

In early 1897, an article in the Irish Times dismissed Ballybunion's Old Course as "a rabbit warren below the village, where a golfer requires limitless patience and an inexhaustible supply of golf balls." And only 12 holes existed at the time!

Now Ballybunion Golf Club offers 18 of the most memorable holes you may ever play. With fairways less than 30 yards wide and tiny greens perched in towering sea-smashed sand dunes, Ballybunion is a roller coaster.

Tom Watson, himself no short-game slouch, did some redesign work at Ballybunion and once served as honorary captain. "I love to play Ballybunion. I think it is the greatest golf course that God ever put on this earth. And make no mistake, God put it there."

The wild and wooly golf links run alongside the Atlantic Ocean between castle ruins and a trailer park. The Celtic-cross headstones of a graveyard loom to the right of the first fairway. From there, Ballybunion begins its daring dance with craggy clifftops that slide into the ocean and sends golfers through passages in wind-blown dunes that block the sun. Tangled rough, grass bunkers, and gaping sod-faced bunkers seem to creep closer to the green as you look over your shot.

If you get a chance to play this bracing, natural masterpiece, follow the poetic and sometimes amusing advice of the Irish caddies when reading the tricky greens, which have quizzical breaks and head-scratching invisible undulations. Reaching a green at Ballybunion is only the beginning of playing the hole! Ballybunion requires precision to reach the green . . . and precision after you reach the green. The course is simply a beautiful puzzle.

Threetops at Treetops Resort: Gaylord, Michigan

Threetops is a 9-hole collection of par-3s at Treetops Resort in Northern Michigan. Although the resort features four regulation golf courses, Threetops enjoys the most popularity because of its distinction as the most picturesque and enjoyable par-3 course in the world.

The holes range from 100 to 180 yards, but they have elevation changes of as much as 170 feet from tee to green. Deciding on a club to use is tricky with that kind of elevation change, but you can play most holes with a mid or short iron. Plenty of bunkers guard the steeply undulated greens.

Threetops, designed by teaching guru and architect Rick Smith, is cut through lush forest above the Pigeon River Valley. Each year the course plays host to the "Million-Dollar-Par-Three Shootout," a televised skins game tournament that offers a cool million for an ace. Lee Trevino cashed in once (see Chapter 19). Other players who have competed are major championship winners Fred Couples, Jack Nicklaus, Raymond Floyd, Hale Irwin, Phil Mickelson, Fuzzy Zoeller, and Lee Janzen.

Strategic Fox, Fox Hills Golf Club: Plymouth, Michigan

The Strategic Fox Golf Course opened in 2001 as part of the Fox Hills golf complex just west of Detroit. When noted architect Ray Hearn designed the course, he sought to create a short game course that would appeal to beginners and skilled players looking to hone their short games.

The 18-hole course begins with a user-friendly 105-yard opening hole and then increases in intensity and challenge along the way. Strategic Fox plays to a yardage of 2,554 yards, and its longest hole is its last — the 195-yard 18th.

Hearn designed the holes so that players can choose between pitch and run shots and high lob-wedge pitches. Players have to carry plenty of bunkers and water hazards. Some of the greens have as much as three feet of break, and the holes can be visually deceptive. The greens have false fronts and close-cut collections areas, as well as grass bunkers.

Strategic Fox also offers an extensive practice facility designed with a short-game emphasis — for before or after the round!

Indian Creek Country Club: Miami Beach, Florida

Built in 1927 by golf course architect William Flynn, this classical timepiece of a golf course sits on a private island in Biscayne Bay between Miami Beach and Miami proper. Residents of the exclusive island include Julio Iglesias and Don Shula. Former Masters Champion and short game expert Raymond Floyd used to live on the island, and he calls Indian Creek one of William Flynn's finest works.

Flynn also redesigned the famed Merion Golf Club in Pennsylvania and designed Cherry Hills in Denver, the Cascades course at The Homestead Resort in Hot Springs, Virginia, and Shinnecock Hills in Southampton, to name a few gems.

At Indian Creek, Flynn spiced up the flat tropical terrain with 124 large, sculpted sand bunkers that flash up the sides of the raised greens. Indian Creek's greens are built so that the ball will roll off the edges into bunkers or down a steep slope. Some of the bunkers appear to be in front of the green but actually cozy up along the entire side of the green. The holes are cut to penalize aggressive shots.

On top of that, South Florida's Bermuda grass has a pronounced grain to it. When the grain runs away from you, the ball rolls faster. When the grain leans toward you, the greenside grass can catch and stop your ball.

Indian Creek CC members and guests develop brilliant shot-making skills and short-game strategy by working their way around this waterside beauty.

The Ocean Course at Kiawah Island Golf Resort: Charleston, South Carolina

The Ocean Course has been much talked about since the day it was built to host the 1991 Ryder Cup Matches, which are known as the "War by the Shore." Kiawah also hosted the 1997 World Cup and a World Golf Championship in 2003. The film *The Legend of Bagger Vance* was shot on the Ocean Course.

Pete Dye designed the course along nearly three miles of pristine Atlantic property in the Carolina low country. Americans won that 1991 Ryder Cup despite Dye building the golf course to emulate the links-style courses the United Kingdom is known for. That means Kiawah's Ocean Course throws windy conditions at you, but it also allows you to negotiate the terrain with a variety of short-game options and necessities. The greens are undulating and well guarded. Deep pot bunkers line the course and provide visually intimidating approach shots. The bunkers, rough, and scrub that lurk around the greens inflict severe punishment on players who miss the green.

All 18 holes offer views of the ocean, and the course plays mean and tough to a length of nearly 7,300 yards.

Augusta National Golf Club: Augusta, Georgia

Although the highly private nature of Augusta National (and its short season — the club opens only from October to May) makes it unlikely that you'll ever play there, the world gets a peek inside the gates of the club each year during the Masters. Whether you're lucky enough to score a ticket or you watch the highest-rated tournament on television, you can see that the course Alister MacKenzie and Robert Tyre Jones Jr. designed in the late 1920s is a short-game challenge.

Designers have recently lengthened Augusta National and added a thin cut of light rough, but they shouldn't worry too much about technology ruining this gem: The speedy and undulating greens have undone some of the world's greatest players, including Greg Norman and Scott Hoch. The greens weren't designed to be as fast and severe as they are now, but modern agronomy advancements, plus the change from Bermuda grass to slippery, fast-running Bent grass on the greens, have prompted some players to dub the Masters Tournament "the Augusta National Putting Contest."

Perhaps the most delicate and terrifying shot on the golf course is in the heart of what is known as "Amen Corner." The 155-yard par-3 12th hole, the shortest hole on the course, is known as the "Golden Bell." The shallow, sloped green lies in what looks like a giant flowerbed behind Rae's Creek. Shots hit into bunkers behind the green must be blasted out with the touch of a surgeon to avoid running the shot over the front of the green, down the hill, and into the creek.

What you can't see on TV is how hilly Augusta National really is and just how sloped its greens are. The 9th green, for instance, slopes so severely from back to front that players must hit their approach shots beyond the hole to avoid having the ball run off the front of the green and back down into the fairway.

Club de Golf Valderrama: San Roque, Cadiz, Spain

Designed by the late Robert Trent Jones, Valderrama is known as the "Augusta National" of Spain because of its fast greens, lovely setting, and brilliant conditioning. The 6,356-meter (6,951-yard) golf course has hosted Ryder Cup Matches, World Golf Championships, and the Volvo Masters Tournament. The course attracts such events because it's rich in shot values.

Valderrama's 17th hole, a par-5 named "Los Gabiones," gives even the professional players fits. In 1999, Tiger Woods hit a shot into the slippery, tilted green that spun from the back of the green beyond the hole all the way back off the front and into the water. The club has since changed the hole and lowered some of the mounds that one of the players referred to as "dead elephants." Cork trees planted throughout the course complicate matters. You must carefully position the ball to the openings in front of the greens to have favorable short-game situations.

Index

• *Numerics* •

1-iron, skill needed for, 35
2-iron, skill needed for, 35
3-iron, loft of, 34
3-wood
  chipping with, 150–152
  loft, 34
4-iron
  for chip shot, 61
  loft, 34
5-iron, loft of, 34
5-wood, loft of, 34
6-iron, loft of, 34
7-iron
  for backhand swing, 159
  for chip shot, 36, 55, 56, 57
  loft, 34
  opposite-handed, 161
  for pitch and run shot, 130
  for Runyan shot, 63, 65
8-iron
  for chip shot, 36, 55, 56
  loft, 34
  for pitch shot, 72
9-iron
  for knock-down shot, 128
  loft, 34
  for pitch shot, 36, 69, 72, 74

• *A* •

aiming
  borrow and, 230
  bunker shot, 94–95
  chip shot, 57–58
  mistakes in, 18
  pitch and run shot, 129
  putts, 115–116, 230
alignment, as cause of yips, 145, 147
Anderson, Sparky (baseball
    manager), 48
ankles, stretching, 182

anxiety
  as cause of yips, 145
  ridding, 171
approach shots
  description, 11
  precision needed for, 14
architects, golf course, 98. *See also*
    specific architects
arms, stretching upper, 182–186
The Art of Putting (Ben Crenshaw), 222
Augusta National Golf Club (course)
  description, 255–256
  Masters, 222, 240–241
  skip-shots, 162
Austin, Woody (player), 153

• *B* •

back
  strain, 43
  stretching, 183–187
backhand swing, 159
backspin
  cause of, 37
  flop shot, 163–164
  pitch shot, 73, 76
  with pitching wedge, 37
backswing. *See also* swing
  length and speed for bunker shot, 96
  shape for bunker shot, 96
bag, putter placement in, 49
balance, improving, 204–205
ball position
  for bunker shot, 93, 99–100
  for chip shot, 59, 60
  for flop shot, 165
  for pitch shot, 72–73, 78
  for punch shot, 128
  for Runyan shot, 63
  standardizing, 31
Ballesteros, Seve (player)
  feel of, 218–219
  Masters (1987), 240
  Ryder Cup and, 245

Ballybunion Old Course (course), 252
belly putter, 45–46
bellying the wedge, 155–156
Beman, Deane (PGA Tour
    commissioner), 251
biceps, stretching, 185–186
Bingo, Bango, Bongo (game), 197–199
blade putter, 41–42
blame, 172
borrow, 230
bounce, 37, 155
break, green
    reading, 120–122
    speed and, 142–144
breathing, 171
British Open Championship
    Gene Sarazen and, 39
    at St. Andrews, 242–243, 250
    tournaments, 171, 218, 220–221,
        242–243
bump and run shot, 129–131
bunker
    course architects and, 98
    origin of, 98
    pitching over, 76–77
    practice, 153
    size and shape, 89–90
    waste, 88
bunker board, 208
bunker shot
    aiming, 94–95
    ball position, 93, 99–100
    club choice, 92
    clubface, 92, 99, 101
    description, 11
    distance, 97
    explosion shot, 89
    followthrough, 97
    from fried egg lie, 100–101
    of Gary Player, 219
    goals and expectations, 26, 87–88
    grip, 92
    lie, 90–91
    marking on scorecard, 236
    pitch shot compared, 92–93
    practice, 191, 207–209
    putting, 152–153
    rules, 88
    sand variables, 89–91
    stance, 91, 92–94
    from steep lie, 102–103
    swing, 95–97, 100–101
    from uphill lie, 98–100

• C •

Caddyshack (film), 235
Canizares, Jose Maria (player),
    246–247
The Canyons (course), 220
carpet putting, 231–232
cart path, playing from, 154–155
Casper, Billy (player), 119
chalk line, 209–210
chip shot
    aiming, 57–58
    ball position, 59, 60
    characteristics of, 54
    choosing over a putt, 54–55
    club choice for, 55
    description, 11, 54
    into drapes, 234
    expectations, 176
    goals and expectations, 26, 56
    grip, 61, 220
    as long putt, 230
    marking on scorecard, 236
    one-handed practice, 205
    pitch shot compared, 54, 67–68
    practice, 191
    pre-round warm-up, 192
    Runyan shot, 62–66
    shoulder position, 61
    speed, 62
    stance, 59–61
    steps in hitting, 56–57
    strategy, 56
    swing, 59–62
    with 3-wood, 150–152
    trajectory, 126
    weight distribution, 59–60
chipper (club), 61
choking down
    physics of, 127–128
    for putting with driver, 154
    successful short execution, 128–129

chorus line finish, 97
"claw" grip, 115
cleaning
    putters, 49–50
    tips, 236
Club de Golf Valderrama (course), 256
clubface
    awareness, 215–216, 227–228
    for bunker shot, 92, 99, 101
    for pitch shot, 78
    in putting, 116–117
    for flop shot, 164
clubs. *See also specific types*
    average yardage of, 34–35
    deciding which to use, 39–40
    irons, 36
    loft of, 34
    maximum number allowed, 34
    opposite-handed, 161
    for pitch shot, 69
    putters, 40–50
    shot trajectory and, 25
    wedges, 36–39
collar, green, 134
conceding putts, 109
confidence
    building, 16–17, 23, 28
    in bunker play, 207, 219
    lack of, 146
    practice and, 16–17, 28, 193
    putting and, 46–47, 138
    reasonable expectations and, 28
The Country Club in Brookline, MA
        (course), 222, 245–246
courses
    Augusta National Golf Club,
        162, 222, 240–241, 255–256
    Ballybunion Old Course, 252
    The Canyons, 220
    Club de Golf Valderrama, 256
    The Country Club in Brookline, MA,
        222, 245–246
    Crooked Stick, 220
    Emerald Dunes Golf Club, 136
    Indian Creek Country Club, 254
    Inverness Club, 239–240
    Muirfield Village, 221
    New Course at St. Andrews, 132

Oakmont, 223
Ocean Course at Kiawah Island Golf
        Resort, 254–255
Old Course at St. Andrews,
        98, 154–155, 250
Pebble Beach Golf Links, 244–245
Pinehurst #2 at Pinehurst Resort,
        247–248, 250–251
Royal Birkdale, 218
Southern Dunes Golf Club, 39
Stadium Course, Tournament
        Players Club at Sawgrass, 251
Strategic Fox at Fox Hills Golf
        Club, 253
Threetops at Treetops Resort,
        243–244, 252–253
cover, putter, 49
Crenshaw, Ben (player)
    The Art of Putting, 222
    Ben Hogan and, 15
    A Feel for the Game, 222
    putting of, 222
    Ryder Cup and, 222, 245–246
    on Seve Ballesteros, 218
Crooked Stick (course), 220
curve shot, 18

• ᗭ •

Daly, John (player)
    British Open (1995), 242–243
    drives, 220
    short game of, 220–221
deceleration
    bunker shot, 97
    death by, 19, 97, 228
    punch shot, 129
    putts, 117, 119, 144
    water shot, 157
difficult shot, 22–23
DiMarco, Chris (player), 122
divot repair tool, 84
Donald, Mike (player), 242
donut weight, 215
doubt, dispelling, 176–177
dowel drill, for putting, 212–213
draw, effect of lie on, 70

driver
  frequency of use, 10, 11
  loft, 34
  putting with, 154
drives
  flop shot compared, 163
  relative importance of, 1–2, 10, 14
Dye, Pete (course architect),
    155, 251, 255

• *E* •

easy shot, 22
Edwards, Bruce (caddie), 245
Eight in a Row (game), 200–201
8-iron
  for chip shot, 36, 55, 56
  loft, 34
  for pitch shot, 72
electric putting cups, 231–232
Els, Ernie (player), 150
Emerald Dunes Golf Club
    (course), 136
exercises, strengthening, 234–235
expectations
  bunker shot, 88
  chip shot, 56, 176
  distance from pin and, 27
  flop shot, 166–167
  of Lee Trevino, 221
  pitch shot, 69–70
  putting, 109–112, 175
  realistic, 26, 229–230
  unreasonable, 17
explosion shot, 89

• *F* •

fade, 190
Faxon, Brad (player), 148
fear, accepting, 173–174
feel
  carrying wedge to develop, 233–234
  importance of, 30
  for putt, 113
  Seve Ballesteros and, 218–219

A Feel for the Game (Ben
    Crenshaw), 222
feet, position of, 204–205. *See also*
    stance
First to Make Five (game), 201–202
5-iron, loft of, 34
5-wood, loft of, 34
flagstick, pulling, 134–135
flange, 37, 155
flipping the blade, 160
flop shot
  backspin, 163–164
  ball position, 165
  choosing to hit, 164
  deciding against using, 165–167
  description, 12, 163–164
  downsides of use, 166
  fundamentals of hitting, 164–165
  lob wedge and, 38
  options instead of, 166–167
  practice, 165
  stance, 164–165
  swing, 165
Floyd, Raymond (player), 254
Flynn, William (course architect), 254
followthrough
  bunker shot, 97
  flop shot, 165
  holding finish, 223
  importance of, 229
  punch shot, 129
  putt, 120
footprints, on greens, 112
forearm, strengthening exercise, 215
Forrest, Steve (golfer), 132
four-ball, 246
4-iron
  for chip shot, 61
  loft, 34
foursomes, 246
Fox Hills Golf Club (course), 253
fried egg lie, 100–101
fringe, 134
fundamentals
  ignoring, 18–19
  preferences compared, 18–19, 21

• **G** •

games
  Eight in a Row, 200–201
  First to Make Five, 201–202
  Horse, 197
  Jingles, 197–199
  Pitching for Dollars, 195–196
  Snake, 199–200
gap wedge
  description, 38
  loft, 34, 38
gimmies, 109, 200
ginger ale, for swollen hands, 31
GIR (greens in regulation), 53
gloves, 113
goals
  bunker shot, 88
  chip shot, 56
  pitch shot, 69
  putting, 108
  short-game, 26–27
The Golf Channel, 39
Golf For Dummies (Gary McCord), 3
grand slam, 219, 224
grass
  growth effect on putts, 111–112
  length near greens, 55
  pitching from deep, 79–82
  sand compared, 97
  variation, assessment of, 24
greens
  breaks, 120–122, 142–144
  condition effect on putts, 111–112
  crowned, 133, 143
  hard, 133
  holding, 133
  missing, 24
  pitch mark, 84
  practice, 141, 147–148, 192,
      193–194
  practicing around, 191
  pulling the pin, 134–135
  speed, 143–144
greens in regulation (GIR), 53

grip
  for backhand swing, 159
  bunker shot, 92
  chip shot, 61, 220
  choking down, 127–129
  cleaning, 236
  pitch shot, 74, 79, 220
  pressure, 30
  putt, 50, 113–115
  watching Tour players, 232–233
ground, firmness of, 24
grounding your club, 88, 111

• **H** •

hamstring, stretching, 182, 183
hand-eye coordination, developing
      with other sports, 237
hands
  effect on pitch shot, 77–78
  front hand leading swing, 30
  grip pressure, 30
  position for flop shot, 165
  release of, 204
  soft, 220
  swelling, reducing, 31
Happy Gilmore (film), 174
hazard. *See also* bunker shot
  pitching over, 76–77
  playing from water hazard, 156–157
Hazard icon, 5
Hearn, Ray (course architect), 253
height of shot, 77–78
Heintz, Bob (player), 108
Hoch, Scott (player), 48, 255
Hogan, Ben (player)
  Ben Crenshaw and, 15
  chip shots, 61
  practice, 15, 107, 195
  putting, 107
  secret of, 31
  shoe spikes, 236
holding the green, 133
Horse (game), 197
hosel, 41, 215
Huston, John (player), 108

• *I* •

icons, used in book, 5
indent, pitch mark, 84
Indian Creek Country Club
    (course), 254
inside the leather (putt), 200
Inverness Club (course), 239–240
irons. *See also specific clubs*
  distance with, 35
  loft, 34
Irwin, Hale (player)
  Million-Dollar Shootout, 244
  U.S. Open (1990), 241–242

• *J* •

Jacklin, Tony (player), 221, 246
Jingles (game), 197–199
Jones, Bobby (player), 119
Jones, Jr., Robert Tyre (player/
    course designer), 48, 255

• *K* •

Kiawah Island Golf Resort (course)
  description, 254–255
  Ryder Cup (1991), 245
Kite, Tom (player), 218
knock-down shot, 127–129
Knox, Kenny (player), 110
Kuehne, Hank (player), 217

• *L* •

lag putting, 139, 141–142
landing spot, chip shot, 57–58
Langer, Bernhard (player), 115
launch angle, 36
lay of the land, 25
lead hand (non-dominant), as captain
    of the swing, 205–206, 228
left-handed shot, 157–161
The Legend of Bagger Vance (film), 254
legs
  still, 118–119
  warm-up exercise, 182, 183

Leonard, Justin (player), 222, 246
lie
  assessment of, 23
  in bunker, 90–91, 98–103
  bunker shot from downhill lie,
    98–100
  bunker shot from fried egg lie,
    100–101
  bunker shot from steep lie,
    102–103
  bunker shot from uphill lie, 98–100
  downhill, 83, 85, 98–100
  effect on pitch shot, 70
  pitching from a bare, tight lie, 78–79
  pitching from deep grass, 79–82
  pitching from uneven lie, 82–86
  side-hill, 82–83, 84
  uphill, 85–86, 98–100
lip, bunker, 90, 102
lob wedge
  description, 38
  loft, 34, 38
  for pitch shot, 79
loft
  for chip shot, 55
  description, 34–35
  effect on ball travel, 35
long putter, 43–45
LPGA Tour, 202, 222–223

• *M* •

MacKenzie, Alister (course
    designer), 255
make it or break it philosophy,
    139–141
mallet putters, 42–43
Masters
  location, 255–256
  skip-shots, 162
  tournaments, 122, 218, 240–241
McCord, Gary (*Golf For Dummies*), 3
McGee, Mike (player), 110
McGovern, Jim (player), 110
Mediate, Rocco (player), 44
Medinah Country Club, 241–242
meditation, 147

mental aspect
　blame, 172
　doubt, dispelling, 176–177
　fear, accepting, 173–174
　heat of the moment, 172–174
　ignoring results, 174
　over-analysis, 171–172
　phrase, pacing swing with, 177
　of putting, 110–111
　regrouping, 170–172
　self talk, 175–176
　tempo, regaining, 170–171
　visualization, 174–175
Mickelson, Phil (player)
　blade putter use, 41
　flop shot, 163
　Masters (2004), 122
　U.S. Open (1999), 248
Miller, Johnny (player)
　putting by, 223–224
　yips, 146
Million-Dollar-Par-Three-Shootout
　location, 253
　matches, 243–244
miniature golf, 122
mirror, use in practice, 215–216
mistakes
　avoiding common, 16–19
　curve shots, 18
　decelerating club, 19
　expectations, unreasonable, 17
　lack of preparation, 16–17
　over-thinking, 18
　playing without purpose, 16
　technique fundamentals, ignoring,
　　18–19
　too far from target line, 19
　wrong club, 17
Mitchell, Ed (astronaut), 247
Mize, Larry (player), 240–241
moguls, green, 133
moon, Shepard shot on, 247
Muirfield Village (course), 221
music
　for playing in the subconscious,
　　206–207
　tempo, 207

• *N* •

Nary, Bill (player), 110
National Golf Foundation, 10
New Course at St. Andrews, 132
Nicklaus, Jack (player)
　gloves and putting, 113
　putter devotion, 48
　Ryder Cup, 246, 247
　short game of, 224
　U.S. Open (1982), 244–245
9-iron
　for knock-down shot, 128
　loft, 34
　for pitch shot, 36, 69, 72, 74
non-dominant hand, as leader of
　　swing, 205–206
Norman, Greg (player)
　Augusta National Golf Club and, 255
　drives, 1, 2
　Masters (1987), 240–241
　PGA Championship (1986),
　　239–240
North, Andy (player), 110

• *O* •

Oakmont (course), 223
obstacles, assessment of, 23–24
Ocean Course at Kiawah Island Golf
　　Resort (course), 254–255
Olazabal, Jose Maria (player), 246
Old Course at St. Andrews (course)
　bunkers, 98
　description, 250
　Road Hole, 154–155
O'Meara, Mark (player), 146
one-handed shots, 205
1-iron, skill needed for, 35
open stance
　bellied wedge, 156
　bunker shot, 91
　chip shot, 59
　pitch and run shot, 130
　pitch shot, 72
over-analysis, 18, 145, 171–172

• P •

pacing, your swing with a phrase, 177
Pak, Se Ri (player), 202
Palmer, Arnold (player)
  on putting, 152
  Putt-Putt golf franchises, 122
par-3 course, 252–253
Pate, Jerry (player), 251
Pavin, Corey (player), 110
Pebble Beach Golf Links (course),
    244–245
penalty stroke, 156, 158, 159
PGA Championship, 220, 239–240
phrase, pacing swing with, 177
pin, pulling, 134–135
Pinehurst #2 at Pinehurst Resort
    (course)
  description, 250–251
  U.S. Open (1999), 247–248
pitch and run shot
  aiming, 129–130
  club choice, 130
  stance, 130
  swing, 130–131
pitch mark, 84
pitch shot
  ball position, 72–73, 78
  from bare, tight lie, 78–79
  bunker shot compared, 92–93
  characteristics of, 68
  chip shot compared, 54, 67–68
  club preference, 69
  from deep grass, 79–82
  description, 11, 67
  distance, 72, 74–75
  goals and expectations, 26, 69–70
  grip, 74, 79, 220
  hazards, avoiding, 68
  holding the green with, 133
  as long putt, 230
  one-handed practice, 205
  over water hazards and bunkers,
    76–77
  practice, 69, 195–196
  repairing your mark, 84
  from side-hill lie, 83, 85
  stance, 72–74
  steps in hitting, 71

  strategy, 70–71
  swing, 71–75
  trajectory, 77–78, 126
  from uneven lie, 82–86
  from uphill lie, 85–86
  weight distribution, 74
Pitching for Dollars (game), 195–196
pitching wedge
  backspin from, 37
  description, 37
  loft, 34, 37, 74
  for pitch shot, 69, 72, 74, 79
Player, Gary (player)
  bunker shots of, 219
  putter devotion, 48
players. *See also specific players*
  learning from stars, 217–224
  watching on television, 232–233
Players Championship, 251
positive self talk, 175–176
pot bunkers, 90, 98
practice
  bunker shot, 207–209
  chalk line exercise, 209–210
  clubface awareness, 40
  dowel drill, 212–213
  flop shot, 165
  fun, 15–16
  at home, 213–216
  importance of, 13–14
  like you play, 188–194
  making it a priority, 13–16
  mirror use in, 215–216
  organizing, 189
  pitch and run shot, 131
  pitch shots, 69, 74–75
  plan development, 14–15
  putting, 140–141, 148, 209–214
  of Se Ri Pak, 202
  stretching exercise, 213–214
  swings in bunkers, 88
  Texas wedge, 132
  tough shots, 23
  trench exercise, 210–212
  unconventional approaches, 161–162
  variety, 191
  visualization, 174–175
  weighted club, 215
  with wind, 190

practice games
  Bingo, Bango, Bongo, 197–199
  Eight in a Row, 200–201
  First to Make Five, 201–202
  Horse, 197
  Jingles, 197–199
  Pitching for Dollars, 195–196
  Snake, 199–200
practice, off-course
  chip into drapes, 234
  cleaning clubs, 236
  hand-eye coordination with other
      sports, 237
  holding your wedge, 233–234
  homework, 237
  putt on carpet, 231–232
  review scorecards, 235–236
  strengthening exercises, 234–235
  visualize good shots, 235
  watching television, 232–233
practice range
  balance improvement, 204–205
  music listening, 206–207
  one-handed shots, 205–206
  organizing practice on, 189–191
  pre-round warm-up, 192–193
precision
  needed for short game, 14
  of putting, 106
Price, Nick (player), 207
punch shot, 127–129
putter
  awareness, 212
  belly, 45–46
  blade, 41–42
  caring for, 48–50
  choosing, 46–47
  clean and dry, 49–50
  cover, 49
  damaged, 153–154
  description, 41
  devotion to, 48
  grip, 50
  grounding, 111
  handling with care, 49
  individual bag compartment for, 49
  long, 43–45
  mallet, 42–43
  off-green use, 131–132

as Texas wedge, 131–132
  traditional, 41–43
  variability in, 40–41
putting cups, electric, 231–232
putting games, 197, 199–202
Putt-Putt Golf, 122
putts and putting
  by Ben Crenshaw, 222
  best rounds ever, 110
  from bunkers, 152–153
  on carpet, 231–232
  chip shot choice instead of, 54–55
  competitive advantage and, 107
  conceding, 109
  confidence, 138, 141
  description, 12
  downhill, 143–144
  expectations, 175
  followthrough, 120
  freezing head and eyes during,
      119–120, 146–147
  fundamentals, importance of, 18–19
  gimmies, 109, 200
  goals and expectations, 26, 108–112
  grip, 113–115
  importance of skills, 106–107
  by Johnny Miller, 223–224
  lag, 139, 141–142
  learning from, 140
  legs, still, 118–119
  lengthening backstroke, 139
  long, 109–111
  make it or break it philosophy,
      139–141
  maladies, 144–148
  margin of error, 106, 172
  marking on scorecard, 236
  mental aspects, 110–111
  miniature golf, 122
  practice, 140–141, 148, 209–214
  prejudice, 105–106
  pre-round warm-up, 192, 193–194
  reading break of greens, 120–122
  speed, 118, 139–140, 142–143
  stance, 112–113, 222
  straight, 230
  strategies, 137–144
  style, 138–142
  swing, 116–120

putts and putting *(continued)*
  target line, 112–113, 115–116
  two-footers, 109
  variables, 111
  wrists, stiff, 119
  yips, 144–148, 223–224
Purtzer, Tom (player), 153

• R •

ready golf, 199
relief, 45, 154
Remember icon, 5
road, playing from, 154–155
Rocca, Constantino (player), 242–243
Rogers, Bill (player), 244
roll, 230
Ross, Donald (course designer),
    143, 240, 250–251
rotator cuffs, stretching, 182–183, 184
routine, pre-shot
  to turn mind off, 28
  visualization of target line, 29
  watching Tour players, 232
Royal Birkdale (course), 218
rubber band exercise, 213–214
rules, bunker, 88
Runyan, Paul (player), 62–63
Runyan shot, 63–66
Ryder Cup
  history, 245
  matches, 218, 222, 245–247, 254–255
Ryder, Samuel (creator of Ryder
    Cup), 245

• S •

sand save, 88. *See also* bunker;
    bunker shot
sand, soft versus hard, 90
sand wedge
  for bunker shot, 207–208
  description, 37
  invention of, 39, 149
  loft, 34, 37, 92
  for pitch shot, 69, 72, 79
  for Runyan shot, 65

Sandler, Adam (actor), 174
Sarazen, Gene (player)
  career, 39
  grand slam, 219
  sand wedge invention, 39, 149
scorecard
  marking, 236
  reviewing, 235–236
scoring distance, 11
secrets of success
  clubface awareness, 227–228
  expectations, realistic, 229–230
  followthrough, 229
  lead hand as captain, 228
  roll the ball on the ground, 230
  speed, maintaining constant, 228
  straight putt, 230
  subconscious playing, 227
  swing along target line, 228
  swing through the shot, 228–229
self talk, positive, 175–176
Senior Tour, Jack Nicklaus and, 224
7-iron
  for backhand swing, 159
  for chip shot, 36, 55, 56, 57
  loft, 34
  opposite-handed, 161
  for pitch and run shot, 130
  for Runyan shot, 63, 65
Shepard, Alan (astronaut), 247
Shiels, Michael Patrick (author/golfer),
    132, 136
shoes, cleaning, 236
short game
  statistical approach to, 10–11
  swing options, 11–12
short shots, greatest ever
  Alan Shepard on the moon, 247
  Bob Tway at 1986 PGA, 239–240
  Constantino Rocca at 1995 British
    Open, 242–243
  Hale Irwin at 1990 U.S. Open, 241–242
  Justin Leonard in 1999 Ryder Cup,
    245–246
  Lanny Wadkins in 1983 Ryder Cup,
    246–247
  Larry Mize at 1987 Masters, 240–241

Lee Trevino at 2002 Million-Dollar Par-Three-Shootout, 243–244
Payne Stewart at 1999 U.S. Open, 247–248
Tom Watson at 1982 U.S. Open, 244–245
shot variables
  firmness of ground, 24
  gross variations, 24
  lay of the land, 25
  lie, 23
  obstacles, 23–24
  wind, 24
shoulders
  position for bunker shot, 99–100
  position for chip shot, 61
  stretching, 182–186
Singh, Vijay (player)
  music use by, 206
  practice by, 188
  putter preference, 45
6-iron, loft of, 34
Skins Game, 223
skip-shots, 162
slice
  effect of lie on, 70
  from side-hill lie, 83, 84
  wind and, 190
Smith, Rick (course architect), 253
Smyers, Steve (course designer), 39
Snake (game), 199–200
Sorenstam, Annika (player)
  finishing, 222–223
  visualization, 235
Southern Dunes Golf Club (course), 39
speed
  bunker shot swing, 96–97, 101
  chip shot swing, 62
  consistent, 228
  putting, 118, 139–140, 142–143
spike marks, on the green, 112
spinning the club, 78
sports, for hand-eye coordination, 237
St. Andrews
  British Open (1995), 242–243
  New Course, 132
  Old Course, 98, 154–155, 250

Stadium Course, Tournament Players Club at Sawgrass (course), 251
Stadler, Craig (player), 160
stance
  ball position, 31, 59, 60, 72–73
  bunker shot, 91, 92–94
  chip shot, 59–61
  flop shot, 164–165
  mirror examination of, 216
  open, 59, 72, 91, 130, 156
  pitch and run shot, 130
  pitch shot, 72–74
  putting, 112–113, 222
  Runyan shot, 63
  shoulder set, 61
  watching Tour players, 232–233
  weight distribution, 59–60, 74
statistics, 10
steering, as cause of yips, 145
Stewart, Payne (player), 247–248
stimpmeter, 143
Strategic Fox at Fox Hills Golf Club (course), 253
strategy
  chip shot, 56
  defensive, 142
  holding the green, 133
  low trajectory, 126–129
  pitch shot, 70–71
  pitching and running, 126–129
  pre-round warm-up, 191–194
  pulling the pin, 134–135
  putting, 137–144
  Texas wedge use, 131–132
strengthening exercises, 234–235
stretching
  back, 183–187
  legs, 182–183
  putting exercise, 213–214
  upper arms and shoulders, 182–186
  wrists and forearms, 187–188
subconscious, playing in the
  description, 27–28
  music use, 206–207
  as secret to success, 227
  when putting, 118, 146, 147, 148
superstition, 48

swing
  backhand, 159
  bunker shot, 95–97, 100–101
  chip shot, 59–62
  clubface awareness during, 227–228
  distance from target line and, 29
  finishing, 233
  flop shot, 165
  followthrough, 97, 129, 223, 229
  front hand leading, 30
  head down myth, 177
  lead hand as captain of, 205–206, 228
  one-handed, 205–206
  options, short game, 11–12
  pacing with a phrase, 177
  pitch and run shot, 130–131
  pitch shot, 71–75
  practice in bunkers, 88
  punch shot, 128–129
  Runyan shot, 63–66
  tempo, 207
  through the shot, 228–229
  watching Tour players, 233
  weight distribution and, 59–60

• T •

target, focus on, 27–28
target line
  bunker shot, 94–95, 152
  chalk line practice, 209–210
  chip shot, 59, 151, 230
  description, 12, 28–29
  flop shot, 165
  mistakes, 19
  pitch and run shot, 129–130
  pitch shot, 70, 71, 72, 74, 82, 84
  putt, 112–116, 139, 142, 154, 209–210
  standing too close to, 29
  swinging along, 228
  visualizing, 29
Technical Stuff icon, 5
technique
  ignoring textbook, 18–19
  preferences, 18–19, 21
tempo
  music for developing, 207
  regaining, 170–171

tension, 170–171
Texas wedge, 131–132
3-iron, loft of, 34
Threetops Course at Treetops Resort
    (course)
  description, 252–253
  Million-Dollar Par-Three-Shootout,
    243–244
3-wood
  chipping with, 150–152
  loft, 34
Tip icon, 5
Torrey Pines (course), 220
Tournament Players Club at Sawgrass
    (course), 251
Trahan, Sam (player), 110
trajectory
  advantages of low, 126–129
  altering pitch shot, 77–78
  knock-down shot, 127–129
  pitch and run shot, 129
tree, ball against, 157–158
trench practice technique, 210–212
Trevino, Lee (player)
  chipping into drapes, 234
  Million-Dollar Par-Three-Shootout,
    243–244
  short game of, 221
Tway, Bob (player), 239–240
2-iron, skill needed for, 35

• U •

unconventional approaches
  bellying a wedge, 155–156
  chipping with 3-wood, 150–152
  playing from cart path, 154–155
  practicing, 161–162
  putting from bunkers, 152–153
  putting without a putter, 153–154
  water, playing from, 156–157
  wrong-sided attempts, 157–161
United States Golf Association (USGA),
    44, 45
unplayable ball, 102, 158
U.S. Open, 173, 223, 241–242, 244–245,
    247–248
Utley, Stan (player), 110

• V •

Valderrama, Club de Golf (course), 256
Van de Velde, Jean (player), 171
Vardon Trophy, 221
variables
  assessing the sand variables, 89–91
  putting, 111
  short-game, 12–13
Venturi, Ken (player), 173
visualization
  of good shots, 235
  pitch shot, 71
  practicing, 174–175
  of target line, 29

• W •

Wadkins, Lanny (player)
  Ryder Cup (1983), 246–247
  swing speed, 207
warming up
  back, 183–187
  importance of, 181
  legs, 182, 183
  length of time, 192–194
  preround preparation, 191–194
  quick, 194
  upper arms and shoulders, 182–186
  wrists and forearms, 187–188
waste bunkers, 88
water hazard
  pitching over, 76–77
  playing from, 156–157
Watson, Tom (player)
  Ballybunion Old Course and, 252
  U.S. Open (1982), 244–245
  yips, 146
wedge. *See also specific types*
  bellying, 155
  carrying to develop feel for, 233–234
  flipping the blade, 160
  loft, 34, 35, 36

practice, 193
  for flop shot, 164
  use as putter, 154
weight distribution
  chip shot, 59–60
  pitch shot, 74
weight, donut, 215
weight shift, 60, 74, 95
wind
  effect on pitch shot, 70, 72
  effect on putts, 111
  playing ball low in, 126–127
  practicing with, 190
  variations, assessment of, 24
Woods, Tiger (player)
  attire, 149
  Club de Golf Valderrama and, 256
  drives, 1, 2
  practice by, 161
  putter preference, 42
  sand wedge, damaged, 153
  wedge choice, 17
World Golf Hall of Fame, 219, 222
Wright, Mickey (player), 222
wrists
  firm when putting, 214
  in flop shot, 165
  in punch shot, 128
  in putting, 119, 145
  strengthening, 215
wrong-sided shots, 157–161

• Y •

yawn, 171
yips, 144–148

• Z •

Zoeller, Fuzzy (player)
  Ryder Cup, 218
  tension relief, 177
Zokol, Richard (player), 206

Notes

BUSINESS, CAREERS & PERSONAL FINANCE

0-7645-5307-0 0-7645-5331-3 *†

Also available:
- Accounting For Dummies †
  0-7645-5314-3
- Business Plans Kit For Dummies †
  0-7645-5365-8
- Cover Letters For Dummies
  0-7645-5224-4
- Frugal Living For Dummies
  0-7645-5403-4
- Leadership For Dummies
  0-7645-5176-0
- Managing For Dummies
  0-7645-1771-6

- Marketing For Dummies
  0-7645-5600-2
- Personal Finance For Dummies *
  0-7645-2590-5
- Project Management
  For Dummies
  0-7645-5283-X
- Resumes For Dummies †
  0-7645-5471-9
- Selling For Dummies
  0-7645-5363-1
- Small Business Kit For Dummies *†
  0-7645-5093-4

HOME & BUSINESS COMPUTER BASICS

0-7645-4074-2 0-7645-3758-X

Also available:
- ACT! 6 For Dummies
  0-7645-2645-6
- iLife '04 All-in-One Desk Reference
  For Dummies
  0-7645-7347-0
- iPAQ For Dummies
  0-7645-6769-1
- Mac OS X Panther Timesaving
  Techniques For Dummies
  0-7645-5812-9
- Macs For Dummies
  0-7645-5656-8
- Microsoft Money 2004 For Dummies
  0-7645-4195-1

- Office 2003 All-in-One Desk
  Reference For Dummies
  0-7645-3883-7
- Outlook 2003 For Dummies
  0-7645-3759-8
- PCs For Dummies
  0-7645-4074-2
- TiVo For Dummies
  0-7645-6923-6
- Upgrading and Fixing PCs
  For Dummies
  0-7645-1665-5
- Windows XP Timesaving
  Techniques For Dummies
  0-7645-3748-2

FOOD, HOME, GARDEN, HOBBIES, MUSIC & PETS

0-7645-5295-3 0-7645-5232-5

Also available:
- Bass Guitar For Dummies
  0-7645-2487-9
- Diabetes Cookbook For Dummies
  0-7645-5230-9
- Gardening For Dummies *
  0-7645-5130-2
- Guitar For Dummies
  0-7645-5106-X
- Holiday Decorating For Dummies
  0-7645-2570-0
- Home Improvement All-in-One
  For Dummies
  0-7645-5680-0

- Knitting For Dummies
  0-7645-5395-X
- Piano For Dummies
  0-7645-5105-1
- Puppies For Dummies
  0-7645-5255-4
- Scrapbooking For Dummies
  0-7645-7208-3
- Senior Dogs For Dummies
  0-7645-5818-8
- Singing For Dummies
  0-7645-2475-5
- 30-Minute Meals For Dummies
  0-7645-2589-1

INTERNET & DIGITAL MEDIA

0-7645-1664-7 0-7645-6924-4

Also available:
- 2005 Online Shopping Directory
  For Dummies
  0-7645-7495-7
- CD & DVD Recording For Dummies
  0-7645-5956-7
- eBay For Dummies
  0-7645-5654-1
- Fighting Spam For Dummies
  0-7645-5965-6
- Genealogy Online For Dummies
  0-7645-5964-8
- Google For Dummies
  0-7645-4420-9

- Home Recording For Musicians
  For Dummies
  0-7645-1634-5
- The Internet For Dummies
  0-7645-4173-0
- iPod & iTunes For Dummies
  0-7645-7772-7
- Preventing Identity Theft
  For Dummies
  0-7645-7336-5
- Pro Tools All-in-One Desk
  Reference For Dummies
  0-7645-5714-9
- Roxio Easy Media Creator
  For Dummies
  0-7645-7131-1

* Separate Canadian edition also available

† Separate U.K. edition also available

Available wherever books are sold. For more information or to order direct: U.S. customers visit www.dummies.com or call 1-877-762-2974.
U.K. customers visit www.wileyeurope.com or call 0800 243407. Canadian customers visit www.wiley.ca or call 1-800-567-4797.

SPORTS, FITNESS, PARENTING, RELIGION & SPIRITUALITY

0-7645-5146-9 0-7645-5418-2

Also available:

- Adoption For Dummies
  0-7645-5488-3
- Basketball For Dummies
  0-7645-5248-1
- The Bible For Dummies
  0-7645-5296-1
- Buddhism For Dummies
  0-7645-5359-3
- Catholicism For Dummies
  0-7645-5391-7
- Hockey For Dummies
  0-7645-5228-7

- Judaism For Dummies
  0-7645-5299-6
- Martial Arts For Dummies
  0-7645-5358-5
- Pilates For Dummies
  0-7645-5397-6
- Religion For Dummies
  0-7645-5264-3
- Teaching Kids to Read
  For Dummies
  0-7645-4043-2
- Weight Training For Dummies
  0-7645-5168-X
- Yoga For Dummies
  0-7645-5117-5

TRAVEL

0-7645-5438-7 0-7645-5453-0

Also available:

- Alaska For Dummies
  0-7645-1761-9
- Arizona For Dummies
  0-7645-6938-4
- Cancún and the Yucatán
  For Dummies
  0-7645-2437-2
- Cruise Vacations For Dummies
  0-7645-6941-4
- Europe For Dummies
  0-7645-5456-5
- Ireland For Dummies
  0-7645-5455-7

- Las Vegas For Dummies
  0-7645-5448-4
- London For Dummies
  0-7645-4277-X
- New York City For Dummies
  0-7645-6945-7
- Paris For Dummies
  0-7645-5494-8
- RV Vacations For Dummies
  0-7645-5443-3
- Walt Disney World & Orlando
  For Dummies
  0-7645-6943-0

GRAPHICS, DESIGN & WEB DEVELOPMENT

0-7645-4345-8 0-7645-5589-8

Also available:

- Adobe Acrobat 6 PDF
  For Dummies
  0-7645-3760-1
- Building a Web Site For Dummies
  0-7645-7144-3
- Dreamweaver MX 2004
  For Dummies
  0-7645-4342-3
- FrontPage 2003 For Dummies
  0-7645-3882-9
- HTML 4 For Dummies
  0-7645-1995-6
- Illustrator CS For Dummies
  0-7645-4084-X

- Macromedia Flash MX 2004
  For Dummies
  0-7645-4358-X
- Photoshop 7 All-in-One Desk
  Reference For Dummies
  0-7645-1667-1
- Photoshop CS Timesaving
  Techniques For Dummies
  0-7645-6782-9
- PHP 5 For Dummies
  0-7645-4166-8
- PowerPoint 2003 For Dummies
  0-7645-3908-6
- QuarkXPress 6 For Dummies
  0-7645-2593-X

NETWORKING, SECURITY, PROGRAMMING & DATABASES

0-7645-6852-3 0-7645-5784-X

Also available:

- A+ Certification For Dummies
  0-7645-4187-0
- Access 2003 All-in-One Desk
  Reference For Dummies
  0-7645-3988-4
- Beginning Programming
  For Dummies
  0-7645-4997-9
- C For Dummies
  0-7645-7068-4
- Firewalls For Dummies
  0-7645-4048-3
- Home Networking For Dummies
  0-7645-42796

- Network Security For Dummies
  0-7645-1679-5
- Networking For Dummies
  0-7645-1677-9
- TCP/IP For Dummies
  0-7645-1760-0
- VBA For Dummies
  0-7645-3989-2
- Wireless All In-One Desk Reference
  For Dummies
  0-7645-7496-5
- Wireless Home Networking
  For Dummies
  0-7645-3910-8